S P A C E S

DIMENSIONS OF THE HUMAN LANDSCAPE

S P A C E S

S P A C E S

DIMENSIONS OF THE HUMAN LANDSCAPE

TEXT AND PHOTOGRAPHS BY BARRIE B. GREENBIE

NEW HAVEN AND LONDON   YALE UNIVERSITY PRESS

Written with the assistance of a grant from the National Endowment for the Arts.

Published with assistance from the Louis Stern Memorial Fund.

Designed by Sally Harris and set in VIP Janson type by The Saybrook Press, Inc. Printed in the United States of America by The Murray Printing Company, Westford, Mass.

Library of Congress Cataloging in Publication Data

Greenbie, Barrie B.
    Spaces: dimensions of the human landscape.
    Bibliography: p.
    Includes indexes.
    1. Landscape assessment.   2. City planning.
3. Landscape architecture.   I. Title.
GF90.G73   304.2   81-50435
ISBN 0-300-02549-1   AACR2
ISBN 0-300-02560-2 (pbk.)

10 9 8 7 6 5 4 3 2 1

To my wife, Vlasta,
Who shares my territory and makes it home,
And to the memory of my father, Sydney,
Who taught me to see.

Contents

Preface   ix

Part I.   Private Spaces

1   Home Space: Fences and Neighbors   2

2   Street Space: To Go Through or to Go To   36

3   Village Space: Fences and Neighborhoods   70

Part II.   Public Spaces

4   Distemic Space: The Community of
    Strangers   108

5   Urban Space: The Marketplace of Goods and
    Symbols   121

6   Humane Space: Promenades, Parks, and Places
    for Peace of Mind   219

Epilogue   281

Notes   293

Bibliography   297

List of Places Illustrated   301

Subject and Photograph Index   309

Preface

What we call the landscape is generally considered to be something "out there." But, while some aspects of the landscape are clearly external to both our bodies and our minds, what each of us actually experiences is selected, shaped, and colored by what we know, that is, by what we have already experienced. Indeed, some kinds of knowledge seem to be programmed into our nervous system. Our minds are set up to make us *think* we distinguish between what is external (objective) and internal (subjective), but what we actually know and feel about our environment is always a mixture of both.

In this book I shall consider the landscape essentially as a human habitat, that is, as an environment *in* which people act and *to* which they react. In doing so I shall draw heavily on some theories and discoveries from the social sciences and from that branch of natural science concerned with animal behavior known as ethology. I shall also pay due respect to those natural scientists who are concerned with keeping the habitat habitable, but the landscape as ecology has been dealt with so well by so many others that I will take its importance for granted. However, while I will use the work of scientists, and from time to time attempt to assume their objectivity, my basic perspective is that of the landscape architect and landscape planner, of the shaper of environments for human purposes, for human survival, and human salvation.

My interest in the relationship of social behavior to space originated, without my realizing it, thirty years ago when I started professional life as a stage designer. Theater, of course, is concerned first of all with human interactions. But drama, unlike other forms of literary art, presents all experience in a spatial context, and the designed space has meaning only as it facilitates and expresses behavior. Despite the presumption of many people that scenic art deals with flimsy illusions, stage design at its best is far more demanding functionally than the creations most architects have been allowed to get away with. If things do not work in a psychological and behavioral sense, as well as a practical one, an irate director and the actors let the designer know in a hurry. Somewhat later, I found the theater to have been excellent training for design activities in the larger theater we call the landscape.

On the other hand, in real world environments outside the theater, physical design decisions, whether of an aesthetic or technical nature, are rarely subject to such clear authority; they are inevitably enmeshed in political and economic contexts for which there seems to be no director and about which the actors themselves have little to say. The human landscape is not nearly as amenable to artistic composition as the spaces and activities behind a proscenium arch. Nevertheless, the inherent dramatic action of human life, which the theater reorganizes and intensifies but does not create, must remain the basic form giver if that life is to have full meaning.

My half-conscious awareness of this relationship was suddenly brought into focus in the mid-sixties by the discoveries of the emerging science of ethology, which were sprung on the public consciousness by a number of popular and controversial writers. One such writer was Robert Ardrey, a dramatist turned anthropologist. In a book called the *Territorial Imperative** Ardrey suggested that the attachment of animals—including man—to a piece of turf was an innate evolutionary response. It seemed to me that if there was such a thing as a territorial imperative, those of us who spend our working lives drawing boundaries and putting up walls around human activities would do well to find out as much as possible about it. But at that time many American social scientists reacted violently to the proposition that human behavior has anything to do with the behavior of other animals or that it has genetic roots. The reaction was not altogether unwarranted, since Darwinian concepts had been grossly perverted at various times to justify economic exploitation and racism. However, the intellectual battles that raged were largely ideological, not scientific. From the social science literature of the time it was very difficult to know what the ethologists actually were learning and saying. Even more difficult was arriving at a conclusion about what it meant for the organization of human habitats. I decided to go to the source.

With the help of a grant from the National Endowment for the Arts, I set about examining the ideas of prominent ethologists and comparing them with those of environmental psychologists, anthropol-

ogists, and sociologists. The task required a hasty, intensive, and very imperfect education in a number of disciplines about which I had only the most general knowledge. But the resulting intellectual odyssey was one of the great adventures of my life.

The results of my explorations are published in my *Design for Diversity.** Originally I had intended to produce the kind of book I am offering now, an illustrated book about the design implications of these new behavioral ideas. But the subject proved far more complex than I had anticipated, and to my own surprise I wound up with a work devoted largely to social theory. It has taken me another five years to translate verbal abstractions into concrete visual and visible relationships. My social theory is here summarized in chapter 4, preceding a visual exploration of large cities.

In attempting to deal in this book with scientific concepts from a designer's perspective, I have frequently drawn on private experience and have tried to make my personal point of view explicit so that the reader may judge my observations accordingly. But my purpose is not primarily personal; rather it is to generalize from these experiences in such a way that others with different experiences may reinterpret the concepts in their own contexts.

I have also tried to combine as closely as possible verbal and visual modes of thought and communication. Verbal experience is not the same as visual experience, although one obviously influences the other. Visual experience seems to be considerably closer to spatial awareness, although we experience space with all our senses. On the whole, visual communication is probably more important than words to designers, and some of the problems they have in communicating with the nonprofessional public may stem from the relatively greater influence on most people of words, at least in western cultures. As stated in the *Gospel According to St. John*, "In the beginning was the word." But not for the architect, who is more likely to agree with Luke, "If these should hold their peace, the stones would immediately cry out."

There is much evidence from scientific research that in fact our brains are divided on this matter,

*New York: Dell Publishing Co., 1966.

*Amsterdam: Elsevier Publishing Co., 1976.

one hemisphere dealing with verbal and the other with visual and other nonverbal forms of experience. There is also evidence (discussed in more detail in chapter 4) that the brain is not only divided laterally, but is layered, with the centers governing our emotional life lying below and somewhat separated from those controlling our rational thought processes. In any case, spatial experience is acquired by the infant much earlier than speech. It seems to be associated more intimately with primitive needs and desires, especially those relating to territory. The child not only learns to crawl before it can walk, it learns to do both before it can talk. Thus, there is much about our feelings of and for space that is not accessible to the rational part of our brains. Furthermore, we respond to space as a totality, from many directions simultaneously, in what psychologists call *gestalt* experience. Verbal thought seems to proceed linearly, from step to step, from concept to concept, with the possible exception of poetic metaphor.

I will rely here at least as much on visual illustrations as on words. I am not using maps, because I want to retain the ground level perspective with which most of us live most of the time. Where an overview is important, I have used photographs from tall buildings or oblique, low-level air photos. With very few exceptions, I am using photographs rather than drawings for a number of reasons. The most important of these is that drawings usually do not convey a sense of everyday reality to the extent that photographs do. A recent acclaimed book on the subject is Susan Sontag's *On Photography*. Although this book reveals a good deal more about its author's verbal intellect than it does about the photographer's visual one, it is full of interesting insights. One of Sontag's main arguments is that the photograph differs from other works of art precisely because "there is always a presumption that something exists, or did exist, which is like what's in the picture."* She sees treachery in this fact because of course the photographic image is not the reality. The camera can lie, and lie very effectively, perhaps even more effectively than any other form of image, precisely because of this presumption of reality. In the hands of an artist, of course, the camera can interpret, intensi-

*New York: Farrar, Straus and Giroux, 1977, p. 5.

fy, and illuminate reality, as do other arts. But a photograph never replicates exactly, always distorts in one way or another, the experience of being, especially of moving, in a place. The camera lens is not even an approximation of an eye. Even when we ourselves are perfectly still, our eyes are in motion, scanning the field of vision for information, constantly selecting, emphasizing some details, ignoring others. But we rarely experience a real life environment for very long from one place; normally we move around in it, so that our eyes send to our brain a continually unfolding pattern of images. Even when we are sitting in a chair or lying in bed, our head moves. The camera is never as selective as our "eyes" because in fact we don't see with our eyes, which are merely a medium for information flow, but with our brain. That's where the image is put together, not on the retina as on a film.

The camera is most effective in close-ups. It shows detail with a vividness rarely achieved in real life. A flower becomes a landscape, an insect appears to be the size of a dog, a face can be more overwhelming than a crowd. The camera, like a Japanese painting, is at its best when it reveals particularities. It is relatively poor at establishing larger contexts, which are everything in real life environments. And it is virtually worthless in establishing scale, the referent for which is always the human body. But perhaps the biggest problem in using photographs for the purposes for which I propose to use them is loss of three-dimensional reality. Pictures are, no matter what we pretend they are, two-dimensional. This is true partly because we experience space with other senses besides the visual one. Blind people experience it entirely without sight.

Despite their shortcomings, however, photographs are the most effective way of presenting everyday environments for discussion, apart from being in them. Our automatic presumption of reality in a photograph, despite its treachery, is very important in establishing an attitude for examining the visual world as it is given, rather than re-creating it as one thinks it ought to be, as one is likely to do with a drawing. And the photograph has one great advantage even over the reality itself, that of freezing an aspect of the environment in time so that one can contemplate it. Sontag, who says many negative things about photography which I and probably most photographers consider absurd, nevertheless sums up its major virtue very well: "The ultimate wisdom of the photographic image is to say: 'There is the surface. Now think—or rather feel, intuit—what is beyond it, what the reality must be if it looks this way.' Photographs, which cannot by themselves explain anything, are inexhaustible invitations to deduction, speculation, and fantasy" (p. 23).

My objective is to focus on everyday human habitats, for the most part, rather than on the great works of architecture of past or present. For this reason I have tried to restrain, without altogether repressing, the designer's urge to reorganize and intensify aspects of a real place for aesthetic effect, to the extent that doing so would significantly distort the most typical characteristics of a place. Thus, my pictures probably fall somewhere between what John Szarkowski calls "mirrors and windows." My main intent is to use photographs to illustrate various particular embodiments of generalized concepts, without pretending that they represent a completely detached viewpoint. Most of them are limited to the landscapes I know best, those of my own country, with side excursions into places which are sufficiently similar to my own culture that I can comment on them with some sense of confidence.

Almost all of these photographs were taken with the general subject of this book in mind and most were taken specifically for this book. In the past, when I have written something and then sought illustrations for what was written, even from my own files, I have been frustrated by not being able to find the exact image I have in my head while writing. In this case I decided to photograph first and write second, since words are far more flexible than photos. I outlined each chapter in a general way, and then set out to photograph it, quite literally writing it in my head as I peered through the viewfinder. The pictures are intended to serve, then, not merely as illustrations, but as visual statements. Nevertheless, in the process of putting words on paper next to printed pictures, a number of transformations take place, and new ideas emerge which are not anticipated originally.

A few of the photographs I have used are by others and are so credited. I am particularly indebted to my friend, colleague, and fellow photographer Richard W. Wilkie for the pictures identified with his name. I am also indebted to A. C. Scott for his drawing of the Grand Canyon, one of the rare departures from my policy of sticking to photographs. For some visually eloquent departures from my other policy—that of staying as much as possible with ground level views of the landscape—I am grateful to Alex MacLean and Dr. Georg Gerster.

A great many other people have contributed to this book in one way or another through the years, including hundreds of students at the University of Massachusetts, too many to name and thank individually. But I must extend thanks to several people who read all or parts of the manuscript in various versions and provided exceedingly helpful comment and criticism as well as needed encouragement. They are Helen B. Armstrong, Elmer Bendiner, Julius Gy. Fabos, Vlasta K. Greenbie, J.B. Jackson, Paul D. MacLean, John H. Martin, John R. Mullin, Andrew J.W. Scheffey, and Edwarda Van Benschoten.

I feel fortunate to have a publisher for whom publishing is a creative, collaborative act. I wish to express particular appreciation to my editor, Judy Metro, who applied a cool professional eye and a warm heart to my manuscript and greatly helped me to sharpen the focus of both verbal and visual images. My thanks also to others on the staff of Yale University Press, especially copy editor Lawrence Kenney and designer Sally Harris. Mrs. Harris willingly accepted my rather demanding request that printed words follow close by the corresponding photographs and undertook to combine both into a design which is more than the sum of the parts.

Here on my home territory I thank Ruth-Alice Lalliburte, who typed and retyped the manuscript in several versions, as well as others who typed sections of it.

Part of the cost of travel and processing for the photographs was supported by a grant from the National Endowment for the Arts, and that assistance is gratefully acknowledged. I must also acknowledge a grant from my working wife, who contributed substantially to the rest of the cost, as well as adjusting her vacation plans for several years to accompany me on the itinerary mapped for this book.

Amherst, Massachusetts
January, 1981

PART I Private Spaces

Why do they make good neighbors? Isn't it
Where there are cows? But here there are no cows.
Before I built a wall I'd ask to know
What I was walling in or walling out,
And to whom I was like to give offense . . .

Robert Frost, "Mending Wall"

1

Home Space:
Fences and Neighbors

Each of us resides in the center of a personal universe. Our most important boundary is our own skin; the most significant "home" for any of us is within our own bodies, for that is where all experience of whatever larger environments we may encounter resides. Our awareness of the multifold hierarchies of space that constitute our world radiates from that center, like the ripples formed by a butterfly on the surface of a pond, intersecting and reverberating with those of other things and beings.

The newborn infant is apparently quite unaware of boundaries, even that of its own skin. Its own needs and sensations *are* its world. But as children learn to cope with separateness from others in space, they also learn to perceive and to manipulate external objects to form various sets of boundaries within which they can feel secure. Other human beings become part of an increasingly complex environment, and physical structures take on new possibilities for shaping and controlling relations with other people. The very small child thinks of things and spaces in terms of "me"; the older child begins to think more and more in terms of "we." "My house" becomes "our house."

The psychoanalyst Carl Jung placed great emphasis on the house as a symbol of self, and many others have elaborated this idea.[1] Of course Jung considered "self" both in a social as well as individual sense, and in fact the concept of *self* has no meaning except in the context of *others*. Most of us share our houses with some sort of family group during most of our lives, and while parts of an adequately sized house may belong primarily to one or another individual, the boundaries of the home are usually those of a cluster of selves which form a domestic unit. Even people who by choice or circumstance live alone express in their homes the images and traditions formed at one time in a family group.

The architects Kent C. Bloomer and Charles W. Moore view buildings as the projection into space of our awareness of our own bodies. Fundamental and obvious as this relationship might seem, it has been to a great extent ignored in contemporary architecture. A major exception to the rule is the single-family home. Bloomer and Moore sum up the personal situation very well in their book *Body, Memory, and Architecture:*

One tell-tale sign remains, in modern America, of a world based not on a Cartesian abstraction, but on our sense of ourselves extended beyond the boundaries of our bodies to the world around: that is the single-family house, free-standing like ourselves, with a face and a back, a hearth (like a heart) and a chimney, an attic full of recollections of *up*, and a basement harboring implications of *down*.[2]

Many North American tract houses fit this characterization less adequately than they might. But whatever the deficiencies of domestic and other kinds of contemporary architecture may be, they are as nothing compared to the shortcomings of most urban design. A good deal of excellent literature exists on the requirements of interior personal and family space. Far less thought is given to the out-of-doors relationships of one living space to another. This book will focus on the hierarchical structures that extend from the "skin" of the family home to the street and beyond.

As with the living body, the crucial elements of the building are the openings, through which life-giving exchanges take place with the outside world. The poet refers to the eyes as the windows of the soul; the architect should view windows as the eyes of the life within the house. The doors permit the exchanges and cohabitings that support and renew that life. The life of the home is of mind and spirit as well as body, a fact that so much mass housing, especially "public" housing, has overlooked. Through the eyes of the windows in photo 1 the poet Emily Dickinson observed an entire universe centered in, but not limited to, her garden. From the doorway in photo 2, leading to a street she rarely appeared on physically, she sent her letter to the world. Despite her self-imposed confinement to house and yard, her vision was so outreaching that the world, which largely ignored her physical existence in her lifetime, corresponds with her spirit today.

By contrast, a house a short distance away from Emily Dickinson's and roughly of the same era presents to the world a very different spirit (3). Children in any town where such houses are found will call them "haunted," even if they have never seen a Charles Addams cartoon. The spookiness of this

house is certainly enhanced by the evidence of abandonment and decay, as well as by the stark bare trees, but it does not derive from those details entirely. The landscape is full of dilapidated buildings which can be seen in the bleakness of winter, and yet we do not think of them as haunted. Something in the form of this particular kind of house, despite its wide veranda, conveys a quality of menacing withdrawal. Mansard roofs are frequently described as "brooding," and they continue to brood even when reincarnated as modern apartments (4). The

5

4

outer shape of archetypical Victorian houses, reinforced by the dark furniture and heavy drapes inside, undoubtedly expressed for many of their residents a relation to the world governed by the latently hostile energy of repressed libido. Literature abounds in references to the facades of houses as a means of delineating the character of their occupants; for example, the description of Manderley in Daphne Du Maurier's *Rebecca*, Tara in *Gone With the Wind*, and Poe's House of Usher.

The way human beings present the walls of their abodes to the world around them bears the same relation to family identity as clothing, hair style, and makeup do to the individuality of the person. In Amsterdam, Holland, the eighteenth-century houses of the burghers traditionally had elaborately decorated gables called *halsgevel* which were the personal emblems of each family (5). The forms and shapes, the symbols and meanings we put forth and read back from the facades of our homes are expressions of our individual personalities combined with those of our class, culture, and time. The often deplored "look-alike houses" of North

American suburbs are as much a function of the physical and social mobility of the modern middle class as of mass taste and mass production. Houses that are really lived in for long do not look alike, any more than do the people who live in them.

The openings in the walls enclosing a space make the difference between a boundary and a barrier, between an enclave and a prison. As the house walls present our social face to the world, so they let the world come in to us. The important thing in both cases is the degree of control we exercise in the interchange. The environmental psychologist Irwin Altman considers all privacy as a matter of regulating interaction with other people.[3] He distinguishes between "desired levels of privacy" and "achieved levels of privacy." In his model, if we desire less privacy than we have, we are lonely; if we desire more privacy, we feel crowded. This simple formula seems very useful when it comes to laying out and designing all aspects of the man-made landscape, but particularly that encompassing the home. Of course, we interact not only with other human beings but with the elements of nonhuman nature, and these too the walls serve to regulate. Windows of our houses let in air and sunlight; they also let in cold and wind. They reveal to us the events and forms of life outside; in the country the shade of trees and the sounds of birds (6), in town the moon and stars and the shapes of other people's houses. The landscape seen from the window is not the same as that seen from the street outside; the difference is precisely that one is revealed through an opening that is framed and that may be closed at will (7, 8). Especially in the city, the activities of others may impinge on us too ur-

6

7

8

gently for comfort. Indeed, for modern city dwellers
the problems caused by unwanted interactions with
other human beings are usually far more severe than
those dealing with predators and weather, which
historically has been a main function of shelter.

However, the fenestration of the house, important
as it is in architecture, does not comprise the entire
gestalt of the home defined by Bloomer and Moore.
That house, "free-standing like ourselves," must, as
they note, have a patch of land to stand free on. It is
almost heretical among professional architects and
planners these days to extol single-family homes
because from a "Cartesian" point of view they are an
inefficient way to distribute physical land and services. Some social engineers also deplore them because they aggravate the problem of housing the
masses massively. But the evidence is strong that
the patch of land on which a house sits is psychologically almost as important to the quality of life as
anything within the walls of the home, and large
numbers of people continue to pay any price they
can afford to have some piece of physical turf. This
sense of a home as much more than mere shelter, as
the center of a territorial space which includes the
outdoors as well as the inside, is beautifully expressed in a song by David Mallet, "I Knew This
Place":

I knew this place, I knew it well,
Every sound and every smell.
And every time I walked I fell
For the first two years or so.

There across the grassy yard
I, a young boy, running hard.

Brown and bruised and battle-scarred
And lost in sweet illusion.

From this window I can see
The fingers of an ancient tree.
Reaching out it calls to me
To climb its surly branches.

But all my climbing days are gone,
These tired legs I'm standing on
Would scarcely dare to leave the spot
Upon which they are standing.

And I remember every word
From every voice I ever heard.
Every frog and every bird,
Yes this is where it starts.

A brother's laugh, the sighing wind.
This is where my life begins,
This is where I learn to use
My hands and hear my heart.[4]

In photos 2 and 3, the spirit, the presentation of human personality, in each case resides as much in the yards as in the houses themselves. Historic preservation societies, preoccupied with buildings, often ignore the environments around them and, failing to preserve those, fail to preserve everything. If one's ability to control interactions with the environment is limited entirely to private life *inside* a house, then all transactions that take place outside it become public and must remain under public, rather than private, control. No continuum, or gradation, of relationships is possible. The private self disappears and the public self emerges at the doorstep, and vice versa. This is the problem increasingly faced by modern apartment dwellers. But it need not be inherent in urban life at all. For the best parts of older cities, especially the preindustrial cities which still form the nucleus and set the pattern for the cities of older nations, it has been and often still is solved very well. I would argue that a satisfactory hierarchy of transition zones between private and public is the fundamental task of anything that can be called community development or urban design.

I have found very useful the theory of the ethologist Paul Leyhausen, who distinguishes between two types of status, or dominance, hierarchies among social mammals.[5] One is what he calls the "relative hierarchy" because it depends on whether or not the individual is on home territory. The other he calls "absolute hierarchy" because it depends on personal characteristics which do not change with place, except that they are most effective on neutral ground, that is, not on another individual's home turf. The neutral grounds for human beings in the urban landscape are the public places, the streets, the plazas, and the parks, controlled more or less impersonally by law. Our private yards, as well as semipublic spaces under the surveillance of a limited group of residents, provide an important transition zone to our homes, where we as individuals are, or should be, in control of all aspects of our environment.

The psychological advantage which accrues to being on one's own home ground is well known to invading armies, as Americans found out to their sorrow and pain in Viet Nam. On the domestic scene, anyone who has engaged in door-to-door selling or canvassing for a cause becomes aware of the instinctive diffidence that is felt as one crosses a yard and enters a front porch. Fred Fischer, a Swiss medical doctor and psychiatrist, has observed that a physician on a house call will doff his hat and treat his patients with considerable courtesy, while the same doctor may enter a hospital ward with his hat on and is likely to be far more impersonal and brusk. The hospital is his territory, the patient's home is not.

Recently the U.S. Law Enforcement Assistance Administration reported that a study of the emotional effects on victims of burglaries were as severe as those of street muggings.[6] Since muggings and holdups involve assaults on the person, with greater evident danger to life and health, police have assumed that victims of such crimes have good reason to be upset and tend to be more understanding. Their reported tendency to see evidence of psychological trauma in housebreaking cases as unreasonable is reflective of the general tendency in our culture to view the use and possession of space only in utilitarian and economic terms. And yet, the assault on one's house is perhaps the most threatening of crimes because in fundamental terms it is the main line of defense. Consciously or unconsciously we probably expect to be more vulnerable in public places, even in those where crime is not common, an expectation that may reflect the Leyhausen phenomenon.

In the public places of towns and cities we are largely on our own as individuals; we exercise control over others to the extent of our position in the "absolute hierarchy," which is based on personal capacities derived from social or economic status, physical or psychological strength, or simply the possession of knowledge, that is, being "street-wise." If we do not rely on these, then we must rely on laws created and enforced by persons who do have such dominant characteristics in one way or another: the police, judges, and legislators. The implicit authority that derives from personal territory is a function almost entirely of ownership or possession of a particular piece of space. This authority, which home turf gives to all of us who are not homeless, is the most basic of human rights. It is recognized, at least in principle, by law in almost all societies, as suggested by the saying "a man's home is his castle." In a world which appears increasingly out of control to the ordinary citizen, the home at least still offers a bastion where every man can be king and every woman queen.

If this authority is confined to the spaces enclosed by building walls, feelings of influence over, and responsibility for, the larger public landscape are likely to be seriously diminished. If this authority extends outward in relative degree through transition zones into the public street, the street is much more likely to be an attractive, secure, and civilized place. The degree to which the rise of crime in American cities and in the cities of many other countries is related to their spatial design can only be guessed at. But at least one student of the subject, the architect Oscar Newman, has made a convincing case that the relationship in public housing is very strong. His observations, supported by data which have been the subject of some controversy, suggest that where large apartment buildings provide transitional spaces, which are perceived by residents and visitors alike to be under the proprietorship and surveillance of the occupants of the adjacent units, robbery, muggings, and all forms of street crime are greatly reduced. Newman calls such space "defensible space."[7] The unfortunate realities of life in contemporary cities, especially in the pluralistic United States, make the

term vividly appropriate. But it puts an unduly negative emphasis on the universal relationship between fences and neighbors.

Where crime is not a problem the existence of transition zones and the sense of enclave appear to be related strongly to a general sense of "community" and to the maintenance and general attractiveness of a residential area. A number of studies have shown that the degree to which residents of various types of housing know their neighbors is significantly less on through streets than on dead-end, or cul-de-sac, streets.[8] While the shape, size, location, and degree of enclosure by fences or shrubs and trees will vary considerably with the style and period of the place, as well as with the culture of the residents, the structuring of transitional spaces between private and public places, allowing for different degrees of publicness and privateness, is important to all. The greater the degree of diversity in the outlook and life style of neighbors, the more important such structuring becomes. Adequate spatial organization of the urban landscape is the prerequisite for social and cultural diversity. Expanding clusters of fences and gateways, of openings and closings, can give coherent and legible form to complex social behavior.

The transitional spaces between the house and the street have two different but related aspects. One is the transition between the inside and the outside of the home envelope, the "here" and "there" polarity that governs all human experience. This occurs first in the relation of the rooms to the house, and then in terms of house to yard, yard to street space, street to neighborhood, and so on. These establish the boundaries or extensions of "skin" between us and the material environment. The second aspect of transitional space involves the continuum between private and public. For those who seek surcease from interminable interactions with our own kind, the most important aspect may be the transition between oneself and nonhuman nature; windows may look out over small walled gardens or distant views of mountains or sea. For those who find stimulation and creative satisfaction mainly in human interactions, the important transition between inside and outside, between our personal here and the larger there, may be in terms of the private built environment of our house or apartment and the built

9

10

environment of the urban scene. Probably most of us seek some measure of both, but the proportions and priorities vary widely. Creative urban design will maximize free choice in all directions. Thus, we can look at transitional space as being between one level of physical enclosure and another, and simultaneously as being between one level of social enclosure and another. On the one hand it establishes a relationship between interior and exterior architecture, on the other between private and public life.

The egalitarian attitudes of American culture have led many people to think of fences entirely in terms of exclusion, of keeping something or somebody out. But more constructively, they should be viewed in

terms of inclusion, of protecting something within. J. B. Jackson has stated it especially well, defining a boundary as "that which binds together."[9] Apart from weather and serious crime situations, that something to be protected from within is largely psychological. It makes a difference whether we view the fence in terms of an intruder or visitor (9), or as lord of our own domain (10). Only the chronically homeless should see fences per se as exclusionary.

Aesthetically, fences provide form and texture in the urban landscape. Kinesthetically, they define the path space and serve as guides to our body orienting sense (11). The environmental psychologist J. J. Gibson has defined what he calls the "haptic sys-

11

tem," a combination of the several tactile senses with information from our own muscles as we move. Bloomer and Moore, in their discussion of *Body, Memory, and Architecture*, have used the word *haptic* to describe that mentally extended sense of touch which comes about through the total experience of living and acting in a space.[10] While Gibson distinguishes between the haptic system and the visual system, what we see is in fact blended with conscious and unconscious memories of what we have literally *felt* in past associations with the scene before us. Therefore it is appropriate to use the term *haptic* in connection with visual experience, as Bloomer and Moore have done, and as I will do throughout this book. But it is important to remember that it applies to seen objects which at one time or another have been touched and acted upon. For example, we cannot visualize a stairway as a stairway unless at one time or another we have climbed a stair. If we have never done so, it will be merely an abstract form. Strictly speaking, only the astronauts who have walked on the moon can have haptic associations with that object, which has for so long been visualized in different ways. If the moon has haptic meaning for the rest of us, it is only because we associate it in our minds with something like a marble or the face of a man. Actually, because we have no physical, haptic associations with it, we can imagine it to be anything we want. Because we experience our earthly environment with all our senses, including smell and sound, the haptic system puts us in imaginative physical contact with places and objects we once touched but now only see, hear, or smell. This haptic sense is conveyed splendidly in the verse by David Mallet quoted above.

The concept of haptic experience is particularly important in considering fences because not only do they have texture in themselves (the pickets in photo 11) which we can reach out and feel, but they define the kinds of spaces through which we have at one time or another moved. In the human landscape, fences of the type shown permit us visually to enter spaces which we cannot, ought not, or wish not to enter physically; such fences enable us to experience vicariously other people's life space without involving ourselves with them or they with us. *The essence of civilized life is sharing space with others without intruding or being intruded upon.* All sorts of social conventions assist in this endeavor. Fences are high among them. Hold a hand over the shadow in the lower part of photo 9 and the scene becomes one of a tranquil domestic yard. When the hand is removed, the human form of the shadow immediately suggests an intruder. The shadow is even more menacing than an actual figure would be, for reasons that are beyond the scope of this book. The point here is that the fence creates a permeable boundary which controls but does not isolate.

The variety and aesthetic richness of fence designs in various landscape compositions, old and new, here and there, the world over, is limitless. At their best they rival any design form of which the human race is capable (12 a−k). Architecture has been called the mother of the arts. Surely, then, landscape architecture is the father of the arts. Perhaps the terms should be reversed to allow for "mother earth." In any case, both begin by confirming the boundaries of living space.

Photo 13 shows a group of houses quite typical of new suburban developments throughout North America, although the larger landscape in this case is quite special. These are essentially boxes, sitting on, rather than in, a generally undifferentiated space, the emptiness of which is only increased by contrast with the visually rich environment beyond. Real estate merchants call these buildings "Cape Cod" houses. Photo 14 shows a real Cape Cod house. It is on Cape Cod. It occupies a place, not merely a space. In time, of course, the scene in photo 13 will also become a place because the people who live in it will make it one. The trees will grow, shrubs and flowers will emerge, and, depending on the local culture, fences may appear. One way or another the void between the walls of the houses will become elaborated into transitional subspaces, defining both the family yards and the community street. Photo 15 presents a similar house but a very different environment. Although it will take no prizes in landscape architecture, it provides a living space outside as well as in. The prototype of contemporary subdivisions was Levittown, Long Island. Photo 16 shows it as it appeared when newly constructed just after World War II. Today the bleak rows of look-alike "Cape Cod" houses have been transformed into a varied and

12

a

b

d

c

e

f

g

h

i

j

k

13

14

15

sensually rich environment, full of interesting yard spaces and individual details. Photo 17 was taken in 1976. In the intervening thirty years, not only had the street trees grown, but shrubs had been planted, extensions added, and yards defined, each in its way expressing as well as enclosing a unique personality. Unfortunately the physical and social landscape around these now pleasant streets has not developed in the same way, and reportedly Levittown residents have been leaving for more secure, if not necessarily greener, pastures.

In the hierarchy of spaces between internal rooms and the street, a most important area is the threshold, which traditionally has been enhanced by some sort of porch. The porch is transitional, structurally as well as spatially, between inside and outside, offering shelter overhead and a raised floor below, but open to the sides. The feeling of being outdoors under a sheltering roof (18) is quite a different spatial experience from that of being outside, exposed to the sky (19). Most animals, when approaching an open place, stop at the edge of the woods or whatever environment has sheltered them, a phenomenon well known to cat owners, who are forced to let summer flies or winter winds inside while pussy pauses between the jamb and the open door. Environmental sociologists and psychologists, and some landscape architects, are well aware of the tendency of human beings to congregate at the edges of an open space rather than in the center. Most of us feel much more relaxed with a wall at our backs. These impulses had obvious evolutionary survival value. The feeling of pleasant security given by an overhead roof or canopy very likely originated in the arboreal environment of our primate ancestors, and of course there is a present basis for it in the protection it offers from rain or excessive sun while we enjoy the feeling of being out-of-doors. A terrace or deck without a roof also enables us to be out in the landscape but above it, securely connected to our house (20). The porch on the street or approach side offers an extension of the built living space out into the social environment, and generally it is also a welcoming transitional area for visitors. On the porch one shares one's house with nonfamily members in a way that is much less intimate than inviting them inside. It is a much more pleasant way of dealing with salesmen, canvassers,

16   Anonymous

17

18

19

20

and neighborly conversations, especially when the house is not in shape for visitors. Aesthetically, the porch presents to the person entering a visible architectural space rather than the sometimes forbidding side of a perforated box. Porches, porticoes, terraces, colonnades are as important to architecture as fenestration and as important to urban design as fences. When we think of the Acropolis in Athens we immediately visualize the Parthenon (21), which functionally is a portico surrounding a comparatively insignificant interior space. The Greeks, blessed with a benign climate, seemed to like to look outward from their buildings. Perhaps the most famous porch in the world is the Porch of the Caryatids on the Erechtheum, near the Parthenon. It is just as memorable as the Parthenon though not as typical.

Until quite recently, almost any respectable house in America had some sort of porch. Nineteenth-century houses were especially rich in verandas on all levels of scale and affluence (22, 23). An economical and at the same time aesthetically rewarding way of creating porch-type transitional spaces is to project the roof and upper floors of a house outward, thereby suggesting its inner structure while uniting it with the outside environment. A superb example of such porches is the Bradley House by Louis Sullivan in Madison, Wisconsin (24). Here an interesting and complex hierarchy of spaces is achieved. The upper balcony, supported on prominent and extremely decorative brackets, is powerfully connected to the building. The lower, less prominent stoop area below, roofed by the balcony above, is a masonry

21

22

23

extension of the foundation, uniting the building with the land on which it sits. In a much more modest way I tried to combine both principles in the approach to my own house (25, 26).

In the American South, porches were traditionally an important part of the urban landscape. Antebellum architecture is the architecture of verandas and gardens at least as much as of interior space. But porches are not confined to homes we consider "architecture" because there the need for shelter from a hot sun and access to cooling breezes was a basic requirement of almost any building in the era before air conditioning. Photos 27 and 28 show two sets of

24

25

26

little girls in Natchez, Mississippi. The contrast between these settings suggests a social distance that is somewhat reduced in recent times, but still immense; however, they also demonstrate a common relationship of human beings to their habitat. Photo 29 is of one of the most serene transitional spaces I have ever seen, also in a place where shelter from the heat is important, but yet in a very different climate. This is the entrance to the house of a well-known writer on American landscapes, built in the semiarid landscape of New Mexico. He is a transplanted New Englander, and such is the power of the self-image

formed in youth that this porch, while highly appropriate both in style and structure to its region, still conveys something of a New England homestead.

The "capes" and "ranches" and "split-levels" packaged by the building business since World War II in American suburbia do have the free-standing quality described by Bloomer and Moore. But, at least when they are new, they are usually short on porches as well as defined front yard space (30). They really are boxes; one is either inside or out, with the consequences for our sense of privacy and publicness discussed above. Builders and developers will argue

that porches are no longer put on houses because people do not seek to have them there. Fashion is often illogical and capricious, and the relationship of behavior to environment is rarely clear-cut. It is often hard to know if a given phenomenon is a cause or an effect. In contrast, most vernacular houses of the world do have porches of one sort or another,

30

even the most primitive of them. Until World War II, most American houses did, too and a great deal of socializing in towns and cities occurred in them. The "piazza" usually had a hammock and several chairs, and relaxing there, with or without visitors, permitted a pleasant relation to the life of the community which was not as private as being indoors and not as public as being on the street (31). One could enjoy the presence and casual company of neighbors and even strangers without any more involvement than one wished. For children, particularly, porches were fine play areas, and much visiting took place in rain or shine, with considerably less strain on adults inside. Older readers may recall the days when one of the ways of controlling the sexual behavior of adolescents was the convention of turning the front porch over to young people when they were courting. There is a limit to what is likely to take place on a front porch (even today), and as a result a very effective but indirect form of chaperonage took place. At present, some veranda socializing continues in older towns and the more stable older neighborhoods of cities, but the automobile has certainly changed things to a great extent.

31

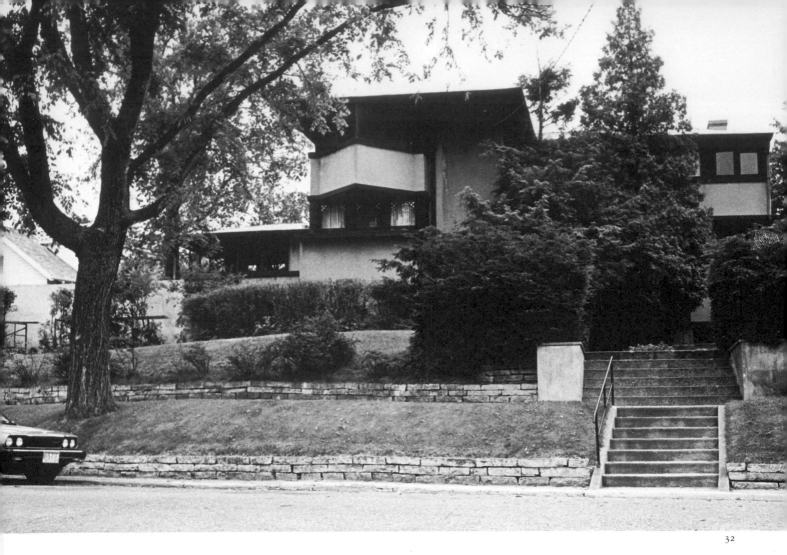

With or without street socializing, the hierarchy of transitions from street through yard to porch makes for experiential richness in the urban environment for house owner and passerby alike. In the hands of a master architect these transitions become works of art. Photo 32, of a house designed by Frank Lloyd Wright in Madison, Wisconsin, is a particularly good example. The vehicular street is separated from the pedestrian street by a retaining wall, a grassy bank, and a set of stairs. From the sidewalk a more impressive set of stairs is flanked by piers which suggest a low gateway and relate the second set of stairs to the mass of the house. These lead to a short paved walk. In the middle of the walk there is a planter (barely visible at the top of the steps) which serves further to separate the house yard from the street, but which at the same time appears to lengthen the walk itself when one is on it.

As with so many of his houses, which take a cue from the Japanese, whom Frank Lloyd Wright great-ly admired, the route to the house is oblique. Passing by and under a shade tree, one may enter a lower level to the left or climb an attached stairway to a second-story entrance. This lies under a projecting room with windows, which in itself almost seems like an enclosed porch and which forms the roof of the open porch below. There is another porch on the left of the house, facing a walled garden, a very private one, and a balcony above on the front jutting out to the street in a sociable sort of way. If the reader will hold a finger or small object from the left over that upper balcony, it will be seen how much more withdrawn the house would·seem without it. And yet this house, like all Wright houses, is exceedingly private. Closer inspection reveals that the front balcony is not now open, although perhaps it once was. In any case, it appears open in a way which permits people to look out on us, but not us in on them.

In contemporary North American towns and suburbs, especially those inhabited by the middle classes, probably the most important yard spaces are not in front but in back.[11] As we turn the streets over to our children and our automobiles, adult socializing turns to the rear, and I found in one study that this is true also in older working-class areas where houses still have front porches. The term *backyard* used to imply a utility area where tools were stored and clothes were dried and children went or were sent. Now the backyard is the first to acquire fences, trees, shrubbery. The porch has been traded for the "patio" (33). The sense of security, pleasure, and pride that human beings find in a piece of private landscape, away from the street, occurs on all levels of scale and affluence, and one can safely conclude that it is found the world over in all climes and times (34). Where space is adequate, the public urban landscape is greatly enhanced if backyard gardens can flow around side yards and are partially visible from the street without being too accessible (35).

33

35

34

36

37

However, in our increasingly crowded and resource hungry world, space is less and less available for such purposes. In attempting to cope with such a world, some planners and architects treat the desire for a single-family home on its own plot of land, no matter how small, as irrational and therefore dismissible, as they do so many other social and psychological realities. Irrational it may be, but dismissible it is not. Failure to consider the human "territorial imperative" has created at least as much hell on the domestic urban scene of most industrialized countries as it has on the international one. If we must learn to live on less acreage, as skyrocketing land prices and dwindling energy supplies suggest we must, the problem is to understand the spatial relationships involved so as to maintain the essentials at increased densities. Other countries which have long had to contend with land shortages, including some of the most affluent countries of Europe, have done this very well, in fact much better than we have with all our space (36). Indeed, poor countries possessing an amount of living space that most of us would consider impossibly constricting manage to maintain these relationships in a way that has considerable aesthetic appeal (37). A venerable and successful way of maintaining front and rear yards, without side yards, is the row house, town house, or, as the British call it, "terrace house" (38). American examples of these are shown in photo 31. It is a type of housing which is particularly adaptable to modern building technology and is used worldwide. The psychological and aesthetic advantages of the side yard, even a very small one, are real, but except on a very large lot it provides little visual or acoustical privacy. Actually, a solid masonry party wall (desirable also as a firewall) provides more, rather than less privacy.

At one time my wife and I lived in the duplex house shown in photo 39, built in the English cottage style that was popular in the 1920s. The twin gables define two distinct living units, essentially three-bedroom houses each, entirely divided by a masonry partition. Each had its separate porch, garage, and entrances on opposite sides. During the year we lived there (on the interior side) we were almost completely unaware of the activities of the family on the street-side unit, but we were con-

stantly aware of the family in the adjacent wooden single-family house. Condominiums, which are usually owned to the center of the party wall, often attempt to maintain the appearance and spatial relationships of single-family homes (40) while permitting more efficient use of land. They are becoming increasingly popular, especially with older people, because they offer some of the advantages of rental apartment units (someone else takes responsibility for maintenance, for example) with the fiscal and psychological advantages of private ownership. However, the sense of family territory is usually considerably reduced unless such units are exceedingly well layed out with that in mind. Collective rules are of necessity imposed on what can be done with the yards. On the other hand, in some cases a sense of *community* territory may actually be enhanced.

38

39 40

When it comes to multifamily rental units, especially those for moderate- and low-income people, the transitional spaces and private territories that are possible for even the poorest of single-family home owners are usually the first things to be sacrificed. In the last fifty years, the worldwide solution to mass housing problems has been high-rise apartment buildings, and almost everywhere the social consequences have ranged from dissatisfaction to disaster. For reasons that will be explored more fully in the next chapter, usually only the affluent seem to be able to maintain spatial and social self-identity in such buildings. To me, the most obvious reason for the generally unfavorable reaction (although it has not been obvious at all to social engineers for two generations) is the separation of interior living space from exterior ground space, or territory. The meager balconies in photo 41 are poor substitutes for yards and porches, or even fire escapes. They may offer opportunity for a breath of freshly polluted air, and sometimes offer interesting, even spectacular, views. But they are not transitional spaces, either to the natural or the social environment. There have been some interesting efforts to humanize tall and/or large buildings, which will be considered later, but for the present I will stick to the low-rise scale which, as is now becoming well recognized, is the most satisfactory human scale.

41

However, even on this scale, the impersonality of decision-making that takes place when a landlord, rather than a tenant, is the client for the architect or builder too often leads to disregard of most of the things that make home-ownership attractive. Consider some of the storage bins that pass for human residences in the town where I live (42). The one illustrated is called Colonial, but it makes the average army barracks look like the home of Paul Revere by comparison. In shape these units are like the little Cape Cod tract houses discussed earlier, only bigger, but size makes all the difference. A group of families living together requires quite another set of spatial relationships from a group of people living together within a family, and little of this is allowed for, at least outside of the buildings. But size is only one of many differences. A more important one is that the residents of these dwelling units have no authority, and little incentive, to act on their own environment by doing such things as putting up fences and planting shrubs. One of my students pointed out that these apartment buildings somewhat resemble the tobacco barns which are such a distinctive part of the landscape in this vicinity (43). But human beings are not tobacco. The apartment buildings do not fit the landscape the way the barns do; the proportions and texture are very different, and the apartments lack the stark simplicity of form which can be beautiful in a barn but which is inappropriate for a house, for reasons already discussed. In any case, one finds Connecticut River Valley tobacco barns only in the Connecticut River Valley; one finds apartment units like these all over the country and, sadly, the world.

This sort of housing is really inexcusable, on any grounds, including economic ones. It is only slightly more expensive, relative to all other building costs, to create rental units like the ones in photo 44, which have interesting transitional spaces and modest plantings, and create an environment more nearly like that of single-family homes. It may actually be less expensive to construct housing like the low-income project in photo 45, which is minimal in terms of architectural details but which has the structured yard spaces that make possible a modicum of personal identity in a collective environment.

42

43

44

45

The economic problems of constructing any sort of housing for people of moderate incomes, to say nothing of poor people, are very real and get worse with each year of inflation. Building architects and landscape architects, with their natural tendency to give matters of aesthetics top priority, are often justifiably blamed for a reluctance to accept financial constraints and deal constructively with them. Designers, for their part, are too ready to blame contractors and developers, whose priorities of necessity begin and end with costs. Much of the bleakness of the residential landscape in our time can be blamed not only on self-interest and indifference on the part of the merchants of living space, but on the statistical averaging that is the basis for so much urban planning in our time and the arbitrary requirements written into statute. Some of what is wrong with both the Colonial apartments just discussed and the Cape Cod houses considered earlier is prescribed by the local zoning ordinance and other land-use laws in the interests of the "public health and welfare." Blame must also be shared by clients, voters, tenants, and buyers in a consumer society whose cultural images are built around objects rather than relationships, on measurable, merchantable things, on codifiable categories and administrable abstractions rather than living human ecosystems.

That the spatial poverty of such habitats is not due primarily either to lack of space or to economic and technical constraints can be seen in the comparison of two planned unit residential developments (known as PURDS) in the same locality. PURD zoning was developed a decade or so ago by architects and planners to provide a legal way of permitting more subtle social-spatial relationships than categorical zoning allows by waiving certain requirements upon approval by appropriate local boards of a *plan*. The PURDS permit designers and developers to do more sensitive and subtle things, but they do not *require* anyone to do them or to approve them if they are planned. And, indeed, it is difficult to imagine statutes that could make such a requirement. Judgment, talent, insight, and empathy cannot be legislated, and planned unit developments require as much of these human qualities in the approvers as in the makers of plans. Both of the PURDS in this case were approved and built at about the same time,

under the same provisions of the same ordinance, in the same town, side by side on former farmland with very similar natural characteristics.

One I will call Rolling Grass, which is similar to but not its real name. In the early years, poor grading abetted by pounding rains and pounding feet caused much of the grass to roll downhill. The other I will call High Hill, also similar to its real name but fictitious. Photo 46a shows the approach to Rolling Grass. Two basic types of building are scrambled into a hodgepodge of shapes and spaces. The two types of building apply the highly developed skills of the packaging industry, as used for such things as soaps, cereals, and engine oil, to the real estate business. The buildings on the far right and in the left center, with the mansard roofs, are the trademark for the "apartments," that is, units limited to a single floor, separated horizontally as well as vertically. The others, with the gable roofs, are the trademark for the "town houses," that is, rental units which combine an upstairs and a downstairs, separated from other units vertically. Why they are arranged as they are in relation to each other is not visibly apparent, if, indeed, there is any reason. The decisions seem to have been made by rolling dice or dropping jackstraws. The grassy yards, which belong to nobody in particular and therefore to everybody in general, are awkward, ugly mounds placed on a once pleasant landform. They were presumably made by the builder's pouring the foundations of one building near the surface, then dumping the fill from the next cellar hole against the foundation wall as steeply as the soil permitted without its falling into the road. The road itself, as a result, seems unpleasantly constricted. "Landscaping" consists of shrubs and small trees splattered here and there, screening nothing, shading nothing, defining nothing, either private or public. One might argue that this environment is somewhat less bleak than the neighboring Colonial units described above, but as we proceed toward the center of the development, we find that it becomes more empty (b). There, the random mixture of gable roofed and mansard roofed units do a sort of country dance around a large, open circle, the unchosen partners bumping into each other rather than holding hands. The space is too large to be a yard and too small to be a football field,

a

b

c

d

e

although it is sometimes used for Frisbee. But it meets the "open space" requirements of the PURD. If one climbs up on somebody's front stoop (no porch) at a strategic point and stands on tiptoe, one can glimpse the surrounding hills, but that opportunity is undoubtedly an accident.

By contrast, High Hill, next door, sits well back from the highway on the hill above a winding road, too far back to be seen and photographed from it. The road enters a series of courtyards, and the rental units there, also called town houses, are grouped in regular and mostly attractive masses, surrounded by a hierarchy of transitional spaces, well defined by planting (c). Some have terraces with garages below. Others have separate garages nearby (d). In either case, the buildings are for the most part formed and

f

g

h

j

k

l

m

fitted to the landscape, rather than the other way around, in some cases very elegantly (e). In Rolling Grass, lack of front yard space is made up for by pretentious doorways facing out on cars parked so that their headlights can bore through the picture windows of the living rooms (f), or out onto the community garbage dumpster (g). In High Hill, town houses face onto small, rather impersonal, but pleasantly defined common yards in the front, with recessed doors forming a miniporch (h). Private yards are either the terraces shown in (c), with cars out of sight below, or patios facing tree shaded open space (i). What in Rolling Grass is considered to be patio is shown in (j). There were fewer groves of existing trees on the original site of Rolling Grass than of High Hill; however, in the former a potentially beautiful wooded bank above a brook was used for a parking lot, not patios (k). In order to create the parking lot, the area had to be filled, adding an expensive storm sewer in place of a natural drainage system. The fill killed many of the remaining trees. The apartment balcony from which photo (k) was taken also looks out on the community swimming pool (l). At High Hill a considerably more lavish indoor pool is part of a swim and tennis club which draws revenue by membership dues and is open to people outside the development. It is perhaps not so much of a community center as the one in Rolling Grass, or as economically accessible to all residents. Still, it is much better located, in an area by itself (m), as the other might have been without loss of availability.

The rents have been somewhat higher in High Hill than in Rolling Grass, but not so much higher as to account for the difference in the quality of the two environments. Even without its more lavish plantings and possibly better construction of houses, High Hill would be a far more attractive place to live. The somewhat more secluded and inward turning atmosphere there might well attract an older and more sedate clientele in a university town, even if rents were equal. But most of the drawbacks I have suggested regarding Rolling Grass are not such as to improve the life-style for any group, although probably some groups tolerate them more readily because they have come to expect nothing better.

Near Rolling Grass and High Hill is a more

recent PURD, which originally proposed to include apartments and town houses along with condominiums and single-family homes (47a,b). Only portions of it have been completed because of problems in the approval of plans having as much to do with social psychology and local politics as with economic, technical, and legal constraints. The units shown were designed to be condominiums rather than apartments, although many are rented. For my taste, they are far superior even to High Hill as regards the fitting of buildings to landscape, although perhaps not in the fitting of people to people. In form and texture they convey a strong regional image, retaining some of the essential qualities of single-family homes. The yards and patios are skimpy even by small lot standards, and in some cases not well worked out from a territorial point of view, but they are well defined and attractively shaped into transitional space (c,d). Nowhere is a resident forced to step directly into a living room from a public way.

However, for multifamily residences in this area, by far my own favorite is a small gem sitting on a grassy hillside overlooking a valley of meadows and a range of hills (48). I like it for the simplicity with which it fits this particular social and geographical landscape. Although it is in the same rapidly urbanizing university town as the others described, its clear intention is to place its residents comfortably in communal relationship to a region rather than to a street. Neighbors are reasonably well buffered from each other in row house fashion with foyers and balconies, but all have equal visual access to a special portion of our unique western Massachusetts farmscape (49). It is an example of good design achieved with great economy of means, both material and financial. Here *landscape* is a noun, not a verb, and it costs nothing. The main problem is a great vulnerability to less sensitive and skillful development that may well occur above and below, but even that cannot threaten its possession of its own piece of hill.

Such residential development will presumably tend to attract people who value such an environment, and to that extent the design will foster a community. Under proper conditions, this can occur in any group of homelike apartment units when residents share common attitudes and when there is the feeling that any investment of energy, time,

a

b

c

d

48

49

money, or emotion in acting upon the environment will not be immediately undone or counteracted by somebody with different needs and values. I recall with pleasure an unusually livable apartment unit in a midwestern city. It was in one of a group of owner-built, two-story apartment buildings, looking out from under shady oak trees to a pretty small park on the shores of a lake (50a). It was located on a dead-end street, separated by a small but well-defined front yard from that most attractive kind of

a

b

Because the service station was well buffered by our pleasant, if not elegant, backyard, it was not only no nuisance but a great convenience. One could leave the car for servicing or repair and step easily into the home; the attendants were known and trusted, and by simply looking out a window one could see if the car was parked and waiting for pickup (c). Across the street was a neighborhood baker and a neighborhood butcher, on the left a small supermarket, and on the right, beyond the gas station, a neighborhood bar. It was on the edge of a commercial zone, on a heavily traveled arterial street, mixing business with residence, in an aging neighborhood, the very sort of

public space, the park, and it had a well-bounded semiprivate social yard in the back (b). Here the landlord planted flowers and some tenants felt free to plant things also, and both collaborated to keep things tidy in a relaxed sort of way. If newspapers or beer cans floated over from the park, someone would pick them up. It was very much what Oscar Newman, as noted, calls a defensible space, but at first there was remarkably little to be defended against. And yet it violated the most cherished dogma of suburban land-use planning. Directly behind it was a gas station, a type of use ordinarily considered in zoning law to be a public nuisance.

c

d

place that used to be scheduled for "renewal," and it was a very good place to live.

However, because it also faced a park, it attracted the forces of progress. A much larger apartment building was built next door (d). Both the scale and the spirit of the street perceptibly changed in a short time. There were many more cars, much more noise,

HOME SPACE: FENCES AND NEIGHBORS   31

and considerably more litter on the streets. There was less tendency to pick it up. The first Christmas morning after the new apartment building was occupied, a tractor clearing the new enlarged parking lot adjacent to the gas station was dumping the dirty snow across the street in the park! Rents in the new apartment building were three to four times those in the older little community. But different proprietary attitudes led to a deterioration of the environment, at least at the beginning. After some years I returned and took the pictures presented here. The scene was tidy and neat and quiet. Perhaps the tenants in the newer units have now settled in and developed an environmental sense for the place. Time tends to stabilize social as well as physical ecology.

Within our local territory, there were most happy relations with the landlord's daughter and son-in-law, who lived on the premises and took care of themselves and us in an easy, competent, and friendly manner. The tenants were mostly middle-class professional and academic types; the son-in-law manager was a sheet-metal worker. The tenants often had picnics in the park and used it in other ways also, but rarely used the yard space except for a little gardening or hanging laundry in the drying yard provided. However, the manager couple held large family get-togethers in the yard in front of the apartment, with portable barbecue equipment and all the works on improvised tables, even though there were ample picnic tables and grills a few yards away in the park. Use of front yard space and even street space in front of houses is common among extended families in many working-class neighborhoods, and in this case it contrasted with the more internalized life-style of the middle-class tenants. But they all knew and liked each other; the family gatherings were relatively few, and there was no resentment. However, contrasts in life-style of this sort are precisely the sort of thing that can cause conflicts and real problems in large, diverse residential projects, where people do not know or do not wish to know each other. The larger and more impersonal the physical environment, and the more diverse the social one, the more fences do indeed tend to make, if not good, then at least less bad, neighbors.

Consistently overlooked in both physical and social planning is the degree to which objective physical activities are shaped and colored by personal and cultural image systems, the most powerful and permanent of which are those acquired in childhood. Although often out of the range of conscious memory, they continue to influence the way we evaluate ourselves, our neighbors, and our environment. Architects and other environmental designers, like all artists, draw on these often unconscious image systems; without them there can be no art. But designers, like everybody else, are too ready to overlook the fact that the image systems of others may not match their own.

The problems of organizing differing social uses of space among differing subcultures in pluralistic societies, where diverse image systems are based on varying life experiences, will be discussed in more detail in the chapters that follow. But I should like to underscore their problematic nature, as well as their importance, by ending this chapter with a personal example of how conflicting images and interests in the use of the near environment cause trouble, even among single-family home owners in communities that sociologists would consider homogeneous middle-class; and of how abstract land-use laws designed to please everybody often please nobody, because instead of fostering structured environments they actually hinder them.

When my wife and I settled down on our own piece of turf several years ago, we acquired part of a sunny, south-facing hillside that was a functioning apple orchard. Our lot included one side of a wooded ravine, which I opened up for an unusually attractive view of a mountain range. The choice was in itself a compromise among conflicting environmental images. I would have selected a mountaintop with a view of three states, which can be had in our part of the country if one is willing to commute far enough. My wife would have liked to be in town. We settled on the urban rural fringe, neither town nor country, but, more rapidly than we had expected, on the way to becoming town.

The stage designer Mordecai Gorelik used to refer to what he called the "scenic metaphor," a visual image which could sum up the essential theme of a play and make it visible on stage. I have found it useful to apply this idea to real life settings as well and have tried to start all design projects with a search for a visual metaphor that will anchor everything in place. My conscious metaphor in this case was the apple orchard. To keep the orchard as intact as possible, we planned to place the house toward the back of the lot, on the edge of the ravine, among some tall pines and oaks. However, the side yard requirements of the zoning ordinance, as the lot was laid out, gave us the choice of either cutting down a number of apple trees or a number of exceptionally beautiful pines. Refused a variance on the grounds that it might "set a precedent" (a precedent we felt *ought* to be set), we worked out with the owners of the house above us on the hill a complicated land trade. This enabled us to stay out of their field of view while maintaining our own, to keep both pines and apple trees, and at the same time to meet the statistical area requirements of the zoning law.

Besides the apple orchard metaphor there were other, less conscious images floating around in our heads. The most important of these for me concerned the hill. I suspect people who grow up in the country or at least spend a lot of time in it have a different sense of the way buildings connect with earth than those who spend their lives on pavement. It is a memory of the way sod feels under the feet and the way frost acts on walls, a kinesthetic, haptic knowledge of the way water runs over and through earth, of the way wind energizes trees, and sun shapes the microlandscape. Frank Lloyd Wright summed it all up by saying a house should be *of* a hill, not *on* it. Photo 51 is the one we used on a Christmas card during our first winter in our new house. In the summer the apple trees largely hid the house. But that degree of enclosure was unsatisfactory for my wife, who yearned for a more urban type of yard with a fence. I resisted, holding, as designers are likely to do, to my own image. Somewhat later in my mother's house I came across a faded Japanese tapestry that had hung on the wall when I was a child. I recalled thinking as a small boy that that was the way a house ought to be, but I had long since forgotten the tapestry (52).

I shall let the reader decide the extent to which that Japanese vision might have influenced my design decisions. In any case, we were not on the side of Mount Fuji. The house above us on our Massachusetts hill changed hands, and people with different

childhoods and different images of what the environment ought to look like and what ought to be done in and to it made decisions of their own. Down came several of the apple trees and in their place rose a tennis court (53). I surrendered my mangled metaphor and put up the fence my wife had wanted all along.

But again the local zoning ordinance interceded, loyal to its obligation to the public health and welfare. After permitting a twelve-foot chain link fence atop a six-foot bank of earth to rise eighteen feet above our house, it allowed us to mask the whole thing with a wood paling only six feet high (54). The quantified and absolute generalizations of the zoning law decreed that the tennis court was behind the

51

52

53

setback line of its lot, whereas our fence would be in the designated "sideyard," since we had backed as close as the law allowed to our property line to save the trees. The assumption behind the law is one which humankind held for centuries and which some politicians and planners hold to this day, that the earth is absolutely flat. However, in its categorical imperatives, the ordinance fortunately did not define trees as structures. We were able to move a large number of pine trees from the ravine to screen us from both the tennis court and northern winter winds. As a result, our private living space has actually improved, certainly from my wife's point of view (55). But in our opinion the public landscape is the loser.

54

55

However, there is no reason at all to assume the public would agree. The brochures for retirement communities and "year-around living" suggest that a large majority might well vote for the tennis court over the apple trees. In matters of this kind, the comfortable statistics of "majorities" and "minorities" are of almost no help. The ecologist Garrett Hardin refers to the Gresham's law of the environment: "bad uses drive out good." But in aesthetics, *goodness* and *badness* are nearly useless concepts. As the Romans recognized centuries ago, *de gustibus non est disputandum*. Across the valley another family in a more rural setting faced a more difficult, more rural, problem which involved the whole town in a political contest over gun control. The next door neighbor there is a skeet shooting range! One would think that constant shooting next to one's home would be considered a categorical "bad." But the issue proved not to be so clear-cut, and was all mixed up with long-standing cultural attitudes and images concerning the right to do what one wants with one's own land and the right to keep and bear arms. Unfortunately, it is much harder to fence off sounds than sights. When people who like quiet contemplation have equal rights in the use of the larger space with those who enjoy noise and intense activity, those who like quiet effectively have no rights. While soundproof (to say nothing of bulletproof) fences are problematic in the extreme, the answer for most life-style conflicts in a mobile, changing, and increasingly crowded world is to attempt to organize the human landscape in such a way that those with the highest probability of having common interests can have greatest access to a particular common space.

I doubt that good fences make good neighbors; neighborliness comes from far more cosmic sources than that. But they can make neighborly diversity more amicable, and they really make it workable. As Robert Frost says, the point is to consider what one is walling in or walling out. In the case of other neighbors on the other side of our own house, a more nearly similar view of what the local landscape ought to look like enables us happily to share a common lawn in what is left of the apple orchard. The only need for fences is to keep rabbits out of the vegetable patch.

2

Street Space:
To Go Through or to Go To

As porches and yards provide transitions between the house and the outer boundary of the living *space*, so the residential street provides the transition between the local and larger worlds. But contemporary streets are even more limited to exclusively "Cartesian" and utilitarian considerations than buildings and lots. They are designed by engineers mostly to accommodate cars, utilities, snowplows, fire engines, and storm water. In modern subdivisions they often include sidewalks for pedestrians but little inducement to walk. Since in most cases streets are built, owned, and maintained by public agencies, they are categorically public places. But the obvious and essential legal right of passage in the public way (which goes far back in English law) makes no allowance for social territory, local proprietorship, and community identity. Municipal highway plans provide for a hierarchy of arterial, feeder, and residential roads based on traffic flow, but have little regard for different degrees and kinds of publicness. Streets are constructed to be conduits rather than places.

However, from time immemorial streets have been centers of social life for many cultures. They are also, of course, always passageways; the difference is whether they are *only* passageways. The architectural anthropologist Amos Rapoport finds two basic traditions stretching from our own industrial era back to the most primitive societies:

> In one the whole settlement has been considered as the setting for life, and the dwelling merely as a more private, enclosed, and sheltered part of the living realm. In the other the dwelling has essentially been regarded as the total setting for life, and the settlement, whether village or city, as connective tissue, almost "waste space" to be traversed, and secondary in nature.[1]

Before the advent of wheeled vehicles, the connective tissue of the settlement was not necessarily linear, and in most primitive villages and cities whatever streets existed were shared by people with animals and punctuated by squares or other nodes. As vehicles became more important, streets became more like corridors. In modern towns and cities, the noise, danger, and physical obtrusion of motor vehicles have made streets less comfortable for socializing than in earlier periods. Nevertheless, in many parts

36

of most modern cities and most parts of some cities, people still look to the street as a place to congregate.[2]

The two opposite attitudes to settlements in general and streets in particular can be traced through modern cultures in the West. Generally the countries of southern Europe tend to be street oriented, while those of northern Europe, and especially Great Britain, tend to be home oriented. Anton Mestan, a language professor at Freiburg, has told me that these differences show up in European speech patterns. Those in the north speak of returning *to* the home *from* the street, those in the south of returning *from* the home *to* the street. American and northern European tourists have long been enchanted by the street cafes and general gregariousness of Mediterranean cultures. Photo 56 shows a very typical Italian street scene in the Roman suburb of Ostia in Italy. One can guess that the group on the left are northern tourists and the group on the right are local residents, not merely by the physical appearance of the people (which is often unreliable as an indicator of ethnic differences) but by the body postures. Those on the left suggest the somewhat more reserved and internalized socializing of the north, as compared with the south. The group on the right expresses the easy camaraderie of people who know each other very well and see each other often in a macho culture centered outside the home.

The northern European outlook has set the dominant pattern for the middle and upper classes of North America, whereas the Mediterranean pattern has most influenced South America. The North American passion for single-family homes on private lots can be traced in particular to the basic British origins of our culture. However, class differences also enter into the picture. Many working-class Americans have come from southern Europe; Greek and Italian Americans are particularly noted for retaining the lively street life of their antecedents. Not even the heaviest motor traffic can deter it, as, for example, in Boston's North End (57). Ironically, on the relatively quiet streets of suburbs and small towns, where street socializing could be more restful, it rarely occurs.

Nevertheless, it is a mistake to conclude that the quiet streets desired and romanticized by middle-class and probably most working-class Americans are not socially important places or that their only real function is as a corridor. On the contrary, in the mythology of our culture, the very quietness of tree-shaded streets with tidy houses set back on green lawns is the epitome of neighborliness, the symbol of domestic tranquility. The term *myth* is often used to mean a delusion, but as anthropologists use the word it means one of the constellations of symbols and attitudes that make up a culture. Myths may or may not be illusions; that depends on the degree to which they fit, or seem to fit, the physical realities of the environment. Regardless of that, they are probably more powerful determinants of behavior than any but the most extreme of physical conditions, largely because they are to a great extent unconscious.

Among the well-traveled and cosmopolitan members of the American middle class (which produces most designers) mythology idealizes the lively social street life of Europe and elsewhere almost as much as the rest of the people idealize the shady streets of Home Town, U.S.A. But these same cosmopolitans overlook the fact that a great place to visit is not necessarily the best place to live, and they themselves are often voluntary part-time residents of the withdrawn neighborhoods, towns, or suburbs some of them look down upon. I will explore the basic cultural factors involved in where one likes to live in the next chapter. At this point, I merely want to establish that there is a fundamental social aesthetic to both kinds of streets and that although the functional requirements in each case are very different, perhaps incompatible, each can be designed well or badly.

Actually, few will argue over the attractiveness of either the socially compact, street-oriented, traditional European village or leafy old towns. The odious comparison is usually made between these and the spread city of suburbia. And there the myth is often a pathetic illusion.

Photo 58 is of the sort of street that makes and fits the myth. This is in one of those coastal New England towns that tourists like to visit and that the northeastern upper middle class loves to spend summers in and retire to. Where similar streets exist in more contemporary and confused towns and cities, they are often the target of historic preservation

57

58

59

groups, but not as often as they should be. This is what many people carry around in their heads when they visit real estate offices in suburbia.

Photo 59 is of a latter-day attempt to match such a street in another New England town which has many streets such as that in 58 but a lot of other things besides, including a large university. The residents of this city of 15,000 permanent residents and some 25,000 transients hold tenderly to the myth that they live in a New England village like that shown in 58, and there is much discussion in the local press about "preserving the character of the town." Among the means of preserving that character is a zoning law which restricts the location of apartments and commercial establishments, and converts once fertile farmland into streets like those shown in 59. I will not argue that such streets are bad places to live; compared with much of our urban landscape they are heavenly. But I do argue that they have little real resemblance to the thing they are supposed to emulate and that the original is far superior from almost any point of view, except availability. Furthermore, its basic form elements could just as well be provided in the new street without sacrificing any of the advantages of economy or modernity. I think the reason they are not is simply because they are not understood by the modern public, neither by the "producers" nor the "consumers" of "housing," and especially by those who make laws to control both.

To begin with, the street in 58 is a coherent and complex space. It is, as all streets must be, a path, a corridor, but it is much more. It is an enclosed space, defined by buildings and plantings as well as by pavement. The space is hierarchical, with the traditional yard spaces discussed in chapter 1 merging into, without being lost in, the corridor. The dominant form in this case is not the houses, however, but the tall trees (which, sadly, are everywhere threatened by Dutch elm disease). These form a gothiclike corridor for the street, without obscuring the buildings or isolating the domestic domain from the public way.

The street *qua* street in photo 59 is defined only by pavement, a path of sorts but not a corridor. Eventually the street trees will grow up to enclose it, but the clear spatial hierarchy of the street in 58 has

not been designed in. It may or may not emerge with time, but there are fundamental problems working against it. To explain one of them, we must resort to some very simple geometrical relationships that have to do with our perception of space, of openness and closure.

As a rule of thumb, an outdoor space is most clearly perceived as being pleasantly enclosed when the relationship of the vertical and horizontal dimensions of whatever forms it, whether structures, trees, or landforms, is less than four-to-one. In other words the "walls" of the outdoor "room" must be at least one-quarter the width of the "floor" space, and no more than twice the width in height. This ratio applies also to yards, squares, and plazas, but in the case of a street, of course, it is enclosed on two sides rather than three or four.

The most clearly defined space is one-to-one, where vertical elements exactly equal the horizontal (fig. 1). But exact equality in proportions or anything else is usually very dull. The most satisfactory ratio generally is a width that is two to three times the height of defining walls or edges (figs. 2 and 3). If the width exceeds the height of vertical elements more than four times we begin to lose any sense of enclosure. If the height of enclosing walls is more than twice the width (fig. 4), we get an unpleasant feeling of being at the bottom of a ditch. We often speak of the "canyons of Wall Street." In rare cases,

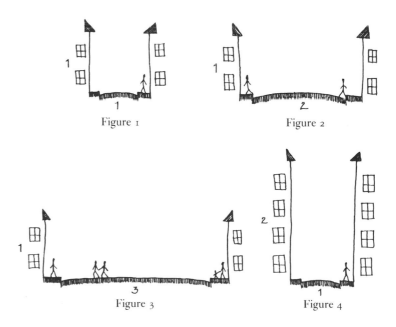

Figure 1

Figure 2

Figure 3

Figure 4

extremes of this sort can produce their own sense of drama, but for daily life they tend to be oppressive and unhealthy. Despite its historic interest, the former Jewish ghetto in Rome (60) was so damp and claustrophobic when we were there that my wife would not go into it with me. The effect of tall buildings in contemporary big cities, where skyscrapers typically rise ten or more times the width of a street, will be examined in more detail in a later chapter. More common and more pleasant for dense urban communities are streets like Hanover Street in Boston's North End (61), where the ratio of building height to street width is less than two-to-one. In these streets there is a strong sense of enclosure and a forcefully defined path, which are conducive, if there are enough interesting things at street level, to a lively street life. A certain amount of compression seems to be needed for real urban vitality.

Of the two residential streets we compared earlier (58 and 59), the first one really consists of two superimposed spaces with different dimensions (fig. 5). In this case the street corridor is defined by the elms, which rise probably 60 feet. The road pavement is about 20 feet with space for sidewalks and shoulders. We have an overall distance between the trees of 45 feet, giving a good width to height ratio of three-to-four. But one sees clearly through the street trees, and the houses provide more of a continuous corridor wall. They are set back from the tree line probably ten to fifteen feet, so we have a total width between the houses of approximately 75 feet. The two- and three-story houses rise 25 to 35 feet, so the general ratio is roughly between two-to-one and three-to-one, nearly ideal. The interplay between the somewhat vertical corridor between the trees and the more horizontal one defined by the houses, which also separates the public and domestic domains, creates a complex and dynamic spatial composition.

Looking now at the newer street in 59, we see small maple trees which may eventually grow 60 feet or more. The street here, laid out according to the local subdivision ordinance, has a pavement 24 feet wide in a right-of-way 60 feet wide, which includes one sidewalk. The trees do not appear to be in the public right-of-way but on the private yards. If they are cared for by their owners and grow 70 feet high, eventually there will be a broad shady street with a

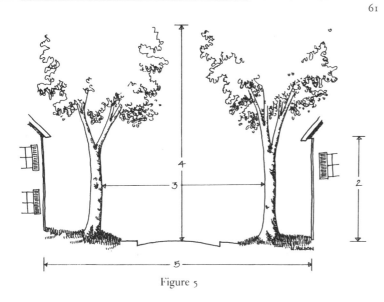

Figure 5

ratio of roughly one-to-one. But that will be more than a full human generation away. At present, and for some years to come, the street corridor is defined by the houses.

The zoning ordinance requires a 40-foot front yard set back to the building line from the public street right-of-way, so we have a total width of 60+40+40, or 140 feet, wall to wall. The height of these "ranch" and "split-level" houses varies from 10 to 20 feet, or a ratio giving us a width to height ratio for the area as high as fourteen-to-one! This is much too great to provide any real sense of street space. Whatever feeling of enclosure the scene in 59 gives is created by the hillside in the background.

A more common type of suburban landscape, based on the same Cartesian zoning principles and the same basic myths, is shown in 62. This is a visual and haptic desert. There is no hierarchical distinction between private yard and the public way. But even from the point of view of the supposedly practical road engineer this street is an absurdity. Pedestrians occasionally cross the street. Children frequently

play on or near it. Posted speed limits are usually twenty-five to thirty miles an hour. If engineers have any training at all in the psychology of perception (and probably most do not), they will know that the wider the space, the less is there a sense of movement and the greater is the urge to travel faster. It is virtually impossible for any driver of a modern car, without considerable effort of will, to keep his speed down to twenty-five miles per hour on the road shown in 62. Except for frequent stop signs, that street is well designed for maximum highway speeds of fifty-five. Here, as in so many cases, aesthetic function and utilitarian function are correlates, in this case, disfunctionally on both counts.

From the psychological and experiential point of view, in such cases the law of the land works not for but against the public welfare. It works against a sense of space and at the same time fails to require the transitional zones between private yard and public street, which can together create a socially cohesive link between houses. Such streets really are, to use Rapoport's phrase, "waste space." Photo 63

62

63

64

65

66

shows another street in that Maine coastal village with which this discussion began, where we have an admirable illustration of an architectural transition between both inside–outside and public–private. Extending from the house near the street is a breezeway (64) which at once serves as a porch leading into the house and as a portico between the public way and a private garden in the rear (65). Passing down the street, one would feel quite free to speak to anyone sitting in the breezeway (as I did in this case, before asking permission to photograph), but would hesitate, and need strong motivation, to call into the garden to somebody one did not know extremely well. And yet this charming house lacks the most basic element which most suburban zoning ordinances consider essential to the public health and welfare, a large front yard. In fact, under a state mandated law requiring citizens of this town to pass a zoning ordinance or have it done for them, an ordinance was adopted which makes almost everything attractive about the town illegal. Illegal, that is, for future development. The street pavement here is only 18 feet wide, and the distance between the houses, shown from the opposite direction in photo 66, is about 45 feet, less than the prescribed roadway alone in the new law. Not only the front yards but in many cases the side yards of these much admired towns are small or nonexistent. How can it be that something so satisfactory can be outlawed in the interest of the public health and welfare in favor of something so obviously inferior? But, of course, this is not obvious.

As in so many cases the answer lies in the assumptions behind the plans that land-use laws implement and the laws that the plans call for. If we want really to become aware of our assumptions, of the "hidden agenda" that all of us follow most of the time, we have to look back to the images of our childhood. Short of psychoanalysis, these are most readily found in the literature (and probably now the video record) of our culture. If we read the urban literature of the nineteenth and early twentieth centuries we find countless allusions to broad streets and stately homes, a reasonable ideal in a land where space was plentiful and people had settled it to get away from the narrow, crowded streets of medieval European cities. They also wished to avoid equally crowded

tenements in the ugly new cities of the otherwise beautiful New World.

For most North Americans the symbolic model was the manor house of the English gentry, neither tenement nor castle, the residence of a free owner of land and a person of importance in town. The term *manor* is attached to almost every conceivable kind of domestic box to this day. If the visitor to the suburban real estate office carries in his mind the image of streets which appear broader but are actually narrower than the ones he will be likely to find, he also carries in his head the model of a house that looks like that in the center of 67. Such houses do indeed call for large yards, although even they do not always need large *front* yards (68). Such houses can be viewed as jewels in a setting, where the setting

67

68

enhances the jewel and in some cases may even exceed it in beauty and cost. But they are usually larger houses, and in any case require broader yards than the 200 front footage which is standard for even "large lot" suburban zoning. The problem of the suburban setting is aggravated because the two- or three-story houses fashionable until World War II have been exchanged for long, low "ranch" houses, which are essentially inconspicuous as the center of any setting. The required large front yard merely accentuates their visual inconsequentiality.

When it is essential to put houses close together, as exploding populations and rapidly inflating land values increasingly dictate that they must be, an entirely different spatial model is called for. Willy-nilly, as side yards get smaller, the houses will tend to form a unit, a wall along the street, and when this occurs it is far more important that they relate reasonably well to each other and define the street as a common setting, rather than pretending a spatial independence they simply do not have. This raises another mythic image, that of individuality, and the bugaboo of look-alike houses. In houses, as in people, individuality and personality emerge through the long slow processes of development that inevitably produce subtle differences in all living things, but always within the context of common characteristics. They are a consequence of living in and acting on the environment. The individuality of the designer can, if he or she is an artist, be transferred to some extent to the thing designed. But the individuality of other persons cannot be designed by any but the people themselves; individuality as such cannot be mass-produced.

Almost all houses today, except the most palatial estates on the one hand and the simplest owner-built homes on the other, are essentially mass-produced commodities. Whether they are entirely prefabricated or what the trade calls stick-built at the site, most of the elements are modular factory products, from plywood siding to prehung doors. More importantly, the designs and plans are mass-produced and mass-marketed through catalogues and magazines. The economics of the construction industry permit only the most modest changes by an owner. Only the very rich can afford to have architects design a personalized home. For that matter, archi-

tects can afford to design custom houses only for the very rich; and even then they rarely make costs but do it for the public relations value, to hook or keep a commercial client.

Nevertheless the need for a feeling of individuality is so powerful that the merchants of housing, like advertisers for other products, work hard at maintaining the illusion, the "personal you" of the TV and magazine ads. To live in a look-alike house is considered the ultimate in depersonalized conformity. But the point is that almost all new houses do look alike, and, as I noted earlier, the only way they can be individualized is through the gradual changes that owners bring about by living in and around them. The developer's attempt to impose a superficial variety by very arbitrary, essentially random changes in materials and shapes usually leads not to individuality but to visual chaos. Since the repertory of arrangements is really very limited, the possible variations are repeated all over the map and lead paradoxically not to individuality but to even greater monotony.

For example, the houses in 69 can be found all over the United States. There is nothing unique about them. In an arbitrary attempt to distinguish one neighbor from another, either the developers or the owners have made one house high, the next low. Beyond there is a poor approximation of a saltbox and beyond that a barn-type gambrel roof. There is no rhyme or reason to these variations; they serve only to create a sense of visual discord. To my taste, the scene nearby shown in 70 is far superior. The houses are frankly similar, and their very similarity unifies the street. Changes in color provide a pleasant variation, but the main source of diversity is in the changes in the landscape from one to the other. These changes may be expected to become much more pronounced over time as people do different things for themselves with their yards. In the meantime the uniform cornice line ties the three houses together, and the two pairs of gables on the near buildings create a pleasant rhythm. Whether or not in this case the unity was accidental or planned, it should be planned, and it costs only a very modest fee to hire a site planner to do it well.

Despite the popular aversion to look-alike houses, the dwellings in New England villages and similar

69

70

71

72

old towns which most of us find beautiful are very much alike (71). In typical pre–Civil War American towns there are at most four or five basic house types. The variety comes from the subtle differences which always accompany handcrafted things, and the unity comes from a traditional way of making them. Such traditions are based on available technology and materials, local environmental conditions, and the collective images that have accumulated over generations of solving environmental problems. The typical New England farmstead in 72 is recognized as being "New England" because house and barns are strung together in a particular way that has obvious practical value in a cold climate. The migration of New England farmers to the Midwest in the mid–nineteenth century can be traced by the existence of similar farmsteads in eastern Wisconsin. The farmhouse in 73 adapts to the environment and available resources and technology in quite a different way. Among other things it is built on stilts because snakes are a problem.

73

machine-made gismos and gimmicks (77). Still, by current suburban standards the street in 77 has a well-defined corridor and considerable unity as a street. The width-to-height ratios are roughly two-to-one; there are intricate transition zones and reasonably integrated scale and texture. Haptically, the street is very rich. And yet, by comparison with the New England, old England, and Scottish streets given as illustrations above, it lacks individuality despite all the technical variety. One can see streets like this in aging towns and cities all over the country.

Twenty years ago, when I was heavily involved in the design of prefabricated buildings, it occurred to me that because mass production technology had taken over the role of tradition as the great urban

74

75

76

The Scottish stone houses on the street in 74 are quite different from the brick houses in the street in southern England (75), a different but related region. In each street, technically very similar houses exhibit subtle variations with considerable unity in style and structure. This is also true of real nineteenth-century town houses (76).

Mass-produced housing emerged in the United States in the mid—nineteenth century with the invention of the balloon frame, wire nails, and improved sawmill techniques. Even a century ago there was already a loss of harmony in the streetscape as craft tradition gave way to a superficial choice of

77

unifier, a fact that was the basis of the Bauhaus movement, we must look to human activities and the landscape itself, rather than to architectural design, for variety. The great fault of the Bauhaus was that it did not sufficiently allow for this. Repetition is inherent in mass production, but living things and natural processes never repeat anything exactly. I became convinced and remain convinced that the real creative design role for modern architects is the way buildings are arranged on the landscape. Really modern architecture is *landscape architecture* and site planning, combined with industrial design. Except for monumental structures, which are still very important, architects no longer have adequate control over building technology.

79

80

81

78

There are two basic relationships of buildings to land which have to do with whether the structures or the landscape are visually dominant. Where the landscape is visible, interesting, and varied, a considerable amount of structural uniformity is not only acceptable but advantageous (78). On the other hand, if the natural aspects of the environment, whether of trees and plants or landform, are sufficiently strong, a great deal of diversity in structures, even of the superficial type, can be accommodated (79). The hodgepodge of house forms in 80 is actually just as mindless and chaotic as that in 69, but in this place, from this vantage point, a particularly beautiful landscape holds them all together. A more artificial landscape can achieve the same thing (81). Nevertheless, a visually and haptically rich environment can provide ample variation for nearly identical tract houses.

82

83

Out in the open range of the American far west, another environmental problem exists. The grandeur of the larger scenery is hard to spoil, but the lack of vegetation in the near ground does in fact allow it to be spoiled with often junky, shoddy structures and general litter that no plant life covers up. The Main Streets of wild-west movies and the half-empty cow towns or mining towns which fit the most popular of our romantic myths are on the whole cheap and ugly, even though sometimes worth preserving for historic reasons nonetheless. Sometimes the rather shacky buildings fit the environment in their own way and create a unique regional townscape that is interesting if hardly beautiful (82). Occasionally a single building fits this landscape remarkably well (83).

A good fit is even less likely to be found in the towns of the Midwest, where the agricultural land-

scape has a special quality of its own (81), but not one that stands out against urban sprawl. The terrain is flat or gently rolling, and the streets tend to be an unrelieved grid, subdivisions of the mile-square land survey system adopted after the American Revolution, a system which divided the whole continent west of the Appalachian Mountains into the giant checkerboard shown in 84. Nevertheless, some of the best of American domestic architecture was developed for such a landscape, notably the low-lying, earth-hugging "prairie houses" pioneered by Frank Lloyd Wright, which, as I noted earlier, have become bastardized into the ubiquitous "ranch" house of suburbia. The rectangular street grid, however, has an unfairly bad name. Among many members of the public and some professionals, it is the epitome of monotony, equated with the industrialization of our cities. But this too is largely myth. The grid street system is as old as civilization, and while it certainly can be monotonous, it need not be and often isn't.

It has its own visual logic and creates its own order or chaos, which is different from that of the curvilinear road system. One can usually tell what parts of a town or city were planned, rather than emerging over time on village paths and ancient trails, by the degree to which they adhere to a grid. Straight lines in the environment are very apt to indicate the work of man; nature generally works in curves, spirals, and dendrites. This is clearly evident in Boston, where, for example, the Back Bay, built on filled land in the late nineteenth century, follows a consistent grid (85) as compared with the twisting streets of the older city downtown (86). There are both functional and aesthetic advantages to both types of street systems. On hilly terrain, street grades and erosion and drainage problems can be kept to a minimum if streets follow the contours of the land, and curving streets can be very pleasant. But the grid is far easier for strangers to find their way around in, and often land and utilities can be organized most efficiently that way. In San Francisco, one of the most absurd

Photo by E. W. Cole, courtesy of the United States Department of Agriculture, Soil Conservation Service

86

87

grids, laid like a giant net on one of the steepest cities in the country, has nevertheless produced one of the most dramatic urban scenes in the world (87). It creates fantastic vistas and some rather scary traffic situations. It makes San Francisco relatively easy to get around in, but parking is problematic, to say the least.

Because of the reputation of the grid for monotony, suburban developers in the 1950s began to lay their subdivisions out with curvilinear streets (88), a policy advanced a century before by the great founder of landscape architecture in America, Frederick Law Olmsted. If the streets are truly laid out with a sense for landform, the result can be both beautiful and efficient. But often they are not, and on flat land the curves can be highly arbitrary and somewhat meaningless. In either case, as anyone who has visited a friend in a strange suburb of this type knows, they can be as effective in confusing the stranger as the streets of medieval cities, which were intended to bewilder invading armies.

One great advantage of the curving street is that it tends to maintain a feeling of enclosure in the background as well as on the sides, as in the picture of the English town (75). However, enclosure can also be achieved with a grid system by using periodic T intersections (89) or by parks or squares. Not only is the grid not inherently monotonous or ugly, it can be pleasing. Some of the most beautiful of our older cities were laid out in that manner, notably Savannah, Georgia, with its checkerboard of parklike squares. As a general rule, it is safe to say that in relatively steep terrain, streets should follow the contours of the land.

But a far less reliable principle states that *buildings* must necessarily line up either with streets or land contours. This works well enough when buildings are widely spaced, but when they are close together it is far better to align the buildings consistently with each other, letting them form a compositional unit which can often enhance both the land and the street by offsetting it.[3] Both man-made and natural forms are thus accentuated by contrast, playing counterpoint to each other.

Even on straight streets an interesting pattern is achieved by placing houses at an angle to the street line rather than parallel to it, as is usually the case.

88

89

STREET SPACE: TO GO THROUGH OR TO GO TO 53

a

c

One of the most attractive little subdivisions I know was built in Springfield, Massachusetts, in the 1940s, with small "look-alike" houses of that time placed at forty-five degrees to the street (90a). One result is that front windows look down the street, *not* into the neighbors' windows, an advantage several residents, all of whom liked the neighborhood, commented on. Most buildings look far more interesting from the corner, where perspective is accented (b), than they do head-on (c). The angled houses also make for interesting yard spaces (d) and a much more haptic streetscape. As in Levittown (built in the same era), people have added individuality to their homes through the years through different plantings, colors, fences, and extensions.

The sawtooth arrangement of housing units is particularly good for partially achieving the effect of single-family homes with attached row houses, whether for expensive condominiums (91) or for low-income housing. They not only enhance the texture and haptic vitality of the surrounding space, but offer large possibilities for transitional zones.

In the area between yard and street, the position of the sidewalk becomes very important. For single family homes or row houses, it makes a difference whether the sidewalk is located on the road side of the street trees or on the house side. If the sidewalk is on the street side, it is within the travel corridor, and pedestrians have a far less personal relation to the houses they pass by (92). If the sidewalk is on the house side of the trees, it is within the corridor formed by domestic front yard space, and the pedestrian, for better or worse, is placed in a more intimate relation to the residences (93). If the community is so located that the street is full of transients and strangers, probably the former is preferable. If the area is one where people feel secure with each other, know and like their neighbors, or at least trust them, and enjoy the sense of belonging to a neighborhood, then the latter may be very desirable. Certainly it increases the opportunities for seeing and being seen. Elderly people, in particular, seem to enjoy being so located that they can see the world around them. If the sidewalk is on the house side of a busy street in an established district and the house owner prefers seclusion, the solution then is to enclose the private yard with fences and hedges. This can provide the pedestrian with a very pleasant corridor of his own, separated from both houses and vehicles.

93

94

But when we come to multifamily housing, a much more complex sidewalk hierarchy is in order. In the public housing project shown in 94, the interior sidewalk, which is perpendicular to the street, obviously does not belong to it but to the residential space of this development. Although it connects with the public sidewalk by the street, only people who have business in the residential community have reason to use it. Here again we have an example of a case where good site planning, which is relatively cheap and may even pay its way, combined with the most elementary kind of architectural design, can create humanely scaled, pleasant, reasonably individual housing units at minimal cost. A more attractive but still architecturally modest publicly subsidized project in Springfield, Massachusetts, is built around a cul-de-sac street. In com-

95

96

97

98

parison with the Colonial or Rolling Grass projects discussed in chapter 1, the streets are of good proportions, and the houses have small porches (95), in many cases arranged around pleasantly scaled courtyards (96). All of several residents I spoke to said it was a good place to live.

If the scale and density are modest, multifamily dwellings can be focused around an internal pedestrian street system of their own, which can become a social territory, or "defensible space." Where most residents have cars some provision for internal auto access and parking is in order, but this can be done in a way that does not turn the entire interior over to parking lots, as so many of our residential projects do. The complex shown in 97 in Ostia, Italy, is pleasantly accessible to and from the street, although there is usually some sort of superintendent looking out for things. In many cities, unfortunately, the gateways to such communities are often locked, thus creating physical fortresses; even so, however, they can retain domestic scale (98). A more civilized private—public transition is maintained in various types of cul-de-sac streets or built around public or private squares, as in Ramsay Garden in Edinburgh (99a) or Louisburg Square in Boston's Beacon Hill (b). In many older cities, residences often surround commercial squares, as in Amsterdam (c). This kind of environmental relationship is also something American suburban zoning considers a detriment to the public health and welfare. Amsterdam, one of the world's most delightful and livable cities, has block after block of medium-rise apartments and row houses facing streets along canals on one side and interior courtyards on the other (d).

The interior courtyard is a worldwide urban residential form that goes back to ancient times. The Greeks and Romans built private houses around an *atrium*; these were excavated more or less intact in Pompeii. As an architectural house form, the courtyard was developed with particular elegance in Spain. But the courtyard works as a social space (100),

100

a

b

c

d

whether for a single family or a neighborhood of families, only when it is small enough to be the proprietary concern of the residents around it. High-rise apartment buildings have had even worse effects on interior courtyard spaces than they have had on street space.

Much has been written in recent years about the bad effect of high-rise apartment buildings on residential communities and especially on low-income people. Probably the most bizarre urban drama of our times, witnessed by millions on television, was the deliberate dynamiting of the Pruitt-Igoe public housing project in St. Louis a few years ago. High among the many faults of Pruitt-Igoe was lack of the various spatial hierarchies I have been discussing: the experientially satisfactory and socially adaptive relationship of fences to neighbors.[4] The irony of Pruitt-Igoe is that it had won an architectural prize a few years earlier and is typical of countless others which convert streets into canyons and courtyards into empty holes, leaving spaces which, whatever the ownership in fee may be, are perceived as the territory of no one. Jane Jacobs was among the first of popular writers to draw attention to the social wastelands that result from the impossibility of experiencing a sense of proprietorship, but it took fifteen years for the arguments to sink in.

I think one inherent problem with all high-rise buildings for residential use is that the interior home space is so completely detached from exterior land space. The technological villain of the piece is the elevator. One leaves the earth encapsulated in a small container, is propelled upward a distance which our senses have no way of measuring, and is deposited in a somewhat more extended capsule, the hallway, down which one propels oneself to home. There are usually no transition zones between the door of the apartment and the public corridor, except for the peephole through which one can peer like a mouse watching for the cat. If the apartment windows face outward from the upper stories, one can often have an interesting and sometimes spectacular view of the surrounding world, but it is only a *view*, not landscape one can feel *connected to*. If the apartment windows face into a courtyard, even one that is elegantly patterned with architectural geometry (101), one has little personal relation to it. Parents of

101

102

103

104

105

young children, in particular, have no way of supervising or keeping track of them, even when the courtyard is policed and patrolled for them by guards. The lower stories of such buildings may be even worse; one is closer to the ground but overwhelmingly aware of those many *other* human beings. The psychological effect of being *below* everyone else is hard on most people. From the street canyon, such apartment units tower anonymously above, visually and haptically inaccessible (102).

One can live for years in such buildings and be unable to pick out one's own window, unless something spectacular is placed in it. Flowerpots may adorn the inside, but are meaningless, as well as potentially lethal, from the outside. Gone are cornices and decorated spandrels which in older, lower buildings distinguished one tier from another. Gone, too, are the often messy but haptically interesting steel fire escapes, exterior staircases which, however infrequently used, nevertheless give us the vicarious feeling of accessibility between home and street (102).

Too often in big, dangerous American cities homes are literally fortresses. One enters past guards, and the visitor must be identified to be allowed across a psychological moat via an electronic drawbridge. For the poor, who have no guards and whose buzzers often don't work, neighbors too often include thugs who patrol, after their own fashion, corridors and elevators. Photo 103 is of a residential fortress on New York's increasingly fashionable upper East Side; the towers beyond the battlements are of low-income public housing in East Harlem. At a distance there is little to distinguish between them, but the social boundary on 96th Street (now pushing northward) is more of a barrier to travel and public intercourse between these populations than the boundaries of most civilized nations.

Of course, in many parts of even our most troubled cities things are not necessarily so dreary and hostile. In outlying sections and smaller cities, moderate high-rise buildings are not physical fortresses to this extent, but unless carefully designed, they tend to remain psychological ones. I once passed the building in 104 with a well-known ethologist who said it reminded him of the mouse habitats designed by Dr. John B. Calhoun for his famous studies of crowding (105).

106

Since World War II, which left the world with an unprecedented housing shortage, the "slabs in fields" architectural theories of the international school were adopted as the most efficient means of providing shelter for urban masses the world over. Outside Glasgow, Scotland (106), they loom over two-story dwellings. They are prolific in Holland, where Hitler's assault on an already overcrowded land was particularly savage. The Dutch are among the most civilized but also the most individualistic of peoples; they are also of necessity among the most environmentally disciplined. They have accepted apartment living, but they don't like it. The Dutch ideal is the human scale village, such as the scene in 107, and that is what most of us think of when we think of Holland. But 108, taken from the same spot turned ninety degrees, is what most Dutch have to put up with. The Dutch are outward looking people; the buildings have transitional space of sorts, and the heights are for the most part, but not always, low enough to maintain some sense of landscape. But the situation is perhaps symbolized with sad irony by playhouses built by children in an Amsterdam park (109) seen against the towers in the background.

107

108

109

110

111

While it is fashionable to blame commercialism in capitalist countries, communist countries are if anything worse in the impersonal way in which they pack the proletariat into the sky. Photo 110 of old Belgrade was taken from a bridge in the middle of the Danube. It is a charming, leafy, Old World city, and Yugoslavia, the most cheerful and open of European communist countries, has done remarkably well in repairing the damage of World War II in the style and scale of the original. But across the river is New Belgrade, a planned new town (111). Photo 111 was taken from the same spot on the bridge as 110, only in the opposite direction. The highly individualistic, ethnically diverse people who make up that nation are used to village scale houses or the low-rise apartments in cities where Mediterranean street life is the rule (112), with varied rooftops and haptically rich transitional zones, even for those living in upper

112

STREET SPACE: TO GO THROUGH OR TO GO TO 61

113

114

stories. But what their planners offer them in New Belgrade is shown in 113. On an official tour, the sociologist who was our guide took us to a new apartment building on the old Belgrade side which was considerably better than those across the river and (like Pruitt-Igoe) had won a prize for design (114). Compared with the others, it deserved one. She explained to us all the new architectural niceties. I asked about the tenants, if they felt a sense of community. She responded glumly that they did not, that they all went their own way with no sense of community spirit. "We are getting exposed to ideas from the West," she said. I pointed over the parapet to the mosaic of small houses below (115) and asked if there was more neighborhood spirit down there. "Oh, yes," she replied brightly, "those are real communities." Apparently western ideas can penetrate only tall buildings.

Of course, there are those who do not wish to participate in a neighborhood or community where they live. Many people have sufficient relationships, both to the landscape and to other people, elsewhere

115

116

and ask only for security and comfort in their residence. I shall return to this subject in the next chapter, but for the present simply want to note that for such people high-rise apartment units may be very satisfactory or even highly desirable. But they are most likely to be satisfactory for people with money and other resources whose lives are full of opportunity outside of their local community. Indeed, for people whose cognitive worlds are based on close involvement with a large urban landscape, who exercise economic, political, or other kinds of creative power over it, the view from a penthouse may make the whole city into a front yard. Although the amount of power life has put at my own disposal has been exceedingly modest, I confess that my interests and activities, or possibly just my temperament, have often led me to feel that way about the outlook from tall buildings. In any case, really well-designed high-rise residences tend to be expensive, partly because professional managers and guards are usually the means of assuring personal security which can be achieved through social cohesion only on a reasonably small scale.

An innovative and imaginative solution to the problem of dense living, one that retained both transitional outdoor spaces and domestic scale, is the now famous Habitat in Montreal (116), built for the 1967 world's fair but also for continued use as a residence.

117

118

Surprisingly the basic concept of Habitat has not been explored more widely since then, because by all accounts I have heard it is a fine place to live. It was expensive to build, but prototypes of new systems usually are. The architect, Moshe Safdie, an Israeli, reportedly denied that he was influenced in the design of this building by the Arab houses of his native land, but it is hard to believe that he was not (117). However, the building has perhaps as much resemblance to the pueblos of our own native Americans (118). Habitat, like the pueblos, uses the roof of one unit as a terrace for another; forming richly integrated and varied private and semiprivate spaces. Although Habitat has a short elevator run in the main core, it does not have the long double-loaded corridors that are the particular curse of most tall apartment buildings in northern climates.

These corridors are more economical than the exterior corridors which the Dutch use extensively (108), but they do not approximate public streets nearly as well. Even in very expensive buildings, they tend to be bleak and surrealistic tunnels, where one is more likely to meet one's own echo than the half-familiar face of a neighbor. Social life will at most be a brief chat during interminable waits for an elevator. The architects of better buildings make an effort to break up such corridors into bays, with comfortably textured surfaces, as in the hallways of Lewis Wharf in Boston (119). But even the best interior corridor is no substitute for an external street. Too many earthbound humans, whose arboreal ancestors were adapted to enjoy the treetops at the most sixty to a hundred feet in the air, are condemned to ledges remote from the environment, suitable perhaps for eagles (120), but not for a social mammal designed by evolution to get around on legs.

119

120

Human beings are so adaptable, compared with other animals, so governed by their native culture and attitudes shaped in childhood, and our cultures are so varied, that it is difficult and dangerous to talk of any sort of human behavior in absolute terms. Some of us are, in a way, eagles, some of us are moles. But I think the fundamental need for social-spatial orientation is as close to a universal human trait as one can get. It might be called the territorial impulse, and probably, as Robert Ardrey maintains, it is in one way or another a territorial *imperative*. In the next chapter I will examine some of the ways the two basically different culturally determined settlement patterns described by Rapoport (see p. 36) are expressed in neighborhood units, which include one or more streets and which, in their own way, also need fences.

In the meantime, I will end this chapter with a visit to an American city which expresses particularly well both of these cultural poles in the attitude toward and use of street space. As every American schoolchild knows, New Orleans was part of the Louisiana Territory purchased from the French by Jefferson. It was first settled by France, but was alternately controlled by Spain; the French and Spanish intermarried and shaped the eighteenth-century part of the city with both cultures. When the Americans took it over, there were severe clashes in life-style. The local residents apparently made little distinction between purchase agreements among far-off governments and military conquest; we were most probably received as territorial invaders. There was little room for the Americans in the original section, a grid on a small section of high ground above the Mississippi, now known as the French Quarter, the old Vieux Carré. Instead, the Americans made their own settlement across the canal, which bounded the Vieux Carré on the west and is now a main shopping thoroughfare appropriately named Canal Street. The new neighborhood became known as the Garden District. Today, both are historic places, and each preserves, with remarkable clarity, the different relationships between domestic living space and social street space.

The place tourists head for in New Orleans is the French Quarter, famous as the home of jazz. To architects and old house buffs it is almost equally

famous for its cast-iron balconies overhanging the streets (121a). It is less famous for the complement to these balconies, interior courtyards where private life is centered. There are no front yards; the streets are given over to public street life, then and now. Family life turns inward in the Spanish style. The distinction between private and public is sharp, and transitions between them are through gates and corridors. Such a gate can be seen in (b) under the projecting balcony near the two pedestrians in the center of the picture. With the busy street life of contemporary tourism, these are now kept locked, and it is hard for the visitor to get into the courtyards unless he knows someone who lives there. I waited for a resident of this building to come along (c); he obligingly let me into the cool and quiet interior, which was filled with potted plants and was the territory also of a small and not very ferocious watchdog (d). During a recent trip I was able to find only two courtyards which were publicly accessible, although many years earlier I had entered several. One is owned by a TV station (e); the other is a popular restaurant and cafe.

Contrasting with the lively street exterior and the secluded domestic interiors of the French Quarter are the quiet leafy streets of the Garden District (122), where homes face outward. This is the prototype of the kind of American townscape which forms the image behind suburbia. Antebellum columned porticoes replace the iron filigree of the French Quarter; these are not directly on or over the street, but set back of front yards, edged by hedges and fences and shaded by street trees, the sort of spaces I have dwelt on at some length. Here, trees are important not only for shade in a hot, humid climate, but as definers of private—public transition zones. In photo 123 they are minimally pruned to permit passage. Side yards are fenced but visible (124). The Garden District seems to be slipping but is still fashionable; both new construction and renovation are proceeding in some parts of it. Generally, porches are retained when older houses are restored (125a,b). But new houses are being built without them (c). At this writing the energy crisis seems not to be taken seriously in that still oil producing part of the country, and air conditioners make shade and breezes passé. And there are Dixieland versions of the human filing cabinets found elsewhere, with decal filigree on nonbalconies

a

b

c

d

e

122

123

124

to give a regional flavor to the ubiquitous modern box (d). The latter project might be called French Gardens Manor.

The manipulation of stylistic details out of context is not new of course; Vieux Carré iron railings can be found behind lawns in the Garden District (126). In one historic house in the French Quarter, a courtyard built by a young mid-nineteenth-century architect is spatially Spanish but American in detail (127).

When style is manipulated in style, the variety can be pleasant and refreshing, even though it can offend the purists among historic preservationists. In other areas of New Orleans, interior courtyards can also be found surrounded by nineteenth- and twentieth-century American wood houses.

One of the focal points of the Garden District is the Lafayette Cemetery. Old cemeteries can be interesting, tranquil, and thoroughly beautiful places. In residential areas their occupants make very quiet neighbors. The Lafayette Cemetery is particularly interesting because in that soggy delta people must be buried in crypts aboveground. The result is an elegant necropolis with complex and intriguing hierarchies of turf space among a rich variety of architectural forms (128). After a rather hectic day which began in the fleshpots of Bourbon Street, my wife and I found it a very restful place to get our thoughts together. But to our shock we found even this place was not immune to the assaults that befoul so many urban environments in our time (129, 130). It seems there is no privacy, even in the grave, without good fences and/or good neighbors.

125

a

b

c

126

127

128

129

130

3

Village Space: Fences and Neighborhoods

As the individual is to the family, so the family is to the community. But while the concept of community is almost universally recognized as a basic human social unit, actual communities are considerably harder to delineate than are families. Nevertheless, there is reason to believe that fences are just as important to neighborhoods as to neighbors, even though the "fences" are often conceptual or symbolic boundaries rather than physical walls or visible edges.

The great problem with the deliberate planning and design of physical neighborhoods is that any social group worthy of that name is a living thing, and one can no more design it than one can design a plant. The most the designer or planner can do is to play the role of gardener, to provide environments where particular kinds of human communities can, like plant communities, flourish on their own ecological terms, without overwhelming one another, and perhaps to encourage the formation of hybrids.

But designers can, I believe, structure the larger city so that those who seek a particular kind of community can find it; and they can enable a particular life-style to flourish on its own terms without adversely impacting another. It goes without saying that fences or arbitrary boundaries in and of themselves will not create a community. But my hypothesis is that the most clearly bounded areas will tend to attract people who actively seek homogeneity, who are already disposed toward small communities, such as ethnic groups, to the degree that their desire for cultural cohesion overrides other needs and objectives.

When most of us in North America think of communities, we think of small towns, probably.[1] As the single-family home on its own plot of land is the mythic image on which the typical American bases the concept of a good home, so the small town is the model for good community. Just as the name *manor* is attached to all sorts of abodes which resemble manors not at all, so the word *village* is attached to all sorts of residential complexes which have nothing in common with real villages. Most of us do not live in small towns but in sprawling metropolitan regions, in central cities, or in suburbs. On the other hand, when we think of neighborhoods in large cities, we usually think of ethnic districts where Old World customs are visibly maintained in New World, but old building, settings. Actual ethnic neighborhoods and actual small towns are certainly very real to their inhabitants, but they tend to be highly romanticized for much of the majority that does not live in either.

The powerful mythic elements of the American attitude to community are well expressed in one of the famous Thanksgiving Day proclamations of the former governor of Connecticut, Wilbur L. Cross, who had been a Yale English professor before turning to politics:

> Now that our land lies fallow once more under the waning sun, quiet and rimmed with hoarfrost, the summer birds gone southward, and the ripe fruits and crops gathered to comfort and stay us, it is meet and right that we remember benefits re ceived.
>
> I, therefore, appoint Thursday, the thirtieth day of November, as a DAY OF PUBLIC THANKS-GIVING.
>
> I call upon the people of Connecticut to give thanks at this time in their homes and churches for the means that have enabled us through another year to live as friendly members of our beloved community; for hope restored; for renewed will to work and share the wages of labor; for the glorious blessings of Health and Peace; and above all for the gift of Freedom—precious as the breath of life—to think and dream and worship, each after the heart's desire. I call upon the citizens of our State to celebrate that day with good cheer like our fathers before us; and with high resolve to return for the mercies of our lot full measure, pressed down and running over, of zealous effort to establish here in our midst, under God's Providence, the ideal brotherhood of wise, just, and charitable men.

I vividly recall as a boy the holiday when this appeared, and my father hanging a copy of the proclamation on the wall of our colonial era farmhouse, which then served as an exurbanite home. The year was 1933! In gray cities across the land, millions stood in bread lines, sharing soup instead of the wages of labor; for them the only fresh crops were the apples sold by the unemployed on street corners. For us there were indeed fruits and some

crops rimmed with hoarfrost under a waning sun, but that was about all. My father, like most fathers in "our beloved community," was unemployed. As I remember it, the actual community fitted the governor's description only very slightly. It was not congruence between the real environment and the one he described which comforted and stayed us and renewed whatever will to work each of us had, but the poetry of the proclamation itself. And yet, if we had lived in a broken-down tenement instead of a broken-down farm, I wonder if this would have been so. In any case, I still have that embodiment of the American dream on my wall. But, as for peace and brotherhood, that was the year Hitler came to power in Germany.

Physical designers and planners tend to share with some social scientists (other than anthropologists) an inadequate respect for mythology as the shaper of environments. Myths arise in the first place from social activities in physical places; they retain their vitality and validity to the extent that they maintain some congruence with the environment, either social or physical or both, or at least the hope of a return to such an environment.[2] Myths shape the relationship between neighbors at least as much as fences, but the relationship is inverse: the fewer the myths that are shared, the more fences are needed. If such a proclamation as the one quoted were issued today, many urban dwellers and probably most college students would greet it with derision. No doubt even at that time many people struggling to endure a depression world—so different from that evoked and promised by the proclamation—did react with cynicism or bitterness. But Wilbur Cross was a most popular governor and was re-elected in a very industrialized state. His constituents must have included a large number of people for whom this was an impossible promise, but who found it reassuring nonetheless, as did my family.

One useful definition of a community, then, is a place where people live and associate on the basis of certain shared myths, or assumptions about the world. This is the definition used by most anthropologists. A neighborhood may be thought of as the smallest form of the physical community in urban areas which include more than one community by this definition. If the myths of any community are only partial approximations of the actual environment, that fact is less important than that these myths become translated into codes of behavior that enable people to live together in reasonably amicable and productive ways. The behavior that results may be largely social or it may involve actively shaping the physical habitat; usually both to some extent. It is also important that the norms of daily life that result from the myths and symbols be functional for the residents, that they satisfy the basic needs and wants in that community. If they do not, eventually they will be rejected, initially by the young, who replace them with new myths in the process of growing old.

Until the social upheavals of the 1960s, a "good community" in the United States was one in which newcomers from anywhere were initiated into the culture of the dominant middle class, and the price of that initiation was the outward disowning of their native culture. This was nearly impossible in the first generation, and old country cultural enclaves formed anyway. But those of the second and third generations who were successfully assimilated aspired to that walking generalization, the "typical American," a creature without ancestors of its own who honored schoolbook images of Founding Fathers, adopted forbears whose real identities had been painted out with watercolors. Thus was achieved the "mass taste" so much deplored by upper-middle-class intellectuals who still acknowledge, somewhat furtively, and equally ambivalently, a cultural heritage east of the Atlantic. Local communities, as cultural entities, continued to flourish in real small towns and in some sections of cities dominated by descendants of Britain and northwestern Europe, while other ethnic neighborhoods became an important but covert reality. The latter were populated largely by working-class people, and that made them even more of an embarrassment in a society which aspired to be classless.

Although industrialization of other countries worldwide has often led to the obliteration of neighborhood boundaries and the mangling of local cultures, until quite recently this havoc has been the consequence of naked economic and technological events, unsupported by egalitarian myths—except in the communist countries, where the egalitarian proposition that equality equals sameness imposed from the top has generally led only to a new form of feudalism. In Western Europe and most of the noncommunist world that was settled before the industrial revolution, people cherish cultural distinctions within as well as between nations. Except possibly in Scandinavia, even the most advanced democracies have few illusions about the existence of class differences.

In this chapter I will consider the formation of cultural groups as the human social expression of the universal tendency of things in nature to form clusters of like entities, which are thereby distinguishable from different entities. The clumping of objects and events into units with shared characteristics, which differ from other units that share different characteristics, is the very basis of perception, the only way we can find any meaning at all in an infinitely diverse environment. The association in our minds of things present with things past is the basis of cognition, the only way we can cope with an ever-changing environment. The egocentrism referred to in the first chapter is the basis of self-identity, without which one cannot identify others. Ethnocentrism, the tendency of people to value their own native culture above all others, is essential to social identity; it is also the only way we can come to terms with cultural diversity, because without a strong sense of the value of our own culture, the behavior of groups whose norms are different leaves us terrifyingly uncertain of how we ourselves should behave.

Environmental psychologists studying the city have been very interested in a phenomenon they call information overload.[3] When people are faced with more information from the environment than they can understand and interpret, they either become very distressed or they solve the problem by ignoring it (if circumstances allow). In pluralistic societies, people tend to cluster in neighborhoods with people who have similar values and codes of behavior, as a way of reducing information overload. It requires much more attention and often is much more stressful to deal with people whose behavior is unfamiliar and therefore both unpredictable and unfathomable. In addition, certain uses of space by different cultures are mutually incompatible. The two different attitudes to the use of street space identified in the previous chapter and the different front-to-back uses of home space represent two very different kinds of community. But there are many other more subtle differences between one neighborhood and another.

The value of a physical neighborhood has not been generally questioned by city planners here. But what most American planners and public policymakers have not accepted until recently is the need for clearly expressed *diversity between* neighborhoods which are *internally homogeneous*. I am not sure most of them have accepted that idea yet; open housing laws and legal assaults on exclusionary zoning which make no allowance for such clustering suggest otherwise. Diversity is still implicitly espoused in this country as a random scrambling of everybody with rights to everything, without regard to different needs, interests, capabilities, and aspirations on both the individual and group level. And, in fact, not only American mythology, but the U.S. Constitution makes anything else very difficult. Our legal system clearly recognizes the right of private individuals to private property. But everything not private in the *personal* sense is public. There is little allowance for hierarchies of public and private domains and in particular for differences between public property on the neighborhood level, such as a local street or park, and that on a more impersonal scale. This too will be considered in more detail in the next chapter.

Sociologists in general tend to scoff at the idea, long held by architects and physical planners, that social behavior can be determined by physical form. Social scientists note correctly that very different cultural systems can exist in similar physical environments and that very similar cultures can thrive in physically different settings. But to say human behavior is not determined by physical form does not mean that physical environments do not influence it and ultimately shape it. As Winston Churchill said, "We shape our buildings; thereafter they shape us."

All behavior takes place in some sort of space, and from an evolutionary point of view all behavior is an adaptation to a physical environment. Ethologists, scientists who make a specialty of studying the behavior of animals in their natural habitats, have indeed learned most of what they have discovered about behavior by observing how a creature uses space. Among the things they have learned is that most animals, and all social animals, organize themselves in groups of limited size in territories and ranges, the boundaries of which are marked in various ways by symbolic "fences." Human beings are not the only animals to create symbols, but our symbolic systems are much more variable and complex than those of other animals. We can use spoken language as a substitute for physical signs, and the relative ease of asking people what they are doing and why they are doing it, as compared with following them around observing what they actually do, may account for the sociological underestimation of the importance of physical space.

The psychoanalyst/anthropologist Erik Erikson notes that because we are such a relatively plastic animal and are so dependent on learned, as compared with instinctive, behavior, our evolutionary survival required that we be obsessively attached to our native tribal culture. We relate to that as other animals do to their *species*, and for that reason he has called this universal ethnocentrism "pseudo-species." [4] In other words, while we may be freer of instincts than other creatures, the most tenacious instinct we have seems to be identification with our in-group. I suspect that territorial spacing serves the same purpose in the evolution of cultures as it does in the genetic evolution of biological species, by tending to limit associations of individuals to those who can develop characteristics adaptive for a particular environment. In other words, Rome is the place where people do what the Romans do, and if one wants to fully experience Rome, one must do likewise.

The boundaries and centers of ethnic urban villages and other types of neighborhoods in big cities are less clearly defined physically than those of most rural towns. Only influential and affluent city dwellers have significant control over the form of their physical environment. Here behavior counts for everything, and it influences the physical neighborhood mainly in terms of maintenance or artifacts placed on buildings or in the street. But the boundaries of a real neighborhood are well known to the residents, even if they are not obvious to the casual passerby. Urban street gangs will beat each other up for crossing a point on a street that is invisible to the rest of the public, who continually cross such points with impunity if they are not members of one or another of the gang societies. In many urban neighborhoods, boundaries are defined only by street names; to strangers, an area which includes several neighborhoods may appear very homogeneous. The sociologist Gerald Suttles found communities in Chicago that were two blocks long and only one-half block wide; they ended at an invisible point in the middle of the street.[5]

The suburb is a type of community which in important respects is socially quite different from either the urban or rural village, although it often pretends to be the latter. Once revered, now maligned, the suburb has become the most dominant form of community in America, visually and politically. The mythic suburb is a friendly small town, but actual suburbs have few of the social or physical characteristics of real villages; they often grow up around old towns, however, and retain some village life at the core, along with many village illusions at the heart. The suburb is not an independent town at all, but a part of the city. It is a sub-Urb. The suburbs of antiquity were composed of villas for the rich and aristocratic, who had armies of servants to transport and sustain them. Modern suburbs appeared with the railroad and exploded, geographically and demographically, with the appearance of mass-produced automobiles.

Contemporary American suburbs are extremely varied socially and culturally, although they do tend to be monotonously similar in appearance, at least when new, for reasons already examined.[6] They range from semirural communities of owner-built or rebuilt houses on the urban fringe to the exclusive modern palaces of the automobile dynasties in Grosse Point, Michigan. The sociologist Bennet Berger was one of the first to attack the "middle class" stereotype with his *Working-Class Suburb* back in the fifties, but it persists, becoming itself part of the mythology of our time, though transformed from Eden to purgatory.

The chief physical characteristic of most suburbs is not enclosure but accessibility. To the extent that they are bounded at all, the boundaries tend to be that most prized amenity of suburbs, open space. They are crossable moats rather than fences. Suburbs differ from real villages mainly because their purpose is to provide a home for people who are essentially mobile, both physically and socially. They seem to me the clearest expression of what Suttles calls the "community of limited liability."[7] The much lamented lack of active neighborliness, while undoubtedly exaggerated, seems to me quite appropriate for people whose lives to a great extent are focused elsewhere. Suburbs are most satisfactory for business and professional people and skilled workers who commute to another place, who are daily involved in social relationships there, and who come home at night for peace and quiet with their families. The last thing such people want is intensive interactions with neighbors, responsibility for community affairs, and the like. They want to be safe and secure with people who share their conventions and myths. These are more likely to be based on class and profession than on ethnic and religious associations.

Suburbs tend to be least satisfactory to adolescents, whose natural tendency is to want expanded horizons, and to energetic or imaginative housewives and mothers who have not managed to find their way into the local leadership structure (as some do) and who find the PTA and church activities inadequately stimulating. It seems no accident that both the youth rebellion and the women's liberation movement of the present generation drew most of their forces from suburbia and still aim their rhetorical artillery in that direction. But as the new youth and mothers go to work in offices or industries, they also either seek out the suburbs or gentrify old towns or old parts of the central city. They are the last to want to participate in the traditional village society, where fathers are near at hand, where paternal authority tends to be dominant, and traditional sex roles are embedded in local economics.

It is currently fashionable to deplore the alleged conformity and superficiality of suburban life, but I see no evidence that suburbanites are any more conformist than any other type of society. However, their social symbols are indeed different because they are designed to permit the establishment of a community by people who have not grown up in identical cultures and who cannot count on sharing with neighbors the kind of myths and values accumulated over a lifetime of living among relatives and neighbors known since childhood. Social behavior based on total life experience is social behavior taken for granted. In real villages a considerable amount of personal idiosyncrasy and interpersonal conflict can occur without threatening the social stability of the group, because the basic values are unconsciously followed. In pluralistic or culturally diverse communities or situations, people assume that the behavior of those from a different culture means exactly what it does in their own, when in fact it often does not. The conventions of middle-class social life, both the urbane social life of the city and the standardized social life of the suburbs, consist of rituals which can make social responses among people from different cultural backgrounds accurately predictable. Such conventions have the same purpose as diplomatic protocol.

Because suburbia is a community of people who are essentially mobile, neighbors are evaluated by externalities: the size of a lot, the trim on a house, the model of car. Where boats are "in" everyone has a boat; where tennis is "in" everyone has a tennis court. In a suburb, people may practice adultery with an impunity that would not be tolerated in a real village, but a botanist who lets wildflowers grow on his lawn may arouse hostility for "running down the neighborhood." These symbols may seem absurd to those who do not share them and pretentious to those whose pretentions are different, but I cannot see that they are inherently more absurd than any other human conventions. For those who are ready to go along with the externalities, suburbs actually offer more opportunity for private individuality than villages do. One of the conventions of middle class life is that it is taboo to be too nosy about other people's business, so long as they maintain proper outward conventions. With the increasing fashion for self-revelation and public psychoanalysis, this may be changing, but it is unlikely to change very much if cultural pluralism is to continue.

The important point for urban design is the need for adequate spatial separation between groups whose codes of conduct are sufficiently different to prevent formation of a reasonably stable and safe community, of whatever type. The purpose of human territory, in my view, is to prevent one kind of culture from obliterating another or creating conflicts which obliterate both. Just as it is necessary for

ethnic groups to somehow define the boundaries of their cultures in order to continue in the polyglot city, so it is important that middle-class places for people with middle-class conventions be sufficiently distinct from various working-class and ethnic communities that they do not undermine each other's basic integrity. This does not mean that individuals within any of these communities must all be of the same culture or outlook, but only that they be willing to respect the basic public norms. On the other hand, the great advantage of democratically pluralistic societies is that constituencies are not isolated from each other, and also that they share the larger conventions of the state, nation, or region and have reasonably equal access to public resources. This other side of the coin will be explored in the next chapter.

In any case, with or without suburbs, the most interesting cities of the world are ethnically and otherwise diverse. As I will suggest in the illustrations that follow, within the most diverse of these, homogeneous areas tend to be most clearly bounded. A number of years ago, when I began to study the subject of urban territory seriously, I formed the hypothesis with which this chapter started, namely, that clear physical boundaries would tend to attract populations most strongly inclined toward cultural cohesion. About that time an article appeared in the *New York Times Magazine* by a young reporter, Steven V. Roberts, who described his return from adult life in California to Bayonne, New Jersey, for a high school reunion.[8] Bayonne was associated in my mind with that gray mass of urban mold which appears to spread endlessly beyond the Hudson waterfront across from lower Manhattan. Ten years earlier, planner Kevin Lynch had published a now classic study, *The Image of the City*. In that study, Jersey City had been compared with Boston and Los Angeles, and it proved to be the least imageable of the three because, among other things, it was devoid of clear boundaries and landmarks. I had always thought of Bayonne as part of Jersey City—or Newark, or something. But what Roberts described sounded like a very cohesive, ethnic community with distinct but sociably interactive groups of Jews, Irish, Italians, and Slavs. I thought, "There goes my hypothesis," but decided to take a look at Bayonne. I

a

b

c

started driving through Jersey City asking where the center of that city was. People looked at me strangely. "What center?" I got such answers as that there were stores over there or some public buildings somewhere else, and so forth. Nobody could tell me where Jersey City began or ended; Kevin Lynch was right. But my map did indeed show that Bayonne

was a peninsula, and it appeared to be separated from Jersey City by the New Jersey Turnpike. I headed south through Jersey City on John F. Kennedy Boulevard, and as I went along I asked the way to Bayonne. I consistently got the same directions. I asked how I would know when I got to it. "At the underpass." When I got near the underpass I

76   PRIVATE SPACES

stopped on the north side (131a) and asked, "Where is Bayonne?" Everyone I spoke to pointed to the underpass: "There." I said, "Where does it begin?" They said, "There, at the underpass." On the south side, they pointed back to the underpass in response to the same question. There was no doubt in anybody's mind about the boundary of Bayonne, although the actual city line lies slightly north of the turnpike.

The ambience of Bayonne is low-key; the streets are lined with wood frame houses (b,c). Overall it is hardly what most designers would call a beautiful town, but it is coherent and interesting. The commercial center is along Broadway, where nineteenth-century wood buildings with false fronts face a reasonably lively streetscape (d). The eastern side of the peninsula is dominated by shipyards and miscellaneous industrial land uses. On a clear day, the towers

of Manhattan loom dramatically beyond; otherwise, this area is a visual wasteland (e). A railroad forms a hard boundary on this side (f), but with numerous bridges to marginal housing on the east (g). The major nodes and landmarks of ethnic neighborhoods, schools and churches, are visible everywhere (h,i). Presumably Roberts's alma mater is among them. The railroad station forms a commercial node toward the southern end of Broadway. The western side of the peninsula is much more attractive, with a pleasant park facing Newark Bay (j,k). A main arterial street connecting points north with the Bayonne Bridge runs by the park, but, perhaps because Jersey City is so confusing that nobody wants to come from there, traffic was not excessive when I was there. The Bayonne Bridge marks the southern boundary with a strong visual landmark (l).

Later—with the help of Dr. Robert Tuthill, an epidemiologist, and Marilyn Brown, a graduate student in planning—I attempted to test in a more systematic way the hypothesis that there is a relationship between physically bounded neighborhoods, social homogeneity, and general well-being.[9] Among other things, we compared the boundary perceptions of various groups in several neighborhoods in Springfield, Massachusetts. We found considerable variation in the perception of boundaries for most of the areas identified by our respondents, but there was unanimous agreement about both the identity and the boundaries of one area, a small neighborhood in the middle of the city. This also turned out to be by far the most socially cohesive and imageable ethnic neighborhood we found in Springfield. It is an Italian community called the South End, very near and at one point a part of the central business district (CBD). It also proved to be the most visibly enclosed.

On its eastern side a series of mostly residential streets dead-end up against a steep bluff (132a,b). These lead off Main Street, a mixed industrial and commercial avenue leading directly into the central business district (c). The CBD forms the northern edge of the district and was the least clearly defined in the minds of the people we interviewed. On the west the South End is bounded by Interstate 91, which runs along the present banks of the Connecticut River. All our respondents agreed that the south-

ern boundary of the neighborhood was marked by a statue of Columbus at a major intersection (d). One elderly lady identified the statue as "the president." When we asked her which president, she replied, "Kennedy." It seems a hero is a hero, whether he discovers America in 1492, or rediscovers it in 1960 (e). In Springfield's South End, as in other ethnic neighborhoods, the visible symbols of the culture are abundant (f). A number of people mentioned a sub-area called Hollywood as a good place to live. It is an architecturally undistinctive but very pleasant cloistered area a few blocks square (g,h), with its own small commercial center concentrated around the Hollywood Cafe (i). The area very closely fits the kind of physical layout which, as noted, Oscar Newman has defined as a "defensible space" (j). Its defensibility was underscored for us by the considerable suspicion with which we were received until we were able to assure the people we talked to that we were neither real estate agents nor people from city hall.

Five years ago it appeared that the South End might be going into decline, but a citizens' council seems to have turned things around (k). I am told by its members that local people have invested a good deal of their own capital in new enterprises (l), and the general appearance suggests that it is well-maintained throughout, despite some conflicting land uses that in conventional zoning theory are supposed to be deleterious.

g

h

i

The hypothesized self-selection of bounded areas by social groups presumably represents the atavistic impulse most of us probably have to maintain ready access to shelter, even if there is no consciously perceived threat of intrusion. This phenomenon can be thought of as an extension to the outside world of the desire for enclosure in the home. It has been observed that in public parks people tend to congregate at the edges of openings;[10] in restaurants also most people sit at tables by the walls and especially in corners, and only choose tables in the middle of the room if all others are occupied. Where crime has been a problem in modern cities, people erect real barriers and form actual fortresses. This is not a beneficent phenomenon; it may be understandable but is hardly desirable from the point of view of civilized urban life. The kind of "fencing" of neigh-borhoods I am discussing is much more basic and, like house walls in a secure community, at its best rather expresses the desire to encompass that which is within than to deflect something hostile outside.

Perhaps one of the most vivid examples of the way a perceived threat from without intensifies and hardens physical boundaries can be found in the famous cliff dwellings at Mesa Verde in Colorado (133). These villages, tucked into the canyon walls, are believed to have been built quite suddenly by members of the Pueblo tribes, who normally live on the mesa top in settlements like the Taos Pueblo shown in chapter 2 (118). For reasons not quite clear to archaeologists, the Mesa Verde Indians left the open spaces and built their towns into the cliff side, apparently to protect themselves from real or potential enemies. These were so well hidden and inaccessible

that white men wandered over the area for years without discovering them. These highly enclosed but outward looking settlements, with sophisticated buildings hugging the larger rock shelter, are strangely haunting, magical places. Only on the Acropolis at Athens and at the pyramids of Teotihuacán in Mexico have I been so moved by the "genius loci." Strangely, the cliff dwellings were occupied for less than a hundred years, and their inhabitants seem to have rejoined the Pueblo nations on the open plains.

It is interesting to speculate on the extent to which these very different environments may have affected the mythology and behavior of the Indian communities. Unfortunately there is no written record to help us. The Pueblos have been among the more successful of the North American Indian tribes in maintaining their native culture against the pressure of the white man's civilization. Nevertheless, while little assimilation and only partial acculturation have taken place, both their life-style and their physical environments have inevitably been altered. Photo 134 shows the plaza of the Taos Pueblo with the church of San Geronimo, an obvious emblem of the Spanish Catholic influence. However, Catholicism is accommodated within the ancient rituals and beliefs of the Pueblos and does not detract from the more important church for them, the sacred Blue Lake in the

mountains above.[11] But a question hangs over the canyon: Is it likely that a Spanish mission church could have been built in the physical and psychic confines of the cliff dwellings if cliff dwellers had remained by the time the missionaries arrived? Might not the physical isolation of the communities have prevented even this small degree of cultural hybridization?

Even where settlements are sparse, they tend to be bounded by topographic features, such as mountains or shorelines (135). The shantytowns that are constantly growing around the large cities of developing countries as the rural poor migrate to them in search of livelihood often appear in ravines or under the shelter of cliffs (136). These do-it-yourself towns are considered by the upper classes a blight on the landscape, and the sanitary conditions are often lethal. Despite that, and without wanting to understate the miseries of life on this level, it seems to me that they have a social-physical structure, as well as a haptic richness, that often puts to shame the slum clearance projects constructed to replace them. Both their social and physical values have been beautifully demonstrated in Edward S. Popko's *Transitions: A Photographic Documentary of Squatter Settlements.*

In ravines around Mexico City squatter settlements of several thousand people will spring up over

135

136

a weekend. At the time I visited one of these in 1973, the Mexican government had developed a program which not only provided sewers and minimal utilities, but also assistance in legalizing title to the land. Inexpensive materials for simple prefab houses (137), along with technical do-it-yourself instruction, were accompanied by an interesting range of social and cultural services designed to provide not merely habitable shelter but a livable community on its own cultural terms.

137

Planning of this type is in marked contrast to so-called slum clearance projects the world over which pack human beings into initially sanitized, high-rise filing cabinets like Pruitt-Igoe without regard to cultural needs and behavior patterns. As noted in chapter 2, people in high-rise residences are deprived of a sense of personal turf, which is so important to personal identity. This lack also seems to affect the ability of residents to develop a community identity, as suggested in the case of that Yugoslavian tower which proved so vulnerable to "western ideas." East may be east and west may be west, but all human beings spring from a common origin in small groups located in large spaces. And the evidence is overwhelming that we still adapt poorly to excessively large groups in very small spaces unless we can somehow compensate by creating conceptual territories not dependent on geography.

I think that is precisely what is done by middle- and upper-class people for whom high-rise living is often quite tolerable and sometimes ideal. They form communities based on professional or recreational activities which can be carried on among groups whose members are scattered over considerable distances. In such cases the apartment is merely a place to retreat to for the most basic of domestic purposes. Apartment towers for the affluent and near-affluent thus become highly condensed in-city dormitory suburbs, communities of limited liability where maintenance, management, and surveillance of public spaces is done by paid professionals who often do not even live in the building. But for low-income people, or even the relatively well-off whose conceptual resources are bound to the village scale of the familiar culture, cubicals stacked around elevator shafts offer no opportunity either for private yard life or neighborly street life and the kinds of *personal* mutual assistance so important on that level. All societies have mechanisms for resolving conflicts among individuals. This is done either from the outside or the inside. If from the inside, neighbors must be able to recognize neighbors within neighborhoods bounded in some way from people who are not known. As Oscar Newman has shown, public housing for people of limited means works best when it most nearly provides for bounded spaces over which residents can hold a proprietary interest.

Even people as sensible and as used to living creatively under crowded conditions as the Dutch have failed to provide for this elementary need. Outside of Amsterdam they have their own Pruitt-Igoe (138). Immaculate, well-landscaped (139), it is one of the most nightmarish living environments I have ever seen. Photographs can't convey the awfulness of scale in this place. I am told Dutch refuse to live in it, and it was turned over as welfare housing to the South Moluccans, with consequences that can be imagined.

138

139

Such places are fortresses which do not encompass social unities but rather make them impossible. They are prisons, ghettos in the worst possible sense. By contrast, the fortress walls of ancient cities were designed to exclude invaders, but contained within them a variety of spatially expressed homogeneous social clusters which were not isolated from each other but integrated by public centers. This is the case, for example, in the walled city of old Jerusalem (140), which has for centuries contained focal points for the three major religions of the Western and Middle Eastern world. Within its walls are four distinct quarters, a Moslem quarter, a Christian quarter, an Armenian quarter, and the former Jewish quarter destroyed during the 1967 war. The Armenians are also Christians but maintain a culture and a sheltered space of their own (141). Photo 142 shows the Moslem quarter as seen from the Christian quarter. The present precarious situation around Jeru-

141

142

salem demonstrates, of course, that walls and boundaries do not assure peace, security, and stable social relations. On the other hand, it is a good illustration not only of the well-known fact that the violation of established boundaries causes trouble, but also that boundaries which are drawn arbitrarily to serve abstract political concepts, without regard to cultural realities, can be as bad or worse than no boundaries at all. And yet these various groups have shared Jerusalem for centuries, and there is good reason to believe that it is not the diversity of cultures there, but the clash of global economic and technical systems, which know no boundaries, with older mythic systems that is at the root of the present trouble. I shall return to that also in the next chapter.

But Israel itself is highly instructive in the ways in which social form affects physical structure. The ecological border between the highly developed landscape of Israel and the surrounding deserts claimed by the Arabs (143) is also a social boundary, but the concept of boundary itself is different depending on which side of it you are on. The anthropologist Edward T. Hall maintains that when Arabs and Westerners talk of boundaries they mean very different things.[12] According to him, it is what they can see that matters to the Arabs, and the worst thing a neighbor can do to an Arab is block his view. In contrast, the transplanted Europeans who govern Israel, regardless of their mythical heritage, view territory in terms of productivity, its usefulness. One of my Egyptian students disagreed with some of Hall's comments about Arabs, but in any case the differences Hall suggests are clearly shown in the landscape of Israel. Wherever possible, Arab houses face outward toward the horizon, while the family space is carefully enclosed with low walls (144). The

143

144

145

146

contemporary Jewish houses in Tel Aviv represent a distinctive Israeli style. Low-rise apartment buildings on stilts, which architects call *pilotis* (145), offer a shady transition zone between the street and courtyards where windows face neighbors, focused inward on the neighborhood group (146). This is a form quite appropriate for a quintessentially urban people who for centuries were confined to narrow ghettos in the crowded cities of the Diaspora. Both the Arabs and the Jews are demonstrative people who like close, physical contact, but whose social outlook is expressed in different architectural relationships.

The labyrinthian streets of ancient walled cities often followed a vertical as well as a horizontal spatial hierarchy. The streets were well known to their residents and were intended to be incomprehensible to invading armies. Such mazelike passageways are well preserved in the old port city of Jaffa, restored by the Israelis (147, 148).

148

147

149

150

The Jews of Israel, whose ancestors for centuries repudiated agricultural labor as symbolic of ancient slavery, now have a rural, small town mythology of their own in the kibbutzim. These collectives are real, if modern, villages in the sense I have described. Although the members are highly educated and often intensively involved in the larger life of the nation, the kibbutzim are not communities of limited liability like our suburbs, but command firm loyalties and a strong sense of collective order. The ambience of the one I visited was very bucolic. Despite communal ownership of property, the territory of the private home is respected fully as much as it is elsewhere (149). At the other end of the scale, there are habitats in Israel as elsewhere that are being constructed without regard either for territorial instincts or cultural traditions. They are devoid of

transitional zones either for families or neighborhoods (150).

Contrasting both with interactive village and the hierarchically clustered walled cities is the home-centered community Rapoport identifies, as described in chapter 2, which has become the basis for the middle-class culture of many of our towns, most of our suburbs, and parts of our central cities. A most extreme example of this sort of community is shown in the spectacular picture by Dr. Georg Gerster of Kirdi farmsteads in the African Cameroon (151). Here the "waste space" between walled domiciles intensifies the feeling of domestic solidarity but also suggests that neighbors are more distrustful of each other than of people in other villages. The boundaries of this village are apparently the point at which no houses exist.

151

All of these examples illustrate the way physical form at once expresses and influences human culture, even if one cannot say that it *determines* behavior in any immediate sense. In the steep, strong, architectural walls of old Jerusalem we have a clear fortification, but while the quarters within are partly walled, they are relatively permeable. The physical symbols of minarets and church spires identify the quarters also. In Bayonne and in Springfield, physical boundaries define but do not isolate, while architectural symbols, with exceptions, do not distinguish one neighborhood from another in a significant way. On the other hand, physical symbols attached to or in the form of buildings can underscore and accentuate cultural uniqueness, as in the Chinatowns of our cities. The most famous and colorful of these is in San Francisco, and its boundaries are well marked (152). Boston's Chinatown (153) is less obviously bounded, as is New York's, but the street decorations make the identity of these places unmistakable and provide an interesting contrast with the prosaic architectural styles.

153

I will conclude this discussion of neighborhood hierarchies with a detailed visual examination of what is for me the most interesting, ethnically diverse, and well-bounded city in the United States, Boston, Massachusetts. The boundaries of old Boston are not fortress walls but waterfronts which, like house walls with doors and windows, also have points of access (154). Over the past two centuries these have been constantly pushed back. Sixty percent or more of the present city is built on filled land. During the first century and a half, the dominant ethnic group was composed of the descendants of the original English settlers, many of whom became prosperous sea captains and merchants. Then Irish immigrants gained local political power, without, however, dislodging the Anglos from their preeminent social position. The Italians came somewhat later, and to ethnic neighborhood buffs, the Italian North End is the favorite.

Early Boston was built at the end of a peninsula, and the North End is at the tip of this peninsula (155). On the south it is separated from the central business district and the relatively new Government Center by an elevated expressway. It is conventional wisdom among urban planners that such highways have a deleterious effect on local residential districts because they "cut off" the residents from the rest of the city. Certainly the effect of such highways often is very bad, but it is worst when it cuts *through* rather than *around* a neighborhood. In the case of the North End, however, many residents oppose a plan to put this highway below grade because they wish to maintain that boundary against incursions that result from the kinds of changes that have been taking place around them.

154

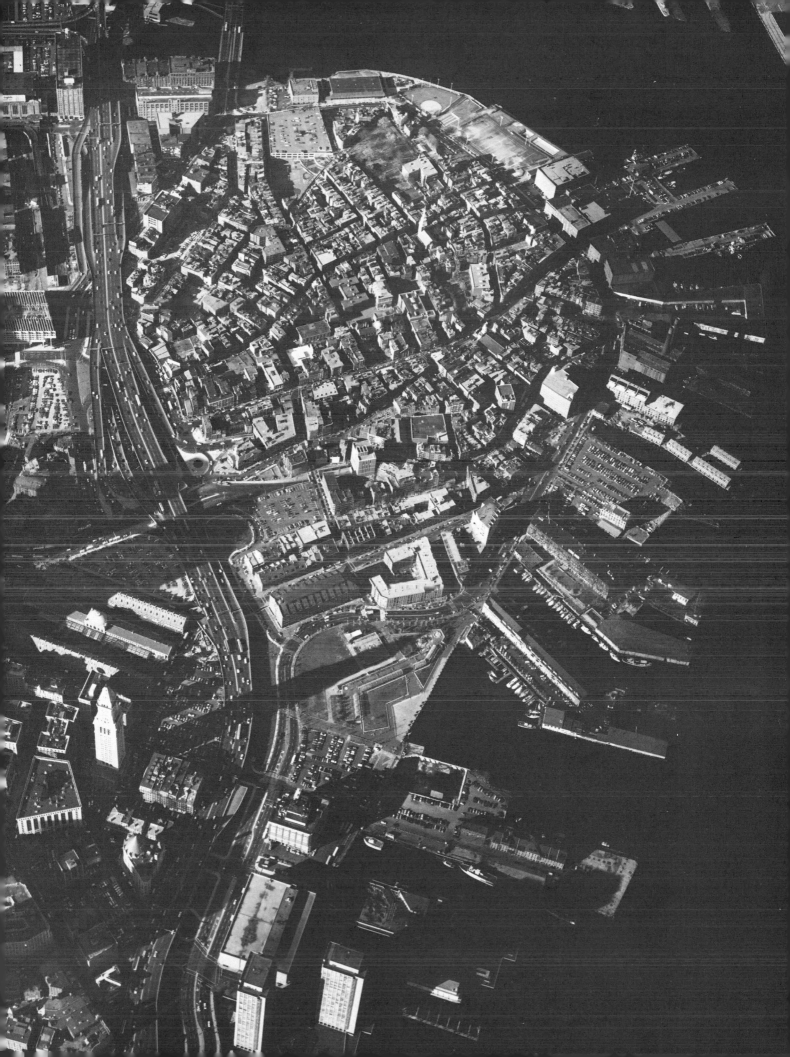

156

On the other hand, the North End incorporates some of Boston's most historic buildings and places, including the Old North Church, from which, as the story goes, the lanterns were hung to send Paul Revere off on his legendary ride (156). Visitors and tourists whose intentions are honorable are welcomed in the North End with considerable hospitality. During the United States Bicentennial, the North Enders converted the highway underpass into a gateway to their urban village (157, 158) and decorated the tunnel with mosaic murals designed by local schoolchildren. The commercial center of the area is on Hanover Street, where historic buildings merge with Italian shops, espresso cafes, churchyards, and

157

158

159
160

161

other symbols of the local culture and life-style (159). At the northern end of the district is Copps Hill Burying Ground (160), from which can be seen the Bunker Hill Monument and the *U.S.S. Constitution* on the other side of the Charles River estuary (161). Eastward on Hull Street the spire of the Old North Church shines its symbolic lantern over the environment (162), and to the south, rising beyond a marvelously enclosed large playground, are the shafts of downtown redevelopment alongside the Old Custom House tower (163). Lively graffiti decorate the old brick walls (164). Men play cards in the park (165) under the shadow of Paul Revere, quite undisturbed by armies of tourists (166).

163

162

164

165

166

Villages in general tend to be hospitable to visitors so long as the visitors don't plan to stay and settle down in large numbers, thereby threatening to upset the local economic and political structure. In the 1960s the North Enders waged a successful war against the danger that redevelopment might bulldoze the old buildings and stores and replace them with high-rise, high-income apartments, as they did in the once similar West End, memorialized by Herbert Gans in his *Urban Villagers*. Having convinced local planners and the general populace that the North End was not a slum, but on the contrary a vital and interesting community, residents now face the opposite problem. The area has gotten such a good reputation as a place to live that all sorts of upper-middle-income people have moved in or would like to. This threatens to drive rents up and drive the local residents out. The process has been encouraged by imaginative, but expensive, redevelopment of the waterfront on the harbor side. The old wharves have been converted into luxurious condominiums (167), old warehouses into boutiques, and an extensive waterfront park has been built (168). The old Italian Haymarket, where vendors sell fresh fruit and vegetables on the street, still draws large crowds at the edge of the Government Center (169), but it is considerably constricted. The once dilapidated Greek revival Quincy Market, behind Faneuil Hall, which Italian vendors of fish and meat formerly used, has now been lavishly and famously restored (170), competing in interest, if not in prices, with what is left of the old Haymarket. The traditional North Enders are worried and have every reason to worry because there is apparently no legal or practical defense against this type of economic invasion. As with natural landscapes, so with social landscapes: their very attractiveness brings large numbers of people, whose presence there endangers the very qualities that draw them in the first place.

Irish South Boston is not so glamorous in the public mind these days. It is farther from the city center and somewhat more isolated, and it lacks the numerous points of historic interest that draw tourists to the "Freedom Trail" which runs through the North End. However, it commands the same fierce ethnic loyalties on the part of its inhabitants, and, for insiders at least, it seems also to be a safe and

a

b

c

interesting place to live. It too is on a peninsula,
bounded on three sides by water. South Boston can
be seen in the far right center of 171a. On the
northern side there are naval yards and a conglomer-
ation of industrial land uses, very like Bayonne, and
to the east and south there is a waterfront park and a
sandy beach (b). On the westerly land side, the area

d

is isolated by a canal as well as by the Southeast Expressway. The residential landscape is composed mainly of the "triple-decker" wood frame houses that, like those of Bayonne, are typical of so many American working-class neighborhoods. The lines of the houses are pleasantly punctuated by church spires (c). The ambience is much less dense and much less intense than in the North End, but there is a strong sense of community life nevertheless. The overall environment has texture and variety and symbols of its own mythic culture. But, as happens in so many other ethnic constituencies which gain political power, its inhabitants impose some of these, visually and politically, on the larger urban environment, where they are not so widely shared; in fact, they are fervently opposed by many (d).

On the Charles River side of the city is the most prestigious, venerable, and affluent of Boston's ethnic neighborhoods, Beacon Hill. Beacon Street, facing the Boston Common (172), is still among America's most fashionable addresses. Beacon Hill also includes Charles Bulfinch's famous statehouse, which together with legislative office buildings forms the southeastern corner of the neighborhood (173). North of that area, the high-rise apartment buildings which replaced the West End of Gans's urban village

172

173

(174) cut off the view of the river and Charlestown. But toward the west, Beacon Hill's quiet streets with red-brick sidewalks and elegant town houses (175) slope down to the Charles River Basin (176). A particularly charming nucleus of Beacon Hill is Louisburg Square, patterned on the London model (177). Compared with the streets of both the North End and South Boston, these streets are relatively quiet and empty. They express the house-oriented, internalized life-style referred to earlier, but Beacon Hill is no less a community for that, and there is the distinct feeling that anyone with bad intentions would be observed. One can imagine genteel elderly ladies peering out behind lace curtains, although in fact there is a younger population there now, and increasing numbers of students are moving in, especially on the lower side.

174

175   176

177

178

179

Boston's Back Bay, stretching southwest from the Boston Common and Public Garden along the Charles River Basin on filled land, was the center of late nineteenth-century affluence (178). Down the center, like a spine, runs Commonwealth Avenue. This area, still physically a neighborhood, has become a center of student life (179).

Perhaps the most interesting of Boston's neighborhoods in terms of boundaries and ethnicity is the South End, the outwardly unspectacular area adjacent to South Boston (but not to be confused with it). Part of the South End is shown in the foreground of 171a. This area contains a number of neighborhoods within a neighborhood. Its overall boundaries are in fact so sharp and hard that until quite recently it remained a low-income pocket, despite the fact that it was built in the mid–nineteenth century as a planned community with elegant bowfront town houses for the wealthy, like the Back Bay. It was isolated from the central city on the north and west by a railroad (180) and this barrier was augmented in mid–twentieth century by the Massachusetts Turnpike (181). The eastern boundary of the South End is the Southeast Expressway and the canal which divides it from South Boston (see 171a). The southern boundary is less clear; it shades off into Roxbury and Dorchester in the vicinity of Massachusetts Avenue, a major arterial street. Since initial construction of the community in the 1850s, a succession of working-class immigrants who have lived there has included Irish, Jews, Syrians, Greeks, Italians, Chinese, Portuguese, West Indians, American blacks, and Puerto Ricans. It is a fine example of the persistent tendency of people in a socially diverse community to form culturally homogeneous clusters, or subneighborhoods. It strongly supports my hypothesis that healthy urban diversity depends on such clustering and not on indiscriminate and involuntary mixing based on "representational" statistics. According to one lifelong resident, the ethnic villages, while remaining more or less separate, got along reasonably well together, united in a community of poverty. As this resident is quoted by the Boston Redevelopment Authority, "They were all together. . . . You didn't have any more than me. That made you equal."

180

181

182

At the turn of the century, the South End had become the largest lodging house district in the United States, with more people than the entire 1970 population of South Boston crowded into rooming houses, especially along Tremont Street (182). As a result, the whole area gained an unfair reputation as a red-light district and general den of iniquity. Actually, large sections had remained stable working-class neighborhoods which, like the North End, were regarded by planners of the time as slums because they were crowded and failed to meet the visible standards of the middle class. By the 1950s the physical environment had become badly deteriorated, despite strong loyalties among its residents. The changing public outlook toward low-income communities of the innercity which emerged in the next decade, combined with strong local efforts, led to massive renewal programs of various types, both privately and publicly funded, some successful, some

183

185

184

186

187

not. The Christian Syrians maintain a strong ethnic identity in their area (183). As in the North End, the church is a visible source of community cohesion. At the northern tip of the South End, across from official Chinatown, is a Chinese residential section (184).

A great deal of publicly funded housing has been built. The Castle Square project, rammed between the Syrian and Chinese communities of the South End and Chinatown proper, seems bleak and cold (185,186). But a pleasantly scaled project south on Shawmut Avenue inhabited largely by Puerto Ricans, designed and managed with local participation, appears to be very successful and well liked by its residents (187, 188). A less successful project near the southern end of the district stands like a prison in a virtual wasteland (189). Here the church has been vandalized and does not look like a unifying community symbol.

190

188

191

189

However, the South End is beginning to encounter the problems of success which have been experienced by the people of the North End. Middle-class people who enjoy ethnic diversity and urban liveliness discovered the elegant nineteenth-century town houses and began to rehabilitate them (190, 191). At first they were welcomed by local people as a sign of a new interest on the part of the city in their complex community. But now many local people are having second thoughts, as economic pressures make it increasingly difficult for the working-class residents to stay in their own neighborhoods. The term *gentrification* has emerged to describe this process in a not very favorable light. This is the dilemma that results from all successful attempts to rejuvenate old cities. The efforts of urban planners in the 1950s and 1960s to stop the so-called flight of the middle classes to the suburbs have to a surprising extent been successful in the 1970s, despite recession and retrenchment of federal programs. The results led Vernon Jordan, one of the major spokesmen for inner-city blacks, to lock horns with President Jimmy Carter very early in his administration over his urban policy. Jordan claimed that federal programs which once ignored old neighborhoods, leaving them in squalor to the poor, now rehabilitate them for the rich and simply push the poor somewhere else.

It is difficult to know how to solve this problem, so long as free-market forces operate at all. Perhaps it is time to look at certain types of social neighborhoods the way ecologists look at valuable natural areas and historic preservationists look at physical neighborhoods and buildings, including them in the National Park Service Register of National Landmarks. Perhaps, too, some system should be worked out to provide special proprietary rights, with subsidies as needed, to lifelong residents of stable communities. Most federal help to low- and moderate-income people is aimed at those who cannot help themselves. I am not questioning the need for such help, but more effort is needed on behalf of those who would help themselves with a little more protection against invasion by outsiders who can afford to outbid them for the results of their own efforts. It is time to view community cohesion and self-identity in and of themselves as major urban resources. To this end we should be much more careful about obliterating neighborhood boundaries and spoiling neighborhood scale.[13]

Of course, it is important to distinguish between boundaries which are crossable, especially by those within them, and barriers which imprison. If the former can facilitate the existence of a community, the latter by definition constitutes a ghetto. Directly to the south of Irish South Boston is another peninsula, Columbia Point, which until the 1950s was a filled marsh containing a dump. It is isolated from predominantly black Roxbury and Dorchester by the same Southeast Expressway which forms the boundary between the South End and South Boston. In the 1950s and 1960s a large public housing project was built, along with a shopping center, some schools, and a bank computer center. The shopping center was a commercial failure. The housing project has become another Pruitt-Igoe and a social failure. In 1970, the University of Massachusetts began construction of its "Boston Campus" on Columbia Point. It seemed an unlikely location for what was billed as urban university. At this writing Columbia Point is an outpost containing a residential ghetto and an academic ghetto in uneasy propinquity (192). However, the Kennedy Library, denied access by the

192

193

citizens of Cambridge to its originally planned site, has now been constructed next to the campus. As a result of a number of ambitious plans, the area may well emerge as a viable and interesting cultural center, but how this will be integrated with the poverty-stricken and crime-ridden housing project is yet to be determined, although there are the usual proposals for mixed-income groups. In time a real community could develop there, but if so, it seems unlikely that it will be primarily a low-income one. Meanwhile, the residents of Roxbury and Dorchester have watched these developments with some anxiety, in fear that demand for housing may drive their rents up and begin the process of gentrification there.

Many of the neighborhoods in Boston, as elsewhere, began as suburbs, and, of course, contemporary suburbs are continually being incorporated into the spreading megalopolis of today. Despite a new tendency for some middle-class people to look once more to the central city for a good living environment, even the most conservative population estimates suggest that suburbanization of the countryside will continue unless the energy crisis becomes so severe as to bring all urban expansion to a stop. Evidence from both developed and developing countries also indicates that most people, if they can obtain a patch of land of their own and private vehicles to reach it, will do so. It seems to me essential that new suburbs and new infilling between old ones respect natural social-spatial hierarchies.

194

If I have concentrated on city neighborhoods in this chapter rather than on suburban ones, it is partly because I have earlier stressed mainly low-density design and partly because the contrasts show up more strikingly in situations of high density. The boundaries of U.S. suburbs are often harder to define than those of city neighborhoods. Their very lack of clear edges and centers gives rise to the character called urban sprawl. Differences in the size of lots, the style of houses, and landscaping are likely to distinguish one from another, to the extent that they are distinguishable. Older American rural towns, on the other hand, are more easily identified by centers than by boundaries (193), in contrast to European towns, where land-use controls have been more strictly followed, and both towns and suburbs often have very clear edges (194).

However, I will end this chapter with a brief description of a small suburb in which my wife and I once lived which expressed the relationship between boundaries and community identity as well as any of the foregoing neighborhoods. It was a small, unzoned residential community on the rural—urban fringe near Madison, Wisconsin. The larger environment was not the most beautiful that region has to offer. It included a major highway with heavy truck traffic, paralleled by a railroad, across from which was a dump and sand and gravel pits. On the near side of the highway there were mixed industrial and commercial land uses, including a parking lot for construction equipment. But the suburb itself was tucked into a cul-de-sac up against a pleasant agricultural hillside with a clear beginning, middle, and end. Being unzoned, it had narrow streets without curbs or gutters, relatively small yards, and a mixture of single-family houses and a small apartment building, including a mobile home. The population was mostly working-class, but there were a few professionals and a handful of students. Despite its violations of planning doctrine, it was a very pleasant, villagelike place. People did not visit back and forth very much, but there were friendly over-the-fence type relations, borrowing of tools, and so forth; we had the feeling that in the event of trouble the community would come together and that anyone could count on help in an emergency. People fixed up their houses mostly on a do-it-yourself basis, planted gardens, and fenced in lawns. I returned after eleven years on a hazy summer afternoon and took photo 195. The neighborhood seemed to have stood up well with time. Nothing much seemed to have changed, except the trees had grown considerably, hiding most of the tidy, varied little houses.

The general feeling—the sense of place—of this relatively new and apparently spontaneous little suburb really seemed to fit the myth of the American small town. There was no particular ethnic quality to it, other than that, no sense of being either a minority or a majority. Despite the noise and pollution, the ugliness and confusion on its approach side, there was a pervasive sense of seclusion and the tranquility of unique ordinariness. It was the sort of neighborhood that can be at once familiar and interesting, where a small person and a small dog can be simultaneously safe and free.

It was exactly the sort of place that zoning boards and planning commissions are likely to plan out of existence in the interest of the public health and welfare, social justice, equality, orderly development, and an improved tax base.

PART II Public Spaces

But all he did was spread the room
Of our enacting out the doom
Of being in each other's way,
And so put off the weary day
When we would have to put our mind
On how to crowd and still be kind.

Robert Frost, "America Is Hard to See"

4

Distemic Space: The Community of Strangers

If the neighborhood is to the family as the family is to the individual, it would follow that the same relationship holds between the city and the neighborhood. But does it? I think not, not exactly. I think, also, that failure to understand why it does not is the source of many human woes, past and present. Although fences of some sort remain important to neighborhoods, it is only as urban life is able to flow beyond city walls that human culture is able to expand. For its most important functions, the real city has that something which Robert Frost says "does not love a wall / That wants it down."

For some time there have been two opposing views of what a city is. One view is that the city is indeed a larger community which calls forth the highest expressions of human nature and of responsibility for the development of mankind. This is the classical view of the city as *polis*. The opposite view, one that has been quite prevalent in the United States and is often, I think wrongly, attributed to Thomas Jefferson, is that cities make community life difficult or impossible because large numbers of people who are strangers to each other hold no sense of responsibility for each other's welfare and remain isolated from "natural" ways of living and relating to each other and the environment. From my perspective, both views are right and both are wrong.

These opposite outlooks affect not only the form of human settlements but the myths that shape our attitude to the environment and to mankind. In the world's religions, the larger view is expressed in the idea that we are all children in God's cosmic family, but this is foiled also in most of them by the belief in a limited "community" of chosen people who alone can reach heaven. In philosophy and politics, the humanitarian goal of the brotherhood of man has constantly been frustrated by communities of special interest. As for the conscious organization of modern cities, the ideal of "comprehensive planning for the public health and welfare of all citizens" has given way to advocacy planning for an ever-expanding array of minorities, often with mutually exclusive interests. The industrial slogan "bigger is better," applied both to places and populations, is being replaced by the postindustrial dictum "small is beautiful."

The recognition of small-group identity as the

mainspring of human society, and the new respect for cultural pluralism that this recognition represents, is certainly a welcome corrective to the proliferation of increasingly impersonal and unmanageable large systems under the control of fewer and increasingly fallible managers. But it is no panacea, either for city planning or world politics. There is, on the contrary, a real danger that we may be throwing out the 5,000-year-old baby of civilization with the dirty bathwater of the industrial era.

In this chapter I will explore the second part of a double hypothesis. The first part of it is that the strong impulse to adhere to relatively small social territories is quite closely related to our sociobiological history as a mammal, and that the sort of community structure described in the previous chapter is a necessary human accommodation to this evolutionary fact. The need for small-group identity will not go away, and all attempts to eliminate it are doomed to failure and will add to rather than reduce the sum of human miseries. The second part of the hypothesis is that we also have the capacity to transcend, *under the right conditions*, compulsive small-group loyalties and territorial defensiveness. The opportunity to make this transcendence is essential to the full flowering of human personality. Provision for the right conditions is the main historic function of cities. Those conditions require that we not mistake cities for villages or allow cities to be governed by village ethics.

Ten years ago when I began my intellectual journey through the scientific landscape of the new science of ethology, the idea that we have inherited behavioral characteristics from lower animals, much as we have inherited physical characteristics, was anathema in the liberal and humanistic social sciences, and not without some reason. Darwinian ideas had been perverted in the late nineteenth and early twentieth centuries to justify the most rapacious and brutal forms of economic exploitation, racial repression, and imperialistic warmaking. Ironically, however, war, racism, and slavery seem to be largely human behaviors and do not follow from Darwinian theory in any direct, predictive sense. Darwin's idea of the survival of the fittest pertains mostly to species, and it is becoming increasingly clear that, while some of our more violent and warlike behaviors

might have been adaptive for us at one time, at present they most certainly are not. Curiously, the debate still rages in some quarters, not over the biological necessity for "dog-eat-dog individualism," but over the idea, as advanced by Edward O. Wilson in *Sociobiology*, that cooperative human behavior may also have been an evolutionary inheritance. Apparently there are people who cannot bear the thought that anything so noble as sacrificing individual needs for the good of a group can have any but human origins. Yet cooperative behavior among other animals is probably just as widespread and just as significant as competitive or aggressive behavior. The fact is that dogs rarely, if ever, eat other dogs, even though they are well known for defending their own and their human masters' turf.

In any case, as I began to talk to scientists and read their writings, the evidence that the social and territorial behavior of other animals does indeed resemble much of our own behavior became overwhelming. But the realization that such behavior does not explain *all* of our own and in fact contradicts some of it was also overwhelming. Not until I came upon the work of two scientists in the U.S. National Institute of Mental Health did the riddle begin to appear solvable to me. The theory of city structure I developed, using their ideas as a catalyst, has been presented in some detail in my book *Design for Diversity*. I will present a brief summary of it here before trying to illustrate it with images of some of the best cities I have seen and known.

Anthropologists have observed that human society evolved through family clans of perhaps a dozen individuals, in tribes of fewer than one hundred. They generally agree that our basic physical characteristics, including the structure of our brains, have changed little if at all since the Stone Age. In other words, we are a creature originally adapted for survival in small, intensely cooperative groups in large spaces. But today, having the same basic biological equipment, most human beings are forced to live in very large groups in small spaces. And yet that change in our social ecology is also a product of the human mind as it began to develop its potential in Paleolithic times. Most anthropologists will agree also that the peculiar capacity of the human brain to form abstract concepts and to develop language represents the quantum leap that permitted the evolution of animal society into human culture. Many social scientists argue that in making this great leap *Homo sapiens* left behind the behavioral constraints that bind other animals. But my reading of evolutionary history is that nature leaves nothing behind. It continues some characteristics unchanged, it reforms many characteristics to meet new ecological conditions, and simply stores others out of sight in the genetic pool, waiting for the time when environmental events may make them useful again.

In all animals above the order of vertebrates, the control of behavior centers in a brain. Dr. Paul D. MacLean, a physician who is chief of the laboratory of brain evolution and behavior at the National Institute of Mental Health, has been studying brains for nearly forty years. He believes that those of higher animals have evolved with three distinct areas that are different in neural structure and influence, somewhat independently, different types of behavior (fig. 6).[1] The oldest and lowest of these he calls the

reptilian brain because its basic structure and function are similar among all vertebrates. It mediates behavior that facilitates survival, such as fight, flight, mating, searching for food, and the defense of territory, all in the most primitive ways. Surrounding the reptilian brain is what has become known as the "limbic system," which is found only in mammals. In humans (and presumably in other mammals) this area mediates emotional feeling. In theory, the emotional responses attached to various experiences provide a memory bank which is larger and more complex than that of lower species. They make possible a far more diverse repertory of behaviors, and enable mammals to develop more complex and adaptable social organizations by allowing much finer distinctions between familiar and unfamiliar members of the same species.

Around the limbic system is an outer layer called the *neocortex*, which increases in complexity as we go up the evolutionary scale (fig 7). The neocortex is highly developed only in the primates and its devel-

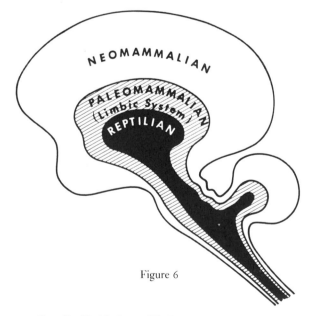

Figure 6

From Paul D. MacLean, "The Brain's Generation Gap: Some Human Implications," *Zygon* 8 (1973): 113–27.

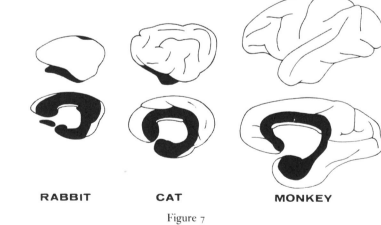

RABBIT   **CAT**   **MONKEY**

Figure 7

opment culminates in humans. In man this area includes the centers that control speech and make possible language, technology, and abstract thought. In healthy persons, these various areas work together and pass information around. Because they do, some scientists question the validity of the theory; but according to MacLean the new cortex can be more or less out of phase with older parts. In particular, the neocortex seems to be without emotion in and of itself. This theory offers a physical explanation for the well-known fact that we can indeed think one thing and feel another and that our emotional responses are often at variance with what we "know" in a logical sense to be true. Supporting the theory is evidence that people who have suffered strokes or injuries to the outer cortex can lose their ability to act, to speak, or to think logically, but still retain intact emotional lives (often painfully so).

It would appear that our small-group identity is mostly a product of our emotional limbic system and that it is in terms of our emotional attachments to *familiar* persons and places that our behavior is most like the social and territorial behavior of other mammals. There is a severe limit to the number of people we can know intimately, probably no more than the number of the original hunter–gatherer band. This is our tribal identity, Erikson's pseudo-species (see p. 73). But we can conceptualize abstractly much larger numbers of people, and thus our new cortex enables us to invent the world community of man. Indeed, as a result of our space explorations, we are already conceptualizing intelligent beings on other planets, which, significantly, but implausibly, look very much like us.

MacLean, in noting the differences between his three mental levels, stresses that in the functioning person they never work wholly alone, and to underscore their interdependence he calls the whole the "triune brain." In order to allow any abstract concept to become emotionally meaningful, we must integrate it into our feeling brain. The problem is that some of its objectivity is lost in the process. In other words, we project (to use a psychiatrist's term) onto the large, grand conceptual brotherhood the emotional attributes of our own friends and family. Thus, sadly, we do not eliminate the ancient tribal ethnocentrism but simply extend it to include every-

body else, whether everybody else wants us to or not. Then, when everybody else fails to respond according to our local rules, we read them out of the human race.

MacLean's colleague at the National Institute of Mental Health, John B. Calhoun, is well known for his ongoing studies of crowding in mice and rats. He has demonstrated in great detail how the restriction of territorial space causes a breakdown in social behavior that eventually interferes with breeding and causes a population collapse, even when food is kept plentiful. Not so well known are Calhoun's theories of how humans are able, at least to some extent, to overcome these density barriers. Presumably because of the power of our new cortex to conceive of abstract relationships that reach beyond the boundaries defined by the mammalian limbic system, we are able to reform our social and territorial relationships by extending them into what he calls "conceptual space."[2] We are able to develop roles within the large human society with which we then identify emotionally in a manner similar to Erikson's "pseudo-species." These roles may be based on religious belief, professions, trades, age, sex, social class, and even recreational activities, as well as national or ethnic culture. In high densities we are able to resist being overly stressed through the expedience of interacting personally with a rather small subgroup, to all emotional intents and purposes ignoring other subgroups. This may or may not actively involve the claiming of physical territory, but when it does not we seem to substitute for geographic turf a conceptual territory, such as a profession, which we defend as passionately as animals do physical territory. In academia, for example, the exhortations to faculty to pursue interdisciplinary research, which is the intellectual equivalent of the world brotherhood in international relations, have been hindered in much the same way and for much the same reasons as have the United Nations peacekeeping activities around the world.

In the typical hunter–gatherer villages there are few role differences, and those that exist are usually between the sexes. Variations in cultural behavior seem to have begun rather early *between* tribes, but there were very few within them. It was not until the agricultural revolution that role-playing made possible significant cultural diversity within a population. When human beings learned to domesticate plants and animals, individuals could produce more than they needed to consume. This led to the division of society into various classes, trades, and professions because the surplus value could support people to do other things. The negative effects, of course, are the well-known injustices that have tortured human society ever since: those who did the most work did not necessarily gain the most benefits. But on the positive side, it freed many individuals to explore other activities not directly related to personal survival, and thus made possible science, technology, and greatly refined forms of art. In short, by allowing for specialized group behaviors, it made the evolution of human culture possible. And, as noted, it enabled us to increase our population densities within a given territory by enabling us to identify ourselves emotionally only with that subgroup sharing our social roles rather than with the population as a whole. Division of labor and the subsequent substitution of conceptual territories for geographical ones coincided with the evolution of cities and are undoubtedly both a cause and effect of it.

Cultural anthropologists, who are particularly concerned with the differences between societies and who generally concentrate on small tribal villages, note that each culture takes its values and view of the world for granted. Traditional societies have difficulty visualizing and accepting other traditions. Not so clear to those of us in diverse metropolitan cities is that we also tend to take the norms of our class or other subgroups for granted and assume they are shared to an extent they often are not. This is probably because so much of what goes on in the lower two levels of our brain is not conscious because we have learned what we know so long ago that we have forgotten that we learned it. We take for granted all the various ways we use space, position ourselves within it, and define boundaries between public and private domains. Edward T. Hall has coined the term *proxemics* to refer to the culturally specific ways in which various groups use space. Since he wrote a fairly well known book on the subject, the term has become familiar to some architects and most environmental psychologists, although it is not exactly a household word. As it is often

used, it refers to any personal use of space and to the effect of space on people. But Hall defined it quite specifically to refer to "theories of man's use of space as a specialized elaboration of culture."

I have taken the term *proxemic* as an adjective to describe the various kinds of culturally homogeneous urban and rural villages and city neighborhoods discussed in the previous chapter as well as certain other types of small group associations in space. Obviously, if much spatial behavior is unconscious and taken for granted, there is likely to be less conflict if people of the same culture primarily share and control a given area. But there are large and important spaces in all real cities which are used by diverse people of many cultures and subcultures and cannot properly be considered the turf of any group. The farther we are removed from environments and social relationships which we have known since childhood, the more we must rely on abstract communication and rationally directed activities. Those parts of the city which are actively shared by people with diverse cultural values and codes of conduct must be readily intelligible to all. They must also be governed by codes of conduct which are consciously directed and followed and which are very explicit. For such spaces and places I have coined the term *distemics* to pair it with *proxemics*.[3]

Sociologists use the terms *primary group* and *secondary group* to refer to distinctions between intimate and less personal relationships. But these do not make what seems to me a vital distinction between various levels of intimacy *within* a culture and relations *between* members of different classes or cultures, and they make little allowance for equivalent differences in the uses of space. Theoretically, relationships within any group much larger than family and close friends verge toward being secondary, even in communities which are quite homogeneous by class and other measures of culture. The word *cosmopolitan* is somewhat closer than *secondary* to what I mean by *distemic*, but it suggests a high level of education and sophistication, and many people associate it with an intellectual and social elite. Real cosmopolitans generally share certain attitudes and values quite intensely, and while they are usually adept at dealing with various kinds of people on the secondary level, they are often quite intolerant of people who do not share their tastes. What I mean by distemic places and relationships pertains to cross-cultural behavior on all social or economic levels, including the diversity of social experiences which are likely to be had by any salesperson, sailor, or long-distance truck driver and the kinds of spaces that facilitate such contacts.

A century ago the German sociologist and philosopher Ferdinand Tönnies published his theory of *Gemeinschaft und Gesellschaft* to describe two different kinds of society. *Gemeinschaft* was his word for those primary group associations, based first of all on the family, which are dependent on mutual sympathy and understanding, on shared attitudes and needs. The epitome of the gemeinschaft society was the peasant village, where shared values also included land, or territory. Members of gemeinschaft communities did not act in self-interest alone, but for the pleasure of serving the community welfare. Its essential element was a common will. Gesellschaft, on the contrary, was a form of society which personified the capitalism of that day, in which the individual acted alone for self-interest only, based on rational calculation of the personal benefits to be derived from any transaction. Its essential element was individual will, in conflict with all other wills. While Tönnies was influenced by Marx, among others, he did not condemn gesellschaft, but considered it an inevitable concomitant of progress. However, it seems to have implicitly represented to him a loss of human warmth and psychological welfare; his was one of the first formulations of the much lamented "alienation" which is still alleged to be the fate of modern man. Tönnies was well aware of the complexity of human experience and of the difference between an intellectual *construct* and a slice of life. He recognized that actual people could exist in both kinds of societies. Still, he seemed to have considered them to be opposites and essentially incompatible. In any case, his followers and interpreters seem generally to consider these to be mutually exclusive forms of community.

Despite the obvious similarities of gemeinschaft and gesellschaft to what I am calling proxemic and distemic relationships, I do not consider the latter to be incompatible at all, but complementary. They might be viewed as different stages in Maslow's famous "hierarchy of needs." Because the familiar home culture so fundamentally shapes our awareness of the environment, both social and physical, it is only when we have the security such identity gives us that we can face the uncertainties of real human diversity. On the other hand, it seems to me that one of the more destructive and tragic of modern myths is that the impersonal nature of city life can lead only to loneliness and alienation. Gemeinschaft, or pseudo-species, seems to have an evolutionary device to allow *Homo sapiens* to cope with a degree of environmental diversity few other animals can tolerate. Nevertheless, despite major cultural differences and minor racial ones, we are all one species, with a common sensory system, adapted to a large but not unlimited ecological niche. Although the distemic activities and places of the large cosmopolitan city can indeed be bewildering, frightening, and dangerous if one is not psychologically or economically equipped to deal with them, at their best they offer us a sense of oneness with the rest of humanity that small-group culture, by its very nature, prevents. As I will attempt to show, distemic relationships can both underlie and override ethnic and class differences. But my hypothesis is that we cannot expect one ever to replace the other. The purpose of cities, as compared with villages, is to provide both. Diversity between neighborhoods which are internally similar should be accommodated in adjacent public places in which various people can interact, both as individuals and as groups, in order to develop those possibilities in human beings which transcend local differences.

Of all distemic public places, probably the oldest and most effective in accommodating social diversity is the marketplace. One theory holds that the primary psychological mechanism for overcoming the natural xenophobia of the primitive tribe was the exchange of goods and services. In order for members of different tribal cultures to make peace through symbolic exchanges of objects and to engage in nonlethal competition in the marketplace as a substitute for war, they had to make bargains which necessarily were more explicit and contrived than the local understandings which were taken for granted. A contract had to be devised, and it is the characteristic of workable contracts that the most significant matters are not taken for granted. In the law of Western countries, everything must be spelled out. I have been told by a lawyer who has spent much of his life trying to devise contracts between members of different cultures that this is not true of many other societies, especially those of Asia and the Middle East, where much is taken for granted or taken to mean different things. The well-known problems of international relations are evidence for this. But to the degree that contracts work at all in such situations, it is their *rationality*—that is, the conscious decisions of all parties to attempt to see things as the others see them—which makes amicable social diversity possible. The development of trade, the exchange of goods and services which could stand as measurements of values more objective than the common will of Tönnies's gemeinschaft led eventually to the development of complex legal systems and civic institutions. On the other hand, it does not follow, as Tönnies suggests, that under such situations individual wills need be in continuous conflict. Trade and the institutions that follow from it can be a means of peacefully resolving both individual and group conflicts which under tribal conditions are most likely to be resolved by war. Furthermore, individual personalities as well as group cultures can be enriched by the very diversity trade and its bargains make possible.

In his book *The Social Contract* Robert Ardrey reworks a concept made famous two centuries earlier by Jean Jacques Rousseau. Rousseau was one of the most influential of theoretical egalitarians, even though he was in practice one of the most intractable of individualists. Rousseau's argument was that in order to approximate the blissful natural equality of Eden, human beings must renounce property and personal interests and form a contract which would bind them in a communal society. As Karl Marx, another archindividualist who preached universal communality, claimed to have turned the philosopher Hegel on his head, so Ardrey turned Rousseau on his head. Ardrey argues that it is a contract to form a social order of independent *individuals* that enables mankind not to eliminate but to transcend the instinctive behavior patterns that bind other animals to familiar groups and familiar territory. Instead of viewing man as he says Rousseau did, as a

"fallen angel" who must be restored to "natural" communality, Ardrey sees man as a "risen ape" who has achieved individual consciousness. From my point of view, what makes the rise possible is our rational capacity to deal with members of our own species whose behaviors may be greatly different from our own.

Twenty years ago, Jane Jacobs, in *The Death and Life of Great American Cities*, a book which in its time and way was as controversial as Ardrey's books, suggested that the city differs from the small town because, among other things, its essential function is to make the streets safe for strangers. I would go farther and assert that the city in its essential character is itself a *community of strangers*. It is no less a community for that, but it is a very different kind of community from the neighborhood or village.

On the neighborhood, or proxemic, level we distinguish those who belong from those who do not by observable characteristics. We are also limited to habitats small enough to permit such observations to be made. The subtleties of human facial expression begin to drop off beyond 30 feet, and conversation becomes difficult. Facial features become hard to distinguish beyond 300 feet, and normal conversation is impossible. The human body cannot be seen clearly beyond half a mile and is invisible to the naked eye at a mile.[4]

In the proxemic community, where strangers are readily recognized both by feature and behavior, policing is accomplished largely by social pressure. The punishment for violations of group norms is ostracism, which can be so psychologically painful that it can be as bad as physical torture. I am told that if an Australian aborigine is driven out of the tribe he will simply die; he cannot conceive of life outside of it. In the homogeneous proxemic village or neighborhood, both the social and the physical environment can be extremely complex and yet understandable to its residents because they have learned to know it over a longer period of time, they share its cryptic symbols, and, even when newcomers, they can count on friends and kin to help them get around in it. In fact, under conditions of external threat, as in the medieval city, the unintelligibility to outsiders of a local landscape may be its greatest asset. Because it can be more complex and is the product of special relationships, it can be unique, and the more it reflects the special life of its residents, the more interesting it will be to insiders and outsiders alike. To insiders it will appear logical and proper, no matter how illogical it may be to outsiders; outsiders may, however, find it delightfully picturesque if they are not threatened by it.

The situation is reversed in the socially diverse, distemic spaces of the cosmopolitan city. Because such spaces must accommodate people with differing values, myths, symbols, and cognitive attitudes, society cannot rely primarily on the standards of behavior in one subculture without infringing on the rights of another. Behavior must be controlled mainly by objective, impersonal authority: police, judges, and legislators. But the important point is that, in distemic as compared with proxemic surroundings, far fewer kinds of behavior are subject to control, ideally little more than physical assaults on persons or property. Thus the law, standing above rather than arising from within a society, is an inevitable concomitant of urban diversity, and it must be applied arbitrarily and impartially. The punishment for breaking the law is physical or economic restraint. Because it is not necessary to distinguish stranger from friend in distemic places, they can accommodate large numbers of people, often huge crowds, and consequently the scale can be great. Although such places do not necessarily have to be large to perform distemic functions, they are more likely to be comfortable if there is sufficient room for maintaining personal distance, and ready egress if things get too stressful. On the other hand, since the function of such places is to accommodate people who are not only strangers to each other, but who may be travelers and thus strangers to the place itself, the environment must be far more predictable and legible, at least as regards those details and landmarks that serve for orientation. Both the rules for behavior and the cues for getting around need to be much more explicit and also simpler than in the local proxemic neighborhood.

Perhaps the clearest example of what I mean by a distemic space is an automobile highway, where anyone with a driver's license is free to travel more or less as desired, provided a few relatively simple rules are followed. Even a bank robber in a getaway car will follow the most basic of such rules, such as driving on the proper side, because it is impossible to use the space for long without doing so. On a more demanding level, an airplane pilot from America and one from Japan can agree readily on the design of an airport, while each will have very different requirements in the design of a home. Here again, the rules of conduct and the means of communication are much more explicit in the distemic than the proxemic situation. The point is, they continually involve rational, conscious processes that presumably originate in MacLean's new cortex, even though they may, and usually should, become habitual with practice and eventually become embedded in the unconscious. But they can be learned consciously and relatively fast in adulthood, as compared with attitudes acquired over a lifetime. Anyone with the right physical and mental abilities can become an airplane pilot as an adult, but one can be wholly an American or a Japanese only by being born one.

Nature rarely follows classifications as neatly in reality as in theory. But even in theory, proxemic and distemic places can turn into each other; and a single place can perform both functions depending on what activities we are looking at and who is primarily in charge. The ethnic urban village or historic rural town can be highly proxemic for its residents and distemic for tourists, and it will be distemic even for residents who perform services or sell commodities to visitors. On the other hand, most really interesting cosmopolitan public places, while distemic in function, express the proxemic cultures of the societies which initially brought them into being as well as those of the people that most strongly influence decisions in the present. These relationships are subject to evolutionary processes also. What is distemic in one generation may become proxemic for the next, and I believe that is just how cultural evolution proceeds. Also, what is proxemic in one *context* can be distemic in another. In his book *What Time Is This Place?* Kevin Lynch has observed that urban spaces change form with time. A shopping district or civic center which is full of life and activity on Friday becomes a dead place on Sunday, while many parks come to life only on weekends. Modern transportation technology as well as certain concepts of city planning intensity these fluctuations.

In many older cities, commerce, institutional activities, and recreation all take place in more or less the same spaces, sometimes at different times, sometimes all at once.

Nevertheless, while proxemic communities are at least to some extent territories in the ethological sense of a defended space or, as Oscar Newman puts it, a "defensible space," distemic places should not be the territory of any individual or group. To serve their purpose, they can exclude only those who would deprive others of personal life, property, freedom to come and go, and pursuit of whatever legal goals led them to be there in the first place. The distemic spaces of the city are the domain of the individual because they accommodate a degree of nonconformity that few proxemic communities will allow. In the typical village, everybody minds at least some of your business. In the city, your business is nobody's business except that of people you choose to do business with, so long as you stay within the law. As noted, all cohesive social groups seek consensus.

Villages can tolerate a considerable amount of personal idiosyncrasy among known residents, provided they do not rock the communal boat. But genuine innovation is resisted strongly, and most people with the "gumption" to try something new find they have to leave town. They head for some sort of city where there is a higher probability of meeting up with other individuals who share their visions and potentialities. It is precisely a milieu which permits people to interact with each other as individuals, rather than as members of a group, which distinguishes the urbane public spaces from neighborhood streets and village commons. The very anonymity of city public life, which is so often deplored as alienating, is what makes the city preferable to the village for many people, at least part of the time. The price, of course, is a certain amount of personal insecurity (which always accompanies opportunity) because the formal law imposed by police and the courts is much less dependable than the social law of the small group. Among other things, lawmakers and law enforcers tend to territorialize their professional domains like everyone else, interpreting the law through the filter of their own cultures and interests. This is the more likely to occur

the less personal contact they have with those they are supposed to protect. In the cities, the problem is always to keep the cops honest. In the village, cops are not necessarily more honest, but they are more discriminating in all senses of the word because they are much more likely to be held accountable by members of their own society. This was well summed up by the retiring police chief of my own community, who had seen it change from an elite college town into a diverse academic city. In the old days, he said, "you had to watch out who you kicked in the ass; he might be the next secretary of state!" On the other hand, it is easier for professional criminals to function in the distemic city because behavior is not observed so closely and consistently, and other people are less likely to intervene personally in the event of trouble for someone else.

While proxemic local communities and distemic public places serve opposite social functions, the latter are likely to work best if they are surrounded by neighborhoods whose various members have a common interest in the use, safety, and maintenance of the more impersonal center. If, as in many of our own large cities, the public places serve primarily an external or commuting constituency, they are much less likely to be safe. Members of neighboring groups who feel no stake in the larger community of strangers may enter distemic places only as marauders. This is epitomized by political hijackings.

Airways in particular have become vulnerable to proxemic warriors who know no law but that of their own tribes, just as sea lanes were once menaced by pirates and stagecoach routes by highwaymen. At this writing a neotribal chieftain in Iran has led what purports to be a national government into an unprecedented hijacking of the most basic vehicle of world civilization, the time-honored system of embassies and diplomatic immunity. On a more local level, cities from Belfast to Rome are being ravaged by such tribes. One of the most cosmopolitan and beautiful cities on earth, Beirut, has been virtually destroyed by members of its own proxemic neighborhoods. In democratic industrial countries, a currently fashionable political concern with minorities, coupled with inadequate practical concern for their interests, continually escalates the threat to distemic institutions and places.

In his book *The Fall of Public Man* the sociologist Richard Sennett has observed that public life depends on conventions and rituals which to a great extent separate it from private life. He views urbane public life as a kind of theater which enables strangers to interact with each other on the basis of relative equality precisely because many individual characteristics and personal interests remain hidden. According to Sennett, this sort of public life thrived in the eighteenth century as urban mercantile capitalism brought masses of strangers into the city from outlying areas. People could no longer depend on the rituals of class and caste to determine who was who. In Sennett's view, the public behavior which developed was an art very much like that of the stage actor, expressive because of its universally recognizable form rather than because of its idiosyncratic contents. One may suspect, also, that, like the actor's art, public behavior involves a considerable degree of conscious self-control and reliance on MacLean's new cerebral cortex to a greater extent than domestic and village manners do. Sennett believes that this art of city behavior has been eroding during the past two centuries because of an excessive preoccupation with private personality, to the detriment of both public and private life. A somewhat similar idea was expressed two decades ago by August Heckscher in *The Public Happiness*.[5]

I myself believe the contemporary erosion of public life, especially in the United States, has been as much a consequence of the blurring of boundaries between proxemic and distemic zones of influence as between public and private domains as such. Sennett notes that public life enables various constituencies with common interests to form alliances for their mutual benefit, but that the tendency is for these to become frozen into ideologies which become the badge of membership in a new group society. When this occurs, negotiation and compromise become impossible. He calls this, very aptly, "dangerous gemeinschaft." With the increasing ability of latter-day tribal warriors to command powerful weapons, uncontrolled gemeinschaft may indeed be the most dangerous social phenomenon on earth.

However, Sennett, like so many literate and sophisticated cosmopolitans, seems to overestimate both the need and the desire of large segments of the population for social diversity. Other sociologists have pointed out that the urban villagers very often do not participate in much of the public life of the city, and often are unaware of the existence of many of its public areas and facilities. Many, but certainly not all, distemic zones are of greatest interest to the middle classes and tend to be underutilized by both the very rich and the very poor. It is a new, educated elite, the young professionals with few or no children, who are primarily responsible for the gentrification discussed in the previous chapter. In the city, as in the wilderness, a disproportionate amount of space and public investment often goes to meet the values of a relatively small segment of the population. When the larger public is served by this small population it is primarily because of the indirect benefits of its activities.

I think the distinction between proxemic and distemic zones of influence in a world that is increasingly mobile, both in physical and social terms, is not academic. I believe the distinction is very basic to the successful implementation of planning on any level that involves people with conflicting outlooks. For example, I wonder that so few, if any, social scientists, jurists, and legislators seem to have pondered the fact that Martin Luther King, Jr., and his supporters were able to integrate the *public* places of the U.S. South within a few years, after two centuries of deeply held racial prejudice on the part of the white population, while two generations of schoolchildren have been bused back and forth, north and south, in a largely unsuccessful effort to achieve school integration. Open-housing laws and policies north and south have also led to uncertain results. In all cases racial integration was enunciated as a fundamental American principle of justice, backed by new laws and Supreme Court orders, spurred by determined black political organizations and sympathetic white ones. King was aiming at distemic places and institutions: buses, restaurants, and public accommodations. But in the case of "neighborhood" schools (no matter how much that term is distorted and manipulated by self-serving political interests) and residential areas in general, fundamental territorial, or proxemic, impulses are at work. The fact that they are often very "irrational" makes it more, rather than less, important to recognize them. This is not to suggest that matters of social justice and general fairness and decency are not relevant on the proxemic level, but that any sort of change on that level is likely to be far more problematic than it is on the distemic level. In this sense I hope my multidimensional model of social landscape can be useful as a predictive tool: wherever innovation is called for, it will be more acceptable in the distemic domain and meet most resistance in the proxemic one. Also, from the point of view of real social justice, proxemic needs become more urgent the less privileged people are, economically and otherwise. The initial movement toward racial integration in this country was essentially in the distemic direction, enabling black people who had previously been barred by color to enter the American mainstream. But the more successful the movement became, the more those blacks not able or willing to take this direction held onto their own proxemics and developed the idea of "black separatism." This was predictable because distemic relationships—cooperative social diversity and free cultural coexistence—will tend both to foster and to benefit mainly a middle class.

To suggest this is neither to idealize nor to condemn the middle class but simply to identify its historic role in cultural evolution. The conventions of middle-class life, which often appear superficial because they must mask as well as accommodate differences, can cover up human vices as well as virtues. It is true that if one wants to know another person in the wholeness of character, one must know that person intimately. On the other hand, distemic public life can reveal dimensions of the human personality that are often inhibited or denied entirely by the demands for compromise and conformity on the part of families and close neighbors. One characteristic of the public personality is the capacity to understand, tolerate, and enjoy different personalities, to rise above local conceptions, and to adjust one's own life to change.

None of us welcomes new situations unless we feel able to cope with events, and the ability to cope with large and more impersonal environments is the particular characteristic of the middle class. This is partly the result of access to economic and conceptual resources through education, but not entirely. Many highly "educated" people are very narrow

conceptually, and many very wealthy people inhabit constricted cognitive and geographical worlds. Both may travel extensively and see nothing but what they wish to find, which is usually more or less what they have at home. On the other hand, many of the world's greatest thinkers and leaders have come from poor origins and have educated themselves. But whatever their route, they arrive in the middle class. The blue-collar philosopher Eric Hoffer may not like the idea, but even he speaks primarily to the middle-class intellectual.

I am indebted for some heightened insights into middle-class life, which came at a time when it was most fashionable to denigrate it, to my friend and colleague Richard W. Wilkie, a geographer who is also an anthropologist. Wilkie has spent many years studying a rural village in Argentina which was settled by members of the so-called Volga Deutsch, German colonists who in 1760–61 migrated as a group to southeastern Russia on the Volga River and who, after 1880, fled the near-famine conditions prevalent in that semiarid part of that land. One branch settled in South America, keeping its original village relations intact throughout. By the economic standards of developed countries, this entire village would be considered by sociologists to be lower-class. But Wilkie has found not only that it divides into characteristics of upper, middle, and lower classes, but there are two kinds of middle class. The upper and lower classes are basically conservative, the upper because they are relatively well-off and do not wish to risk what they have, the lower because things are, in effect, bad enough at home and there is reluctance to risk making them worse by going somewhere else or trying something new. Both classes tend to lack faith in their ability to act positively on the environment, and child-raising tends to be restrictive and authoritarian. Members of the upper class do not generally migrate; those at the bottom are sometimes forced to in search of a livelihood, but go no farther than they have to and return home if they can. In addition, a portion of the middle class, as defined in his study, resembles one or the other of these groups in some respects. But another part of the middle class, about one-sixth of the population, is what Wilkie calls the "dynamic" group. These are people who feel most confident of their ability to cope with the environment: they are most likely to seek and welcome change, they are most willing to migrate voluntarily, to travel farther and settle in larger cities, and to assimilate into the new environment when they do. Among this group, child-rearing tends to be more permissive, and children are consequently more adventuresome. But Wilkie's theories do not lead to the long-range supremacy of the members of any class. In little over a decade he has found people in the village shifting from one class to another, rising or falling, and children do not necessarily stay in the slot of their parents.

Thus it is both the geographic and social accessibility of distemic places and relationships that gives dynamic people their opportunities in comparison with physically and conceptually more fenced in neighbors and neighborhoods. On the other hand, the social openness of distemic and urbane spaces requires that they be readily understandable. In most modern urban design the clarity of proxemic neighborhoods relative to the city at large is the reverse of what is needed. Architects and planners have concentrated on the design of single buildings or clusters of buildings on the residential or district level, and as a result standardized forms have been imposed on people who might be permitted much more opportunity to shape their local habitats in their own way. Distemic, public centers are also often overdesigned and monotonously predictable in appearance. However, the larger urban landscape has become a bewildering catchall of discordant elements, without perceptible structure and clear means for orientation for the traveler, as anyone leaving an expressway to enter a typical large city for the first time knows very well.

In Kevin Lynch's *Image of the City*, which I mentioned briefly in chapter 3 in connection with my Bayonne experience, the middle-class professional people whom he interviewed identified five basic elements which contributed to the imageability of the three cities he studied. They were *edges, nodes, districts, paths*, and *landmarks*. The clear presence of these contributed to what Lynch called the city's "legibility." In my classes in urban design I have combined Lynch's system of urban analysis with the work of environmental psychologists Stephen Kaplan and his wife Rachel, who have studied pre-

ferences for various landscapes, urban and otherwise. The Kaplans have found that those environments which have legibility are greatly preferred to those which do not. But Stephen Kaplan has also found an aspect of the environment that is equally important to people and that he has called "mystery." It is present when a given view promises more information than it actually reveals. This promise of information causes a response which the Kaplans call "involvement," while legibility enables people to "make sense" of the environment.[6] In other words, to feel secure at any point we must know generally where we are in relation to where we were and where we want to go, but there should be sufficient complexity (or even ambiguity) to keep us interested as we go along. The degree to which ambiguity is a positive or negative feature is a matter of debate among environmental psychologists, but as far as I am concerned some measure of it is essential to the experience we call art, as it is in the experience of life itself, and to the extent that any landscape is aesthetic, it cannot be so understandable as to give our minds nothing to do as we pass through.

Returning to Lynch's five elements of imageability, we find, of course, that in different cities they are expressed in a great variety of ways and are perceived in combinations which, at best, make each environment unique. The most obvious kind of edge that comes to mind in a book which begins as this one does is a fence or a wall, but in modern cities edges of that type are the least likely to be significant on the large scale. Historically there have been three geographical features which contribute to urban boundaries, the land–water edge, the edge formed where a valley floor meets a steep hill or range, and the rural–urban edge. Perhaps the most persistent and significant is the water edge, partly because human beings have a particular attraction to water and partly because waterways were the most efficient means of travel; so usually water edges have also been activity nodes as well as pathways and thus combine three of Lynch's elements into one. Districts, as Lynch's subjects saw them, were simply areas that seem to have common characteristics or a separate visual identity from the rest of the urban landscape. They may be proxemic neighborhoods or they may be distemic centers, such as "business districts." Landmarks can be any prominent features which serve for orientation and which are different from things around them. A tall building may be a landmark if there are no other tall buildings nearby, no matter how undistinguished it is. On the other hand, an elegant work of architecture placed among other elegant works of architecture in the same scale will likely not be a landmark. A single tree on an otherwise treeless street, even if relatively small, may be a landmark. But landmarks are more likely to be significant if they contain a measure of symbolic meaning for the observer. It will be recalled from chapter 3 that in the Italian South End of Springfield a statue of Columbus was unanimously agreed upon by the residents as marking the edge of that neighborhood, while an equally prominent statue of a World War I soldier at a major node in the Puerto Rican part of the North End was mentioned by no one.

Even though distemic places transcend local mythology, they and their landmarks do not lack symbolic meaning of their own. On the contrary, the development of more comprehensive social symbols is their prime function. As the peasant village represents a higher order of development than the hunter—gatherer tribal village, with symbols appropriate to its particular ecology, and the city-state represents a higher order with broader symbols than the village, so those of the nation represent yet another level of cultural evolution. Hopefully the United Nations, whose boundaries are the surface of the globe, will eventually transcend, without obliterating, nations.

Until the mass use of automobiles, the emergence of distemic activities, places, and symbols usually required city densities. With the mobility offered by the car and the conceptual mobility offered by electronic media, the city can now be spread out, as I noted in the discussion of suburbs in chapter 3. Whole international communities now exist which are maintained by air travel and telecommunications, although the tendency is for worldwide cultural differences to become increasingly blurred in a very dull sort of way. Mass media may simply be replacing one kind of small-group culture with another. Actually, the television screen, which, like other forms of photography, is most effective as a close-up medium, tends to emphasize individual personality and private relationships at the expense of larger social and environmental contexts, encouraging not a world city, but, as Marshall McLuhan has suggested, a "global village." Epic relationships of people to each other and to the environment, which the art of the stage expressed so well, have been replaced in cinematography by a kind of collective introspection and public psychoanalysis, as exemplified by the films of Ingmar Bergman. In politics, charisma has replaced heroism. This is a form of gemeinschaft, and it is certainly dangerous in the face of problems which cannot even be conceived of, let alone solved, on the level of the local tribe, whether the "locality" is a geographical village, the board of a multinational corporation, or the inner circle of a government bureaucracy. It is well known that no one is a hero at home; heroes are conceptualizations that expand our capacity for concerted action by standing for something both *larger than* and *other than* that with which we can be intimately familiar.

The current design and planning fashion for "human scale," which is to say small scale, and the consequent hostility to monument builders does not bode well for cultural evolution. Small scale is mammalian scale, a sociobiological necessity but not a noble aspiration. Really human scale is the magnificent large scale made possible by the new conceptual brain. Historically, it was mostly barbarians who toppled monuments. The relevant question is not whether we should have monuments, but what constitutes meaningful monuments for large numbers of people in our time.

5

Urban Space: The Marketplace of Goods and Symbols

In organizing the images with which I will attempt to illustrate what I mean by distemic places, I will begin by returning to Boston, which in recent years has become as good an example of the community of strangers as it is of neighborhood ethnicity. Since we rarely, if ever, perceive the environment in terms of parts such as Lynch's five elements, but rather as a variety of continually shifting wholes, I will try to treat central Boston as a comprehensive urban composition. On the other hand, for analytical purposes it is useful (even essential) to deal with parts. Thus, I will also examine a number of other cities, first in terms of their waterfronts as edges, nodes, and pathways, next in terms of commercial centers, and then in terms of modern interurban path systems and the nodes they connect. I will subsequently examine three capital cities, which in and of themselves tend to be nodes and landmarks for the regions or nations they symbolize. The three I have selected were originally *designed* cities, and as such come as close to being works of art in the sense of consciously organized artifacts as it is possible for cities to be. Finally I will close this chapter with a place which is not a city in the ordinary sense but is yet an urban environment, a proxemic community of a sort which is at the same time a distemic center. In all of these, the physical forms the centers, the boundaries, the paths, and the landmarks—define spaces where people who are not intimate exchange goods, services, ideas, and myths.

Boston

In Kevin Lynch's study of Boston, Jersey City, and Los Angeles, Boston stood out as the most imageable of the three. At that time, in the late fifties, Boston was just beginning its metamorphosis from a rather dowdy, dingy, economically retarded but nostalgic and picturesque seaport to its present status as one of America's most chic urban centers, the equal of San Francisco to the cosmopolitan mind. It is as imageable as ever, probably much more so, but the image is in important respects very different after nearly a quarter of a century. The proxemic neighborhoods I described in chapter 4 were there then, plus another, the Italian West End, which was bulldozed and "renewed" shortly after Lynch's

study. As I have said, such neighborhoods give any city vitality; they probably add strongly to Boston's current image, but they do not account for it. In the fifties ethnicity was not fashionable at all, and older neighborhoods were considered by most planners to be reactionary nuisances and impediments to "orderly development." In fact, many of the neighborhoods I have identified had rather low imageability for Lynch's middle-class subjects. From my perspective, the great achievement of the planners of Boston's reincarnation as a lively American city is that they restored its distemic places, symbols, and functions without altogether obliterating proxemic ones.[1]

The pervasive symbolism of Boston, both for its residents and to its visitors, is that of U.S. revolutionary history, perhaps most universally expressed for Americans in the figure of Paul Revere. "Listen my children, and you shall hear . . . ." Come to Boston and you shall see. You shall see that legendary horseman riding forever through the North End (196), close enough now to the Old North Church to have gotten the message by a call rather than by lanterns gleaming across a river. It is no matter that ancestors of the present population of the immediate area knew nothing of the "shot heard round the world." As I have said, the distemics of one era become the proxemics of another. It is no matter that two-thirds of today's Boston were under salt water in 1776, making the signals necessary. It is no matter that dense buildings now make the Old North Church invisible from the next block, let alone the other side of the river. The symbolism matters, and symbolism makes a good city as much as bricks and mortar, glass and steel, and shade trees. We are probably all instinctual ancestor worshipers, and we worship the idealization of the past, not its reality, which is mostly lost to us anyway. Symbolic landmarks may be proxemic or distemic; the best urban landmarks are both, and Boston has many of them. But it has been unusually successful for an American city in being able to erect powerful symbols of the present without obliterating those of the past.

Symbolism resides in places, in spaces, in nodes or districts as well as in landmarks. For New England towns and small cities, the common was both a functional node and a symbolic nucleus which gave

form to the surrounding community, both socially
and physically. Few large cities in New England
have retained their focus on a common because large
cities have many centers which usually express different functions and different social meanings. Modern Boston has several centers as well as many nodes,
but its famous Common, which, like so many other
parts of old Boston, is a registered historic district, is
still the heart of the city, as it has been for three
centuries (197).

The Boston Common is the clearest example I can
imagine of what I mean by a distemic urban center.
It is bounded on the north by fashionable Beacon
Street and the residential district known as Beacon
Hill (upper left in 197), one of the most long-
standing and elite of proxemic neighborhoods in the
country. To the west (lower left in 197), across from
the Public Garden, is the Back Bay district, diverse
but not as socially diverse as it likes to think of itself

(198). It has become a center of student life. On the
north corner is the statehouse, designed by Charles
Bulfinch, the first native American architect. Since
1799 it has been the seat of government for the
Commonwealth of Massachusetts. Further east of
that are the new Government Center (not visible but
located behind the buildings in the top center of 197)
and new skyscrapers of the financial district. These
have not yet quite obscured what was once the major
landmark of the port of Boston, the U.S. Custom
House (upper right in 197). On the southeastern
flank of the Common is the central business district
(generally right in 197), now rapidly being revitalized
(199).

199

200

201

People with business in all of these districts cross the Common and diverse people without any particular business at the moment enter it for the sheer pleasure of doing so (200). On a good day one can find manifestations of every conceivable American attitude and life-style (201). The statehouse, appropriately for a distemic place, is the most visible and significant landmark, although its visibility has been greatly diminished by some of the most inappropriate new construction in the city. Fifteen years ago it was the most prominent feature of Beacon Hill; today, it is overwhelmed by inelegant and dull, square-topped office towers (202). From most angles, the new structures have inexcusably spoiled the ele-

202

gant silhouette of Bulfinch's masterpiece (203), but as of now, from Park Street it presents a powerful and unifying terminus (204). In many capital cities, notably Washington, D.C., and Madison, Wisconsin, ordinances forbid the construction of buildings which would rise above the capitol dome.

203

204

The contrasts of scale in modern downtown Boston are violent, but in the best cases they create a dynamic aesthetic by that very fact. The effect is a kind of architectural distemics, where almost mind-boggling diversity is accommodated without loss of unity. The little Old State House sits like a piece of child's toy village among the grown-up furniture in the heart of the financial district (205). I once complained to a class in urban design about this absurd violation of scale and the inversion of symbolic importance it represents. One of my students argued that to her, the tall buildings around the Old State House actually enhance rather than detract from its importance. I have never seen it the same way since; she may be right. In Manhattan it would have vanished long ago; the only equivalent I can think of there is Trinity Church near Wall Street.

Walking down Tremont Street from the Common toward the Government Center, one finds wedged in among the neo-Bauhaus towers the Granary Burying Ground, where lie more Founding Fathers per square foot returned to dust worth more per pound than in any other cemetery in America (206). If John Hancock could rise from his grave there to catch a glimpse of the sleek and bedeviled new skyscraper erected in his name, the shock would undoubtedly send him back again instantly.

Nostalgia is in style today, and it is equally stylish to deplore "growth" and massive construction. Yet we are a constructing animal, and there is a fascination in construction for its own sake. Any building project will have its fences pierced with peepholes for sidewalk superintendents. We admire the Roman aqueducts, yet intellectual fashion now disparages the skills and courage of the designers and builders of the new landscape, where drama is a daily event (207). Even if the world were to achieve zero population growth, the urbanized area of the earth must increase vastly to accommodate children now living. The problem is not whether to build but where to build and how to build well. Boston has not by any means always built well, but taken as a whole it is a reasonably good model of how it can be done. Destruction of the best building of the past has not been avoided, and is still not, but in Boston, as compared with most other American cities, it has been minimized.

206

207

208

no city that does it better, at this time, than Boston, which is not to say that it does it perfectly or, for some, even tolerably.

The catalyst for Boston redevelopment was the Prudential Center, built in the late fifties. In my opinion it is the least satisfactory of the new landmarks, but it is certainly a prominent one (210).

The symbolic and aesthetic icing on the redevelopment cake came with the bicentennial celebrations of 1976. Even the schoolhouse theatricals contributed to the physical and symbolic unity-in-incongruity, where your friendly neighborhood minuteman could be counted on to help a stranded visitor with an ailing twentieth-century nag (208). The characterization of the city on a plaque at the top of an escalator in the Prudential Building defines the city as a song (209). This may be stretching things a bit. There are songs to be heard in a healthy city, even in a sick one, along with the cacophony, but a more definitive word, as Sennett suggests, is *theater*. Classical drama was defined as the resolution of conflict. A good city is a place where the conflicting wills of Tönnies's gesellschaft can find unity of purpose. I can think of

210

209

211

Designed in the bastard Bauhaus style of the so-called urban renewal era of the fifties, it is a geometrical anyplace, conveying no symbolism but that of ubiquitous corporate power. The skin of the curtain wall tower looks as if it had been made out of recycled automobile grills. The surrounding complex is a sleek, brittle assemblage of stores and expensive high-rise apartment buildings (211) that for the most part ignores and shuts out the character of the area it is in. During the Bicentennial the atmosphere was enlivened by a brilliant and beautiful multi-slide show called *Where's Boston?*, produced by a group of architects and designers called the Cambridge Seven. But standing inside of the plaza areas, one could well ask the question which the show answers eloquently but which the Prudential Center does not even consider. One could be in Los Angeles or Houston. There is, for example, only one spot where it is possible to get a partial glimpse of what had been previously the major landmark of the area, the Christian Science Church (212). However, the

212

effect of the Prudential Center was to generate a great deal of other development in the vicinity that has been more fortunate. In fact, it extended the economic center of gravity from the old downtown into what had been a respectable but rather dowdy and deteriorating residential area. This was an area which in Lynch's study had shown up as "chaotic and/or characterless." It is still somewhat chaotic, but it no longer lacks character because of what the Prudential Center has stimulated its neighbors to do.

The Christian Science Church has, in its own way, as much economic muscle as the Prudential Insurance Company. It was not about to allow its Beaux-Arts mother church and publishing house to languish in the chill shadow of its arrogant and soulless neighbor. In terms of my distemic theory, the Christian Scientists have an admirable world view in secular matters. A room-size, concave stained glass map of the world symbolizes this. Their world headquarters is almost as conspicuous a landmark as the Prudential complex, but symbolically and aesthetically it is far superior to it, and it is regionally more unique and appropriate.

Photo 213 shows the Christian Science World Headquarters as it appears from the Prudential observatory. The architects, I. M. Pei Associates, and the landscape architects, Sasaki, Dawson, and DeMay, have created a space as unifying as the other is discordant. They have not only succeeded in the improbable task of uniting past and present architecturally (214a) through forms which happily marry contemporary concrete to the stone ornamentation of the mother church (actually two churches built six years apart which were more discordant in style than they are now). The architects have also managed to unify everything else in view, including the "Pru" (b). The great reflecting pool, which also serves the air-conditioning system, achieves a serenity appropriate for any religious organization. The water spills quietly over a marble coping, disguising its edges, so that Bostonian mortals appear to walk on water (c and d).

Some antimonumentalists have asserted that the Christian Science Center lacks human scale. By that they mean intimate scale, which this place certainly does lack, but so does the plaza of St. Peter's basilica

a

b

c

d

e

at the Vatican. Here, a high-rise secretariat tower focuses on the space without dominating it, saluting rather than upstaging the mother church (e).

As do most large-scale renewal projects of our time, this one raised considerable controversy. Old residences were demolished. The church claims every effort was made to relocate people fairly, but in any case the die had been cast already by the Prudential Center. Something on this scale was bound to occur in the area, and from a distemic point of view, at least, it could hardly have been done better. It is unfortunate that the plan could not have included Symphony Hall (top of 213); however, the plaza is used by its patrons as a promenade during intermissions. Even from a proxemic point of view, the Christian Science Center has enhanced the residential sections of the South End across Huntington Avenue, although probably more for the "gentry" than the low-income residents. Still, people of all sizes, shapes, and colors can be found sitting in the gardens on the eastern edge or playing in the fountain (215). In a window of a building not far away, someone had posted an appropriate cartoon showing a preacher in a pulpit with the following caption:

"And finally, Lord, may Thy wisdom guide and inspire the deliberations of those Thy servants our Planning and Zoning Commission." May that prayer be answered as well elsewhere as it has been in the Christian Science World Headquarters.

On the opposite side of the Prudential complex, separating it from the Back Bay, is Boylston Street, which leads into the Common. This formerly rather dingy street has now become a lively, small-scale commercial avenue, one that, despite the traffic, is remarkably pleasant and easy to stroll on (216). A few blocks away it joins Huntington Avenue at Copley Square, one area that showed up as a prominent node in Lynch's study. It was an important node then because it contained a number of major landmarks which performed distemic functions, among them a once fashionable hotel, H. H. Richardson's still fashionable Trinity Church, one of the most valuable of Boston's registered historic landmarks, and the Boston Public Library by McKim, Mead and White. Although the high-rise buildings that have sprung up nearby have made present-day Copley Square less conspicuous as a node than it was when Lynch studied it, commercial development of

216

the area together with a young and lively population in the Back Bay have encouraged its position as an important distemic focal point.

A few years ago a competition was held to select an architect to redesign Copley Square. Photo 217, taken with a telephoto lens from the top of the Pru, shows the square as redesigned. Photo 218 shows it from the top of the Pru's new competitor, the John

217

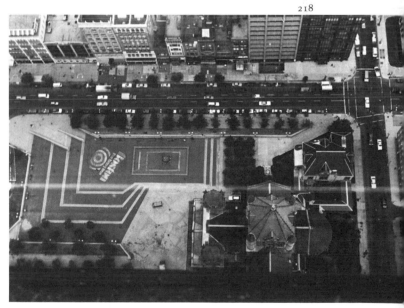

218

219

220

221

222

Hancock Tower. Both views illustrate, I think, the way the drawing board view of a design concept so often fails to work out in three dimensions on the ground. The object of the competition most certainly was to give Trinity Church, which is generally regarded as Richardson's masterpiece, a setting it deserves. But the effect of the rather puny steps is to direct attention away from the church to a fountain (219). This one is not sufficiently interesting to warrant such a detraction from the church. For my taste, Copley Square looks better from the other side of an earth berm as seen from the public library, much as it appeared when it was simply a grassy park before it was "revitalized" in this manner (220).

However, Trinity Church now has even tougher competition from the new John Hancock Building, also designed by I. M. Pei. It is hard to conceive that the synthesizing mind or minds that produced the Christian Science Center also produced this relationship (221). The real sin was not the architect's, of course, but that of the client, who decided to put a tall structure in this small space, and of planning policies that permitted it. Actually the blue, mirror-like building that is there now damages the place visually as little as could be expected, once that decision was made. Indeed, it is probably less oppressive and incongruous than the old John Hancock Building, which ruined the silhouette of the church long before (222). In fact, the fantastic reflection of the church at ground level intensifies the church's effect on the square (223). Taken by itself, the John Hancock Tower is an architectural jewel.

On the other hand, a more serious kind of physical problem for the church has been presented by this skyscraper. Boston, unlike Manhattan, is not built on rock but mostly on filled seashore. Trinity Church, like the buildings of old Amsterdam, was built on wooden pilings, which hold up for centuries if they stay wet. The excavation for the foundations of the John Hancock caused the church to settle, and I am told that now the weight of the finished skyscraper is lifting the church up. There is considerable concern for its structural welfare. But in this case, as in few others, the architectural intruders have had to pay for their hubris: somebody goofed in the design of the windows, with results that will probably keep large numbers of lawyers and judges employed for the rest of this century (224).

223

224

225

226

Looking west from the church toward the Prudential tower, one is aware of the visual syncopation that
is the "song" of modern Boston (225), with melodies
of an earlier era still to be heard in counterpoint.
That is the magic of this strangely chaotic and coherent city. And there are places to get away from
the dissonance, as in the cloisterlike courtyard of the
public library (226). In such places, which all humane cities need, one can have enclosure without
intimacy, privacy in a public setting, and enjoy the
sense of being part of the human race without having
to interact with it.

Boylston Street leads past the southern edge of the
Public Garden, bends slightly to the right, and
crosses Charles Street, which divides the garden
from the Common (see the right side of photo 197).
It intersects Tremont Street almost at a right angle.
But if the pedestrian cuts across the Common, as the
environment invites him to do, and emerges at the

other end of Tremont Street, he will swear that Tremont is in a straight line with Boylston. At ground level the Common is perceived as a rectangle, not a pentagon as it actually is, another example of the disadvantages of the drawing board view of the world. Kevin Lynch's subjects found the route around the Common one of the more confusing of the many confounding path systems in Boston. Even life-long residents can get lost there. Nevertheless, with the powerful visual landmarks that have emerged since the Lynch study, the overall effect is now of a more direct link between the area we have just considered and the older downtown. The distemic terminus of that has become the Government Center.

I have suggested that from the dawn of cities, commerce has been the chief mechanism by which tribal strangers can form a larger public community, and that trade requires laws, and laws spawn institutions to shape and enforce them. The Prudential Center is the embodiment of one kind of *commercial* institution, the Christian Science Center the embodiment of a particular kind of *religious* institution; both are distemic in their different ways, with of course a proxemic culture at the core. Also the work of I. M. Pei, Boston's Government Center, which replaced

the somewhat sleazy but picturesque Scollay Square some two decades ago, is the physical embodiment of the *civic* institution. It is a large, brick-paved, open space focused on the "new" city hall, by Kallman, McKinnell and Knowles, an upside-down ziggurat that started a trend in its time. As one approaches through old Tremont Street, past the Granary Burying Ground and the King's Chapel, the city hall is located off to the side, so that what one sees first is the tower of the Old North Church in the distance (227). Such awareness of environmental context is rare in modern architecture, particularly in the United States. In fact, it makes the difference between architecture per se and urban design.

To emerge suddenly from the constricted space of Tremont Street into the vast open plaza is very dramatic. Civic centers and other single-use complexes have frequently been criticized (the first such criticism was in Jane Jacobs's *Death and Life of Great American Cities*, written about the time this complex was planned) because they tend to become empty, dead spaces when the allotted hours of use have come to an end. The Boston Government Center has been denounced as cold and bleak, and on a winter weekend it can indeed be a drafty, empty place. But during a weekday, when it is full of people, it can be

228

229

230

very lively, especially in summer (228), and at any time of year it makes a grand stage for public events (229). The planners of this space were faced with the interesting design problem of fitting a circle into a square, and it was obviously decided to preserve the elegant Sears Crescent Building (left in 230). By placing another curved building opposite it and repeating the curves in white steps on the brick plaza, a very dramatic mill wheel effect, a visual vortex, is created. Against the curves, rectangular steps and buildings make a dramatic counterpoint, and here the steps, unlike those of Copley Square, are strong and forceful (231) because they reflect real changes in grade and are not merely a designer's attempt to contrive a "space."

But to me the finest thing about the Government

231

232

Center, whatever its faults, is the way it lets in the surrounding landscape through view openings to the most important landmarks. The nearest and most important are Faneuil Hall back of City Hall (232) and the Custom House tower just beyond that (233). These views have been increasingly closed off by ill-considered new construction, such as Sixty State Street shown in skeleton in 234 and now complete. The Custom House, an important symbolic monument harking back to what once was the principal

233

234

port city in the era of the great clipper ships and the China trade, still dominates the area east of the Government Center, including the remnants of the old Haymarket, described in chapter 3 (235). From close up, the Custom House is an architectural absurdity, a late-nineteenth-century stone skyscraper improbably perched on the roof of a mini-Parthenon (236), but the generally convivial commercial redevelopment around it has made close-up views more or less moot. As noted in the previous chapter, Faneuil Hall and the old Quincy Market have been restored into a swinging shopping and social center.

235

236

The famous market and warehouse buildings designed by Alexander Parris and opened in 1826 by Mayor Josiah Quincy were in their time the climax of a two-century struggle by Boston merchants to establish a market worthy of the city. One hundred years earlier Peter Faneuil had donated the building that bears his name for a market, but faced the opposition of farmers who thought they could get better prices selling door-to-door without concentrated and organized competition. The opening date of the original Quincy Market was fortuitous because it permitted the one hundred and fiftieth anniversary to coincide with bicentennial festivities in 1976, after the whole had been glamorously restored by architects Bart Thompson and Tad Stahl. The developer was James Rouse of Columbia New Town fame. For decades Faneuil Hall and the markets had been fixtures in the old Italian Haymarket, surrounded by a skid row atmosphere (237). The restoration gutted the elegant warehouses, leaving the basic structures intact. The result is the commercial success story of the decade, and its success reportedly surprised even its staunchest backers (238, 239). Its distemic qualities

237   238

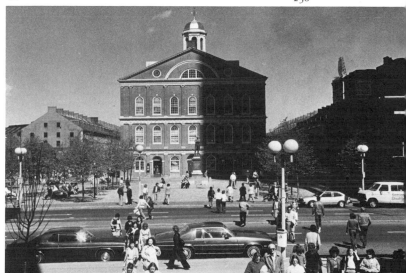

239

are somewhat limited by its high prices and chic atmosphere, and many people still prefer the more authentic street market atmosphere of the nearby North End (240). Still, for tourists, suburbanites, and local residents who can stand the crowds, it is a most delightful bazaar, especially for comestibles (241) which can be consumed standing up indoors or out or sitting down in the shadow of Faneuil Hall or the Custom House. But it's difficult to ignore the reminders that real estate is currently Boston's chief commodity (242).

240

241

242

Despite the rehabilitation of the adjacent wharf area and planned redevelopment of the rest of it and the harbor islands, the waterfront is not the center it ought to be, given Boston's history as a seaport. The Custom House has lost its symbolism, although many New England imports must still pass through its Greek columns. This may be partly because, except for the aquarium and a new park, most of the developed harbor area has been converted into very expensive residences and thus has become proxemic territory, and partly because it is obstructed by a raised highway. But the decay of the waterfront as a whole in this century is also, of course, the product of changes in transportation from ships to rails to highways. Some idea of the changes both in symbolism and shape can be gained from photo 243, a snapshot I took as a schoolboy in 1934 from what downeasters called the Boston Boat and which Bostonians probably called the Bangor Boat. On the East Penobscot Bay we used to be able to set our watches by it. In those days the Custom House was the largest thing in sight, and a lantern could still have been spotted in the Old North Church, to the right in my time-stained picture. As far as I can figure out, when it was taken the boat must have been just about where Logan Airport is today. A contemporary view from there (244) suggests the diversity of worlds that human beings can now pass through in a single lifetime. In that view the Custom House is framed by the large building on the left, and the Old North Church can be seen just left of two chimneys on the right.

Twenty years ago the Charles River edge of
Boston was more imageable to Kevin Lynch's subjects than the harborside, and it probably remains
so for many Bostonians to this day (245). Such river
imageability is not typical of American cities, where
rivers have generally been viewed as highways,
sources of power, and sewers rather than as social
and symbolic focal points. The present Charles River
basin is the result of the foresight of Frederick Law
Olmsted, whose work will be discussed in more
detail in the next chapter, and his disciple and part-
ner, Charles Eliot. It is worth reiterating that a
waterfront can be both an edge and a center. In this
case the Charles River is both the boundary of
Boston proper and a central node for Greater Boston,
which includes Cambridge.

One of the most important kinds of distemic institutions and places are universities, which, in theory
at least, are the marketplaces of ideas. In the forums
of antiquity, the exchange of thoughts and the exchange of goods took place in the same center, even
though the different kinds of traders have always
tended to mistrust each other. Intellectuals have traditionally looked down on "materialistic profiteers"
as philistine, and merchants have tended to scorn

"eggheads" of each period as unrealistic troublemakers. Nevertheless, the relationship is essentially symbiotic, even though clichés, not ideas, sell best in the public bazaar and probably always did. Both clichés and ideas are produced in quantity in some of America's most prestigious centers of learning across the Charles River, the accessible banks and bridges of which make it even more of a center than an edge (246).

If the long-range plans of the Boston Redevelopment Authority to revitalize the entire waterfront and the harbor islands are carried out, the current vibrancy and distemic vitality of the peninsula could be extended to the sprawling former suburbs around it. However, care would be needed to avoid excessive gentrification of such proxemic communities as Italian Charlestown and East Boston, Irish South Boston, and the black Dorchester—Roxbury communities. The trick will be to expand Boston's present charm and vitality without overdoing either chic nostalgia or architectural megalomania. If that could be done the city might once again become the outward-looking trading place in touch with the whole world which it was in the days of the great sailing ships.

246

New England Seaport Towns

Harbors still remain the visual and social centers of the lesser seaports on the New England coast which have become resort communities. The docks swarm with tourists in summer and now are filled with yachts and pleasure boats instead of trading vessels, merchants, and seamen. These communities, like many others that subsist on tourism, have an interesting social and territorial structure that includes at least four segments on my theoretical proxemic—distemic continuum. There are the native, year-round residents, who are largely descendants of original settlers. They usually loathe being called natives, but I shall call them that with apologies because I can think of no other word that adequately distinguishes them from the other three groups. There are the old-guard summer families, who own extensive properties that usually monopolize much of the seashore. The relationship between these groups is strongly proxemic and essentially symbiotic. The summer people have special privileges and territorial rights in the summer, but there is a tacit understanding that they will pay their taxes, not interfere in town politics, and leave the town to its permanent residents during the rest of the year. The old summer families are usually descendants of the nineteenth-century urban elite who began coming in the days when railroad or sea travel was fairly time-consuming. As a group, their economic and political involvements are elsewhere; they look to the summer as a time to get away from responsibilities and have little interest in local affairs as long as their needs are met.

Since the years when the mass use of automobiles began, and especially since World War II, another class has appeared on the scene. This is comprised mostly of college-educated professionals, and their effect on these seasonal communities has been very much like that of the new gentry on ethnic urban neighborhoods. But the real "gentry" in this case are the old-guard summer people. The newer group might more accurately be called exurbanites because they frequently dream of settling permanently and sometimes do. The permanent residents call them "city people," a derogatory term not applied to the old-guard summer people. This group brings with it the latest fashions in progressive political ideas; they "get involved," and they are usually not well regarded by the local power structure. A fourth group is the tourists, who pass through and drop off money for souvenirs and services, staying for a day, a weekend, a week, or at most a month. They are not involved at all in local matters; they simply want to have a good time and cheerfully accept what they can find, including the chain restaurants, motels, and souvenir shops loaded with local treasures made in Taiwan.

The first two groups are extremely territorial; the most defensively territorial are not the natives but the old-time summer people. Both are essentially permanent residents in the sense of having long-standing associations and attachments, and both consider the others transients. Both permanent groups dislike the last two for cluttering up their peaceful world; the summer residents strongly oppose all so-called development. The year-round group is ambivalent on this point; most need the income from tourists, and some of the more enterprising take both profit and pleasure from serving them. But they resent any "outside interference," even planned efforts to protect that which they themselves value. The exurbanites have some distemic attitudes, but the most distemic group is of course the temporary tourists. These relationships and conflicts are presented most dramatically in their essential form in Jane Langton's poetic detective story, *Dark Nantucket Noon*. Nantucket is perhaps the most pristine of the New England seaport communities which fit this model. Because it is an island, it has been less vulnerable than other towns to the kind of future shock associated with automobile travel. It has been protected, rather than restored, not by plan but by physical isolation. But it was originally a wealthy whaling community, and it has so far been preserved with exceptional taste and care, not by alien archaeologists or boutique culture developers but by people who know and love it.

The chief landmarks to be seen as the ferry from Cape Cod approaches this island are lighthouses and church steeples (247), the same landmarks that were symbols of home to the pursuers of Moby Dick. Church steeples dominate the town center with its elegant Federal and Greek Revival buildings, which

247

reflect the great affluence of the whaling era (248).
But the real center of life in all seasons is near the
docks, where the supermarket is located. An inherently functional approach to aesthetics which is basic
to genuine seafarers makes even oil storage tanks
things of beauty (249). During the vacation season,
the permanent residents tend to withdraw from the
harbor into their fenced homes (some of which are
shown in chapter 1), turning over the waterfront area
to tourists from Memorial Day to Labor Day (250).
There is a seasonal tide which ebbs and floods with
people. In the summer the docks and main streets
become a highly distemic place, at peak season
crammed with day-trippers, who come over on the

248

249

250

ferry. In the fall, the descendants of the whalers reclaim their town center, and it once more becomes the heart of a proxemic island village. For the more contemplative tourist, that is the best time to visit. One will still be received with hospitality if one comes as a courteous visitor, and it is then possible to enjoy a long, easy, relaxed chat with people for whom this small sandbar is the center of the world (251). There are unsaid things that I can personally share with them. I spent some impressionable childhood years as a year-round resident in a place of this sort. Perhaps for that reason autumn has remained my favorite season, the time of year associated with sudden fulsome quietude and the repossession of habitat.

251

Near Nantucket is Martha's Vineyard, a much larger island with three distinct towns. There also are found the four distinct groups I have described and the same seasonal flux of people. But the citizens do not see themselves as members of a single island community, as those in Nantucket do; rather they are fiercely loyal to their own towns and reluctant to cooperate on anything. They share mainly a deep mistrust of any "off-islanders" who attempt to meddle in their affairs.

American Port Cities

I know of three large cities in the United States which retain the outward-looking, distemic character of a major seaport. They are New York, San Francisco, and New Orleans. The latter has already been explored here in another context and will be touched on again in connection with rivers. San Francisco was Boston's predecessor as America's most romantically cosmopolitan place and remains its chief competitor. But while Boston has been for generations inherently nostalgic in the New England manner, San Francisco has always been contemporary in design, life-style, and attitude. Its distemic character subsumes innumerable subcultures and cults, but it is also highly intensified by its focus toward Asia.

Because of the city's steep topography, the harbor is rarely out of sight. Its bridges, especially the Golden Gate Bridge, are internationally known landmarks (252). The Embarcadero Freeway cuts off the waterfront near the famous old Ferry Terminal, but it is a measure of San Francisco's outlook that it was one of the first to halt such public crimes, and the freeway was mercifully terminated (253). But even away from the harbor, at Union Square, there is a powerful sense of international comings and goings (254). And even in this relatively sedate business section, the unusual is so usual that it is hard for a poor hard-working nonconformist to get attention (255a–d).

252

a

253

b

254

c

d

New York City is a curious paradox. It is our most cosmopolitan city by far and also one of our most provincial in proxemic outlook. Native New Yorkers tend to consider everything west of Manhattan as the boondocks. Middle Americans (in both a geographical and social sense) do not look upon New York as a symbol of the nation, as the British do London, the French do Paris, the Swedes do Stockholm, the Czechs do Prague. This is surprising in a country that values bigness. New York is one of the major financial capitals of the world and yet its municipal government teeters year after year on the edge of bankruptcy. Many Americans were quite pleased a few years ago that the city was about to go broke, something that baffled Europeans. New York is the intellectual center of the United States as well as the financial center. But while many famous and productive intellectuals work out of New York, most of them come there from somewhere else. New York offers support for the hypothesis that cities express the culture of a region or nation but are not the source of it. Culture originates in the hinterland, in proxemic villages of various sizes from which it flows as water flows from tributaries into rivers and from rivers into the sea, gaining both volume and energy in the process. And, like water, the culture must eventually be returned, transformed, to the regions from which it came.

The hostility of geographical and social Middle America toward New York has many historical roots, going back to the age of Jackson and the opening of the frontier, a time when American economic and political power resided in the East. But it is as a center of art and ideas, of conceptual trade, at least as much as of money, that so many pragmatic Americans look at it with suspicion. This is partly because it is the major port connecting us with Europe. America has never lacked for ideas of its own, but traditionally it has been suspicious of ideas imported from abroad, especially Europe, which American mythology, grounded in considerable fact, has associated with war and oppression.

In any case, recurrent reports of the demise of New York, like those of Mark Twain's untimely death, have been greatly exaggerated. Although it is certainly one of our sickest cities, socially and physically, and large parts of it are unbelievably dilapidat-

ed, polluted, and ugly, at its best it retains a degree of proxemic diversity and distemic vitality which no other place in America can match. Even economically, despite the predictions of recent years, it seems to be staging a comeback. As in Boston and elsewhere, some of the most interesting neighborhoods are rapidly becoming gentrified, with consequences already noted, good for the city but often hard on the neighborhood residents. As America's most international metropolis, strategically placed in a striking natural and man-made landscape, New York is an expression of the United States' worst vices and greatest virtues.

Probably no landmark in human history has been more imbued with distemic meaning for travelers than was the Statue of Liberty in New York harbor during the late nineteenth century and the first half of this one (256). For people who had voluntarily (or involuntarily) abandoned their native cultures beyond a large ocean for a promise of individual self-fulfillment, it must have been an overwhelming sight. So too must have been the first glimpse of that rocky island of Manhattan looming out of the smog like the tip of a man-made iceberg (257). It is ironic that so many of America's new poor were to anchor at Ellis Island in sight of Wall Street, where the power of mammon was glorified by towers outreaching those of the Gothic cathedrals that celebrated the power of God. But for some of them Wall Street was in itself a symbol of hope, perhaps even of God. In any case, the skyline of lower Manhattan has been as unique in form and symbolism as the great churches and castles of old. But in the last decade much of its special beauty has been compromised by the metastasized International School of office building. The twin towers of the World Trade Center have destroyed the scale and made the whole scene lopsided (257). Other buildings in the same period have obliterated the flamelike neo-Gothic quality which not so long ago made that skyline so unforgettable. Some idea of the change can be had by comparing photo 258, taken from the Brooklyn edge of the harbor in 1963, with 259, taken from the same place only thirteen years later. The flat-topped buildings are merely big, but without scale, which is always relative. No wonder the word *square* emerged in the counterculture of the sixties to mean soulless con-

258

259

260

formity. Perhaps more important, the tallest towers
of the earlier skyscraper era, like the Woolworth
Building, were set back from the waterfront, with
lower buildings by the shore allowing views *from* the
interior giving some sense of the interior *to* the
viewer beyond.

Manhattan is an island, its boundaries inexorably
defined by its waterfronts. Approaching by land
from any direction, one must either cross a bridge or
duck into a tunnel. Standard catechism in city planning says that highways destroy cities, but that, like
most other things in life, depends on the point of
view. Actually, the most dramatic way to see New
York is to ride the parkways and expressways that
girdle the island. Approaching from the north on the
West Side Highway, one sees an unfolding panorama
of striking man-made and natural features, the city
on the left, the Hudson River and its palisades on the

261

262　263

264

right. This highway is currently quite dilapidated, like so much of the city, and the lower section is closed to traffic, but grand and controversial plans to redevelop it are under consideration.

At present it is the East River Drive, with its spidery bridges to Brooklyn and Queens, which gives the most dramatic sense of the cityscape (260, 261). The Roeblings' historic Brooklyn Bridge (262), opened in 1883 and now a registered national landmark, started Greater New York by linking Manhattan to Brooklyn at about the same time that the Statue of Liberty took up her station in the harbor. This great bridge combined ancient stone-bearing architecture with new engineering principles of tensile steel to launch the modern era of city design, a design predicated first of all on transportation, both horizontal and vertical. Elevators appeared concurrently, making humanly practical the tall curtain wall buildings that steel made technically possible. In the Roeblings' day, bridges were things to walk on as well as ride upon, and one of the most marvelous excursions I can recommend to anyone visiting New York is to stroll across the bridge on a sunny Sunday morning (263, 264). (When the Verrazano-Narrows Bridge was built in the early 1960s, a planned walkway was vetoed by the authorities on the grounds that people might use it to commit suicide.)

265

266

The dominant inlandmark of New York City is the Empire State Building (265). It remains a strong visual landmark because of its position at the center of Manhattan (in a part called midtown but geographically in the lower end of the island). In this particular spot relatively little new building has taken place. Below the Empire State Building on 34th Street and slightly west of it is old Herald Square, named for a long-gone newspaper but still noted mainly as the home base of Macy's department store. It was a major commercial node when the Empire State Building was built, but seems to have lost some of its former dynamism (although this is denied by an authority on New York, Paul Goldberger). Two bronze blacksmiths continue to herald the hours in honor of James Gordon Bennett, the paper's famous editor (266). An even more famous editor, Horace Greeley, is a somewhat bedraggled, if still defiant, figure as he sits slightly to the south of Bennett in the shirt center of the world (267). A few blocks north is a major node which is still dynamic in its own way, a de facto but unregistered national landmark, Times Square. It has changed somewhat in form in the last two decades but little in spirit, and it remains a dizzy blend of the sordid, the spectacular, and the nostalgic. George M. Cohan still goes on giving his regards to Broadway, which some people find a bit overwhelming (268). The family in this picture appear to personify the problems of information overload combined with illegibility so often found in large cities.

Photo 265 was taken from the top of the RCA Building at Rockefeller Center, eight blocks north of Times Square. North and east of that is the Museum of Modern Art, where, as in the courtyard of the

267

Boston public library, a semienclosed space forms a restful subnode in the city landscape. Even in winter, when it is not physically accessible, the museum's sculpture garden is peopled by the surrogate forms of art (269). One can enter it vicariously through the glass walls of the museum interior without trampling its carpet of snow. The exterior walls enclose a conceptual territory and exclude the casual passerby, but from the inside they do not exclude the city beyond.

268

269

On the proxemic–distemic continuum, people's interest in formal art creates a kind of ephemeral proxemic community based on life-style, education, talent, and intelligence. Both the art and interest in it vary considerably with local culture and changing fashions and tend to be limited somewhat by social class. Nevertheless, even in its most elite and avant-garde forms, it is a community of interest among people who are mostly personal strangers. The conventions of this community permit quite friendly associations and lead easily to more intimate relationships when desired.

At its best, art represents the most distemic kind of community conceivable, reaching into levels of human experience that are universal. It does this by enlarging or intensifying reality, not by duplicating it (270). It unites aspects of a particular culture, place, and time with aspects of all places and times. A cliché of our time is that technology dehumanizes us, but all art is technology devoted to expressing human experience. Some artists turn machines into sculpture (271), and some allow nature and time itself to collaborate on the compositions (272). Art can bridge the generations as well as other human stratifications; it can be as much fun taking children to some art exhibits as to a carnival.

Like art, science and technology can form a distemic community of the mind, reaching across language and age barriers here and now and across the

270

271

272

generations of recorded history. I was privileged to live, at an impressionable time, next door to New York's venerable Museum of Natural History (273), and I learned more there than I have at any school since. Dr. Richard Allen Chase, a psychiatrist at Johns Hopkins University, has made an interesting comparison between the type of learning that normally occurs in schools and that afforded by museums. He observes that the latter have been increasingly successful in recent times as the effectiveness of the former seems to have waned.[2] We are innately an information seeking animal, and we learn by acting on the environment and then watching the effect as the environment reacts. In the dialectic drama of life, the action and reaction sequence may be between people and people or people and objects. When attention is focused on the reaction of objects, conflicts between people are correspondingly reduced. In losing our preoccupation with self and others we can actually get closer to others through a common interest in the environment around us. In a museum of science, we can all learn with firsthand fascination the critical lesson of the moment: how much energy it takes to light a light bulb (274). Who needs a hickory stick in such a school?

Among the private centers in New York that have most energetically stimulated both art and science is the Ford Foundation. Its headquarters on East 42nd Street, designed by Kevin Roche, John Dinkeloo and

273

274

275

Associates, expresses quite forcefully an idea whose time has come. It has come, unfortunately, for a bad reason; as the urban outdoors gets uglier, more paved and more polluted, there is an energy-expensive trend toward bringing the "natural" environment inside. This has been done very expressively in the Ford Foundation Building, where office windows face inward on an enclosed park (275).

Near the Ford Foundation, facing the East River, is the United Nations, a major node which also represents an idea, not new but one whose time we hope has come for good. This is not a New York center or even an American one but a focal point for the world. Unfortunately the architecture of the United Nations headquarters has not expressed its idea more forcefully; it was designed by a committee, an international one, in the International style. It

276

277

278

would be nice to think that a more imaginative form could have produced a more effective symbol and thereby have improved the functioning of that uncertain and essential agency (276). The problem of integrating proxemic cultures in distemic settings does not call for neutral symbols but powerful, super symbols which can reflect what is common rather than what is different in the aspirations of diverse peoples. This was precisely the problem faced by the Continental Congress when the United States emerged as a nation; Thomas Jefferson urged that the new capitol be such a symbol and he was instrumental in creating one in the city of Washington, D.C. We shall consider the capitol later.

From the urban designer's point of view, the most marvelous opportunity was lost at the UN. Even from the water the Secretariat is conspicuous without being distinguished (277). What little distinction it has is derived more from the accident of three adjacent chimneys than anything in the complex itself. There is irony in the fact that this emotionally neutral, abstract generalization of a building has been built to house the penultimate in distemic relationships, a world forum. What was needed for such a global beacon was, first of all, a striking point on the harbor, such as that occupied by the World Trade Center, but one that would have left the ethnic, commercial, and architectural variety of the old downtown intact. Or it might have been located on one of the harbor islands, with a territory of its own; what better place than Ellis Island, where generations of immigrants entered the New World—a world now growing up or growing old? In any case, the United Nations has survived longer, much longer, than any such idea has before; may its star rise and not fall over that slippery surface (278).

The basic pattern of most of the older cities of the world was established when water was the most efficient means of getting around. The role of waterfronts as physical and social centers has been so firmly set in the layout of European cities, and the traditions associated with that layout are so strong, that they have carried through the industrial era far more strongly than in the United States.

An especially good example is Rotterdam, the largest seaport in the world. Its harbor is a landscape of cranes and towers, of barges and tanks, all the technological service apparatus for great ships and heavy resources. But it is the focal point of the city; part of it is also an extended linear park, dramatic, challenging, and in its own way beautiful (279).

279

Visible in the center of photo 279 is a phallic sort of monument to Victory in World War II. Not far away are two other monuments on the war theme which are more powerful as public symbols and works of art (a synthesis which is not all that common in our era). Their significance on both counts as well as their function as civic landmarks can best be presented by quoting that great master of discourse on these subjects, Lewis Mumford. In his book *The Highway and the City*, published in the midst of the reconstruction boom in the period following World War II, he recounts the rebuilding of Rotterdam after the savage blasting of the city by the Nazi Luftwaffe and the grim occupation that followed. A Jewish businessman and art collector who had survived with the help of Christian friends and faithful employees commissioned a leading Expressionist sculptor, Ossip Zadkine, to create a monument that "would remind even those who had not suffered of what the city had gone through." Here is how Mumford described the statue and its location:

> Zadkine's monument, a human figure at least twice human size, stands by itself, toward the waterfront end of an oblong plaza, at a point where the business district and one of the inlets of the busy port meet. It rests upon a granite base, and its long arms, angularly raised to the sky, identify it at a considerable distance. To the right, as one approaches it from the city, a long quay for small craft, with a parked embankment and promenade alongside it, sweeps southward in a slow curve to the outer harbor. Zadkine's dark bronze figure . . . is an image as terrible, in its immediacy, as Picasso's 'Guernica,' yet conceived with a power that promises the resurrection Rotterdam has experienced . . . . The moment that Zadkine's figure recalls is not to be encountered thoughtlessly or remembered frequently, as if it were the sculptured equivalent of background music. Hence the setting of the monument deserves special commendation; though business buildings surround the plaza, a wide thoroughfare and a stretch of verdure insulate it, so that really to see the monument one must go a little out of one's way and visit it on foot. Beyond it, in the port, the uplifted arms of the loading cranes underscore and carry through, with subtle congruence, the pattern of the uplifted arms of Zadkine's Rotterdam.[3]

About fifteen years after I read this I had the opportunity to visit Holland, and Mumford's description was etched in my mind. I immediately headed for Rotterdam to experience visually what he had evoked in words. It was, I'm sad to say, a great disappointment; not the statue itself, but the immediate setting, which had metamorphosed into mediocrity in the intervening years. The transition from the commercial center and the oblong plaza he described was still intact, but behind the monument there was not the slow curve of the outer harbor and

280

281

the echoing uplifted cranes but a rather dreary large metal shed (280). Almost worse than the shed was a collection of spindly plastic rain shelters, without substance of their own but sufficient to shatter the powerful silhouette of the statue. They seemed designed precisely to "encounter thoughtlessly" the moment recalled by the figure, or prevent recalling it at all. There was literally no place on the wide plaza from which I was able to photograph Zadkine's statue as Mumford described it, except by crouching on the pavement below the granite pedestal and focusing up at the sky. Even then the shed intruded into the composition (281).

It is difficult to understand this, really. It is impossible that the citizens of Rotterdam, especially those over fifty, can have forgotten what the statue symbolizes or be willing to recall it lightly. Of course, time mutes even the worst memories (and often enhances the best), and intervening struggles and miseries compete for attention. Possibly for some Dutch people the memory is still so intense that they prefer to have the impact of the monument diffused. And there may be a number of young decision-makers who simply don't care. But more probably Dutch pragmatism overrode all other considerations, as it so often does. The sheds were undoubtedly needed; it rains a lot in Holland. After all, their unsentimental practicality, combined with a stub-

born humanism and blunt kindliness, got the Dutch through the time the monument recalls. They have survived on practicality for centuries in a small land with few resources other than human energy and intelligence. Whatever faults one can find with their planning can hardly be attributed to sheer heedlessness, as it often can in the United States.

In any case, the Rotterdam harbor, with these two monuments to the war, the bland one conspicuous, the powerful one obscured, is the center of life in this city far more than the New York or Boston harbors are in those cities. Nearby in the commercial district is the other monument described by Mumford (282), this one to peace. It was designed by Naum Gabo, the surviving leader of the Constructivists, a short-lived movement originating in Russia which attempted to turn technology into poetry. The monument certainly does that. Here, the original setting Mumford describes is intact. As he says, "no photograph, no static view, no single word can do justice to such a complex form." Its symbolizing of joy, of life is as unmistakable as is the other's of horror and despair. It also celebrates Dutch engineering skill directed to humane purpose. The symbolism was apparently widely recognized at its creation and presumably is still. It was built in a shipyard and trucked to the site in a tense two-day journey which Mumford recounts as follows:

282

On the second night of its journey, two thousand people accompanied it through the cold, windy May night till five in the morning, when the job was over. Not since the high days of the Renaissance, as far as I can recall, has a new work of art drawn so much public interest. The . . . procession [was] headed by Gabo, dizzy with anxiety and elation, dancing in front of his construction almost as David danced before the Ark, sure at last, after repeated inspection, that the men in the shipyard had captured his subtle curves.[4]

Here is a case where a distemic situation led to a very strong sense of common humanity. The two thousand people can hardly have all been close friends, but they must have felt they were that night.

The Beehive department store, next to which the Gabo sculpture stands, was designed by Marcel Breuer, who was responsible for getting the sculpture commissioned. Mumford's description of how this came about is also relevant to the way cities are, or can be, structured. The Dutch planner responsible for the rebuilding of the bombed-out business section had widened the main thoroughfare, so that Breuer's building was set back farther than one old neighbor that had survived the Nazi attack (presumably the building behind the sculpture in 282). The

planner suggested to Breuer that he add a bay to his building at the corner to bring it into line, but the architect had designed it to be square and instead offered the sculpture as a compromise.

A block away from the Beehive is the Lijnbaan (283), which Mumford also praised highly in the book quoted above. It was one of the prototypes of the modern pedestrian street mall, which has become quite fashionable in recent years. At the time Mumford wrote about it, the pedestrian street was a new idea in planning, although old in practice. It is one that will be considered in more detail later. In this case the Lijnbaan focuses nicely on another very important symbol to citizens of Rotterdam, the Old Town Hall, which miraculously was one of two or three buildings in the area to survive the bombing intact.

The Dutch are among the most civic of people, which is to say, the most distemic. The beginnings of western political democracy were spawned there when Holland was a trading center and much of Europe still consisted of feudal fiefdoms. Throughout Holland the town hall, not the church, is the central symbolic landmark. Religion in the Netherlands is a proxemic matter, with two Protestant Reformed churches vying with Catholicism for Dutch souls; there is also a large Jewish population.

283

With one of the highest population densities of any nation on earth, the Dutch have had to learn to live together civilly while retaining their village-scale personal identities. They have almost more seaports than hinterland, and they therefore also have a peculiarly wide world outlook. In addition, the Dutch have a strong and deep tradition of harboring political exiles from all kinds of oppression (except for their own former colonialism), and it was their fierce defense of the Jews that earned them the particular hatred of Hitler. During the war many Allied airmen survived through their courageous help.

If Rotterdam is the modern seaport, Amsterdam is the ancient one. Its famous canals are literally water highways, stretching from the center of the old city (284, 285), which is the subject of careful historic preservation, through the nineteenth-century section that rings it and is now being "renewed," to the old suburbs and new high-rise residences beyond (286, 287). The war had exacerbated what was even before it one of the worst housing problems in Europe. In the postwar period the Dutch, in their no-nonsense way, embraced the slab. Their architects have produced probably the dullest versions of the International School anywhere on earth, but their native sense for scale has allowed them to avoid, with a few

exceptions (see photos 138, 139 in chapter 3), the more oppressive forms of it. On the other hand, they have built new polder towns and have lovingly preserved old Dutch villages. The delightful little port of Hoorn on a lake called IJsselmeer (once the old Zuyder Zee) north of Amsterdam (288) reminded me of Nantucket and other New England sailing towns. On a wall facing the sea are bronze statues of three children, characters from a Dutch story similar, I'm told, to America's Tom Sawyer and Huck Finn (289).

286

287   288

289

One of the most beautiful water-bound cities I know is Stockholm. It is built on an archipelago, really a chain of islands (290), and embraces the nicest blend of history and elegant modernity that I can recall. Waterways thread through the city; most are not canals but broad estuaries and lakes. At the right center of photo 291 can be seen the tower of the Old Town Hall. The ancient historic city where the royal palace stands is an island and is now well preserved as a center for art galleries, specialty shops, and avant-garde living. Its main focus is the old town square with its waterpump, a traditional gathering place, especially for women, in many pre-industrial societies (292).

The Swedes (and Scandinavians in general) have been more successful than most other cultures in using machine technology to produce modern design worthy of the term *art*. This talent extends from

mass-produced household articles to architecture and city planning. Swedish design in furniture has been famous for more than two generations; it represented some of the best of the Art Deco period and was honored with a name of its own, Swedish Modern. Modern Stockholm is as contemporary and pleasantly logical as historic Stockholm is romantically beautiful. The new glass and steel, but low-rise, city hall faces a great courtyard which is a harlequin-patterned stage for civic pageantry (293). The curving mezzanine platform provides an interesting counterpoint to the orthogonal geometry of the surrounding buildings, strongly focused by a glass tower in the middle of a fountain (294).

Stockholm is not really a distemic city in the polyglot way of the other cities we have looked at. Scandinavian culture in general is remarkably homogeneous for modern times. There are national rivalries and old hostilities among the Swedes, the Norwegians, and the Danes, but population densities in relation to total land area are very low, and until recently for most people life was quite rural. Only Copenhagen gives the feeling of being a truly cosmopolitan place. Nevertheless, Stockholm is a very elegant commercial city. It is also the one city I can think of that expertly accommodates both pedestrians and automobiles. While it is remarkably easy to drive in, several of the main streets have been closed to

292

293

294

295

296

automobile traffic and have become pedestrian shopping malls. Photo 295 at first glance gives the appearance of being an enclosed mall, but it is in fact an open street with covered pedestrian bridges connecting buildings overhead. Despite or perhaps because of the short growing season, plants and beautiful garden plazas abound in the summer months (296). Notwithstanding the plethora of elegant shops, informal open-air "farmers' markets" are also well provided for (297). The five slabs which loom over the market shown were erected in the postwar heyday of the International School, a relatively interesting version of this generally dull genre, but their appearance on the Stockholm skyline raised an outcry from citizens, and after that, high-rise buildings were disallowed. Sweden has been one of the most successful of the social democratic welfare states, and in accord with its egalitarian policies has encouraged citizen participation in planning. In the city hall is a model of the central area where proposed changes can be presented for popular debate and approval. Because everything else has been kept low by law, the effect of the five skyscrapers is in fact very dramatic. The five towers can be seen in the far right of photo 290.

As elsewhere in northern Europe, single-family homes are highly prized but expensive and hard to come by. However, the extended shoreline of the city provides marvelous opportunities for apartment houses and condominiums with views, and an excellent highway network, combined with but not replacing a fine rail transit system, has made the central city quite accessible to people who live in

297

298

a

b

c

d

reasonable proximity to nature (298). Around Stockholm are several new towns based on Ebenezer Howard's Garden City model but generally superior to the prototypes in England. The most famous is Vallingby, the first to be built in the postwar era and the most attractive. It has a lively town center (299a) and apartments looking over well-landscaped open space (b). Nearby is a sister town, less elegantly designed but with very attractive public grounds (c) and pedestrian walkways (d). Both are an easy twenty minutes from downtown by car or train. On the southern side of the city a new satellite town, Farsta, represents a departure from the pleasant scale of these two, and also represents a classic worldwide planning delusion that will not fade despite endless failures. The not very new idea in Farsta was to greatly increase housing densities to provide more

"open space" (300). Every Swede I talked to detested this solution, arguing that there is plenty of space in Sweden and no justification for such crowding.

300

301

302

Another Scandinavian port city which combines technology and urban aesthetics in a remarkable way, and which honors the industrial worker with its civic symbols, is Oslo. Norwegians are the equal of the Swedes in craftsmanship; they may even have outstripped them in the international market for fine furniture. Here the city hall and its plaza face directly on the harbor (301). The entrance to the city hall is lined with statues, not of generals or saints but workingmen (302). To the left of the harbor is a park with a museum which in its own way is as powerful a reminder of the horrors of World War II as Rotterdam's Zadkine monument. In front of it is a statue of Franklin Delano Roosevelt. At the foot of this statue, three rather bleary-eyed Norsemen were sharing a bottle as I approached it. As I focused my camera on the statue one said, in slightly slurred but otherwise excellent English, "You're an American." I nodded, not altogether pleased that anyone interested in that monument would automatically be considered an American. They wanted to know what I thought of their city. I told them it was beautiful. They disagreed; they didn't think *any* city was beautiful. They liked nature. I said I had been told that 50 percent of metropolitan Oslo was forest. "It should have been one hundred percent," one replied. Meanwhile FDR, unperturbed, looked over the ships and off-shore oil rigs being built in the harbor (303).

303

River Cities

If American cities as a whole have not done as well
with their seaports as those of Europe and other
older cultures, with a very few exceptions we have
treated our riverfronts abominably by any standard
at all. Particularly atrocious is the urban indifference
to the Mississippi, that great water corridor which
has played such a legendary role in the development
of this nation. Admittedly, it is a difficult river to
deal with, but I have been in most of the cities along
its banks and have yet to find between Minneapolis
at the top and New Orleans at the bottom, a waterfront that does justice to it. Minneapolis has only
recently created a riverfront park, and New Orleans,
the port of entry to our hinterland, has long had its
Moonwalk at Jackson Square in the French Quarter.
But not even Hannibal, Missouri, the boyhood town
of Mark Twain, who immortalized both the form

and spirit of that river for generations of readers, not even Hannibal has a decent riverfront, despite a museum of Mark Twain memorabilia.

There is a small park with some cannon on the bluffs at Vicksburg, Mississippi, to mark the spot where the Civil War was essentially won when Union troops captured the fort there and gained full control of the river (304). But in downtown Vicksburg, while "urban beautification" money has been spent on a trendy pedestrian street mall (305), the tourist-laden steamboat from New Orleans docks at a marginal pier which is probably less attractive and certainly less interesting than it was in Mark Twain's day (306). In Natchez, where the beautiful houses shown in chapter 2 are featured attractions, a grubby little park across from a railroad yard is separated by a chain link fence from the mighty Mississippi (307).

305

306

307

308

The National Park Service developed a splendid concept with Eero Saarinen's spectacular arch, which marks the "Gateway to the West" at St. Louis (308). This is indeed a national landmark with great symbolic value. Its importance as both symbol and landmark is suggested by the visitor statistics, which show this man-made wonder to be the equal of the natural wonders managed by the National Park Service. With our cultural penchant for judging value by size, brochures hail the Gateway Arch as "our country's tallest National Monument," but it is also one of the most beautiful in the modern mode. On this point we have a rare unity of opinion between popular and sophisticated taste (309a–d). However, although the city of St. Louis is billed as a collaborator in its development, the surrounding environment does not live up to the challenge of the concept, either as symbolism or as design. The gleaming, soaring arch is on a narrow, federally owned park wedged between an ugly city and sleazy riverbank concessions. Eastward toward Illinois it looks out on the vast dreariness of an industrialized prairie (310) and westward it overlooks a confused and sprawling city. Saarinen's design lined the arch up to frame the historic old courthouse where Dred Scott initiated his suit for freedom and focused national attention on slavery, the issue which led to the Civil War. But the planners of downtown St. Louis have largely missed a grand opportunity to focus their city on both landmarks. While the courthouse has been preserved as a central node, there are few points in the central business district from which one can see the arch (311), and the only place from which I could get a view that did justice to the gateway was across a parking lot which may soon be (and possibly already is) a tall building (312). Between the city business district and Gateway Park is one of the ever-present expressways that, like the railroads before them, have cut American cities off from the rivers that brought them into life (313). In visual effect, the gate is barred.

b

a

c

d

310

311

312

313

As I have suggested, it is the linkages to other places, not boundaries and walls, that are most essential to the vitality of cities. A good city is a service node, a cultural focal point, and a symbolic landmark for a region or an entire nation. At both ends of the Mississippi, such cities exist. Minneapolis has rejuvenated itself relatively recently, but New Orleans has always been a major port for inland America and has consistently maintained its cultural distinctiveness and diversity. St. Louis, once the jumping-off point for the Santa Fe trail and other routes of the westward expansion, now is a depressed and troubled city struggling to survive culturally and economically. Whether the physical design faults I have just touched on (it has many more) are a symptom or a cause of its social malaise is a chicken and egg question. New Orleans, on the other hand, is now at the center of the energy rich Gulf states, and many of its new faults come from its economic associations with Houston and the oil barons. New Orleans so far has kept the upper hand over its heavy-handed neighbor in cultural matters, refusing to surrender its long-standing ethnic ways, but there are large parts of it that seem determined to emulate Houston and to risk becoming St. Louis.

Many of the great cities of modern Europe emerged from Roman military outposts on the various rivers used by Caesar's armies. Preindustrial cities usually grew up on both banks of the river simultaneously, whereas in America "the wrong side of the tracks" usually meant the wrong side of the river as well, since the railroads generally followed the gentle grades of the river bank. In medieval Europe the dominant urban symbols were the church and the castle, representing secular and spiritual power, which in practical politics were often not that separate. The church was usually in the town square, socially accessible to the citizenry, the castle on a hill, for reasons both of strategy and social status. In Prague, Czechoslovakia, the basic spatial structures of river, castle, and church have remained particularly imageable. This is partly due to the great pride of the Czechs in this most beautiful of cities and partly to the political situation there, which has prevented the kind of modernization that took place in Stockholm. The Czechs are at least the equal of

Scandinavians in combining technical ingenuity and skill with artistic talent. The symbolic role of the river that flows through Prague, the Vltava, has been internationalized for music lovers in Smetana's famous composition by the German name for the river, the Moldau. It can be seen in the background of photo 314. To the right is the dome of the Church of St. Nicholas, a famous baroque cathedral of the Hapsburg era. In this case, both the castle and the earlier Gothic Cathedral of St. Vitus are together on the hill to the left. The St. Vitus cathedral was built in the creative reign of Charles IV in the fourteenth century under the direction of a single architect, Peter Parler, who started the work at twenty-two and died at seventy-two when it was almost finished. Compositional consistency, considered essential in other arts, is difficult to maintain in the arts of architecture and city design, a fact well illustrated by the absurd baroque tower on Parler's Gothic masterpiece, put there when fashion changed. The castle in front of the cathedral had been the seat of power for Bohemian kings through the centuries. It later became the summer capitol of the Hapsburgs, then the office of the ill-fated Masaryk Republic, and is now headquarters of the communist regime.

The Vltava River is not a boundary but the very heart of Prague, as the Thames is of London and the Seine of Paris. It separates what is known as the Mala Strana, or Little City, below the castle and cathedral, from the so-called Stare Mesto, the Old City, on the east bank. Both of these were original settlements of Prague. Linking the two are several

314

a

b

c

d

bridges, one in particular, the Charles Bridge, a work of architecture and a civic symbol of the highest order as well as a major focal point. It is closed to all vehicular traffic and provides a pedestrian way between the Little City and the Old City under a powerful but somewhat intimidating phalanx of saints (315a,b), through a gateway under two towers (c,d). In the other direction, the route over the bridge eventually leads to the Old Town Square, where for centuries people have gathered on the hour before the astronomical clock to watch the apostles parade

317

318

316

319

320

behind small windows above the clock face (316). On the east embankment of the Vltava is the National Theater, now being restored, which is on the site of the theater where Mozart himself conducted the premier performance of *Don Giovanni*, written by him in honor of Prague. Between the river and the Mala Strana is a canal, where old shops and mills are popular with artists and literati, as such places are the world over (317). Under Charles IV was added the Nove Mesto, or New City, by American standards still very old. Around the New City Charles constructed a wall (318). South of the New City is a still newer city, built during the intervening six centuries. Now that is surrounded by block after block of the inexpressibly dreary barrackslike housing typical of communist countries in the Stalin era (319). Beyond that are "new towns" of apartment houses in the sterile International School which differ only in details and quality of construction from examples of that type to be found anywhere else on earth (320).

Florence is another city centered on a river, but nowadays a more distemic and lively city. Like Prague, its former secular and religious nodes are clearly distinguished by architectural landmarks (321). Florence, of course, is the quintessential Renaissance city, the city of Michelangelo and Leonardo. Strangers of genius from villages all over Europe assembled there to found a distemic community of intelligence and artistry. They set off one of these periodic intellectual explosions that have kept human evolution on its course, very much as rocket thrusts keep spaceships headed toward their destinations. Florence was a city-state, a politically turbulent one where the town and the nation were the same thing, a type of social territory that must have particular civilizing power, Athens also having been such a place some two thousand years earlier.

In present-day Florence the Arno River is a market center with a bazaar on a covered bridge. Visible from the arch of the Uffizi Palace, which forms a transition zone by the river bank, is the tower of the

Palazzo Vecchio (322) on the Piazza della Signoria. In front of the palazzo is a copy of Michelangelo's famous *David* (323). The original is inside a museum nearby. At the end of a street blocked off for pedestrians is the famous cathedral with its dome by Brunelleschi and the campanile by Giotto (324), the product of a time when an artist and an architect were the same thing. The entire composition of the cathedral is impossible to photograph at ground level because the church is crowded in among other buildings; one must move around the constricted spaces using the eye, which, because it is connected to a brain instead of to a focal plane shutter, can see at a wide angle without distortion.

Florence is not a big city by contemporary standards, but it is and always was a highly distemic city, not a village, although it undoubtedly has had its share of villagers at the top and bottom of its social hierarchy. On the question of the relation of cultural amenity to population size and density, which is a matter of continuing controversy among both artists and planners, I like the point of view of the American prairie poet Vachel Lindsay:

> Let not our town be large, remembering
> That little Athens was the Muse's home,
> That Oxford rules the heart of London still,
> That Florence gave the Renaissance to Rome.[5]

322

323

324

As for Rome, it too is on a river. The importance of the Tiber to imperial Rome is suggested by the name of Tiberius, one of the successors of Julius Caesar, and it made Rome a port city by linking it to the Mediterranean Sea by way of Ostia. The Tiber also linked Rome to the River Arno and Florence via a canal. Although the Tiber is a very prominent feature and although its embankments are often very dramatic (325), one cannot say that this river is the center of Rome. Rome has so many nodes that it is hard to identify a major one. The Forum, the ruins of which lie right below the present civic center (326), was the focal point of the most distemic institution the human race had known up to its time. But Rome, which once governed the known Western world, can now hardly govern itself. Romans (and the members of other proxemic communities in Italy) seem to be eternally at war with each other. A longtime American resident of Rome, Robert

URBAN SPACE: THE MARKETPLACE OF SYMBOLS 179

Ardrey, has suggested that the Italians' hospitality to visitors, which is delightfully distemic, is in direct proportion to their hostility to each other, and he describes theirs as "the society of inward antagonism," to which he gives the name *noyeau*.[6] Space does not permit me to do justice to Rome, and I will not even try, except to note that it is surely one of the most monumental and symbol-laden habitats on earth. To understand Rome you must understand human history, and you cannot pass through Rome without acquiring a heightened sense of history, however much you know to begin with. For the world's Catholics, and likewise for many non-Catholics, the main center and the outstanding symbolic landmark of Rome is the Vatican. Like the UN headquarters in New York, it is not legally part of the city but a separate nation with its own government. The great oval "square" by Bernini in front of St. Peter's Cathedral is surely one of the grand transitional spaces of the world (327). Like great embracing arms they unite the secular and religious domains, the world of earthbound flesh and of soaring spirit. For help with the soaring, we can again

thank Michelangelo, that superb mixer of mind and matter, who erected the dome to uplift us from without and painted the ceiling of the Sistine Chapel to uplift us from within.

As in the Piazza del Duomo around the cathedral in Florence, one must move through Bernini's square to get the feeling of it. One of the ways we sense perspective is through the changing relationships of objects in the background field which appear to rotate around each other as we move. Bernini's curving porticoes on each side of the square—which is not square but oval—are double rows of columns (328, 329). But if we stand at the center of the radius of each arm, which is marked in the pavement, they appear to be single columns (330). As one moves off this center it is as though a hundred doors have opened simultaneously, inviting—pulling—one into the three-dimensional interior of the cathedral. The Vatican is a distemic religious city for people of a vast array of cultures and at the same time is a proxemic community on a large scale for people who share the myths, the symbols, and the rituals of that religion. The distemics are em-

328

329

phasized by transitional openings like the one just
described, the proxemics by the fact that the
Vatican is enclosed by a very substantial wall (331),
whose portals are guarded by watchmen in the uniform of the Swiss Guard (332).

330

331

332

333

334

336

Northeastward across the Alps are the Swiss themselves. Switzerland is a country that exemplifies my proxemic–distemic hierarchy. This beautiful little nation has been able to make itself a world capital of finance with a highly cosmopolitan culture and yet retain a remarkable degree of proxemic insularity. Not only is it very jealous of its national identity, but small as it is, it is a relatively loose federation of states, or *cantons*, which not only manage most of their own affairs but hold to different languages in several different dialects. Its industrial city of Basel is on Europe's Mississippi, the Rhine, but does much better with it than Americans have with their great river. In general, Swiss towns and cities focus on lakes. One of the most elegant urban settings that I know of is Zurich, a combined financial, market, and cultural node for the country and, especially as re-

gards finance, for the world. The center of Zurich is organized around the River Limmat, which flows between two hills (333) and also around the lake into which it empties. The smaller shops and bistros are along the river embankment (334), where money changers comfortably share space with temples in this still relatively puritanical country. An old Christian church (335) proudly displays to reverent tourists contemporary stained glass windows by Jewish Marc Chagall. At Christmastime the river is a glorious stage set, lit up by unabashedly man-made Christmas trees. Parallel to the river is the main commercial street, the Bahnhof Strasse, named for the great railroad terminal which that street connects with the lake area. Here are the bigger shops with the best that the world consumer society can produce, available at very high prices. At a node in front

335

337

of a popular department store there is a sculpture of a contemporary prefabricated family (336). Above all this, on the hillsides, are marvelously human scaled town houses on narrow streets, where one feels the intimacy of a village (337) while partaking of the opportunities of the world (338).

338

The Environmental Inversion of Urban Public Places

The classic urban function of the marketplace has been seriously undermined in suburbanized societies, especially in the United States. Here, but increasingly in other developed countries as well, the major markets have left the central city and become re-established outside it in the form of so-called regional shopping centers. These have not eliminated the central business district as such but have transferred it from the dense urban core to the spread city of suburbia. This new type of business district is approached almost entirely by car. One consequence is that it has been detached by considerable space from the supporting urban environment. In the near distance, the exterior landscape has been turned over to parking lots, and the townscape brought indoors.

The term *mall*, which used to mean a large, outdoor, public place, now refers to such a place under a roof. In some ways, the good shopping centers have returned the market street to the pedestrian better than have the central business districts of towns because the cars are left outside. A few of these shopping malls are as colorful and interesting as any other bazaars. A number of studies, including one in which I participated, have shown that people go to them as much for sociability as to purchase necessities. Youth gangs, which used to hang out around the neighborhood candy store, now drag race over to the local shopping plaza and hang out there.

The typical design of shopping centers calls for one or more large department stores as "anchors" (really magnets), between which are strung the smaller stores for so-called impulse shopping. The corridors constitute pedestrian streets, which invite considerable window-shopping. Not only are they a place for strolling and people-watching (339), but for many community functions, such as charity fund drives, which used to be associated with central business districts (340). The shops generally do not have the personality of those operated by individual proprietors; most mall developers will rent space only to chains, which are viewed as being more reliable tenants than single-owner stores. The merchandise tends to be monotonously similar, with emphasis on products for youth. Most such emporiums do not offer the unique sense of place and the

sensual variety of an old city center, but they are nevertheless very sociable promenades. Increasingly they have been designed to achieve haptic richness, often by very good architects and urban designers, and the better they are in that respect, the more sociable they become. But their greatest weakness, as compared with lively pedestrian spaces downtown, is that they have no visible relationship to a larger exterior environment. That has been given over to parking. For example, the shopping mall which is the major public node of the "new town" of Columbia, Maryland, is as bleak on the outside as any warehouse, perhaps more so (341). Inside, however, it is

339

340

341

342

343

an elegant commercial plaza, with pedestrian streets surrounded by lively architecture and spaces that can only be described as parks (342, 343).

Our tendency to turn our backs on the outdoor environment in central cities as it gets more confused and ugly, more polluted and congested—as illustrated by New York's Ford Foundation Building—has affected the evolution of another type of contemporary public social space, the large convention hotel. Fashionable and prestigious hotels used to invest considerable money and design talent on imposing marquees and facades that faced impressive and fashionable boulevards, often with elaborate

plantings and transitional spaces between the street and the entrance. Some resort hotels still do. But urban hotels now also turn inward. An example is the Peachtree Plaza Hotel in Atlanta, Georgia. Designed to be a major landmark, it has a round glass tower rising like a chimney above the clutter and congestion of a revitalized downtown. My first reaction to it when I drove into Atlanta was that it was the city incinerator dressed up in stainless steel (344). Leaving the car in a grim bunker of a parking garage, I walked down a bony, claustrophobic street seeking the invisible entrance to this renowned hotel. The entrance from this approach proved to be not very different from the exit to the garage. But anyone who can discover the way in will enter a fairyland. The entire building seems to enclose a lake, from which rises a nicely sculpted concrete service core, surrounded by concrete gondolas, splashing fountains, trees floating in concrete tubs, the concrete terraces softened by cascading hanging plants lit through a glass roof (345).

344

345

Nearby is the Hyatt Regency (346), the prototype of a chain designed by the architect-developer of the whole Peachtree complex, John Portman. He was one of the leaders of the rebellion against "modern" (International School) architecture. Portman refined the ideas of Morris Lapidus, who had turned architectural eyebrows into Gothic arches in the early sixties by formally espousing a new sensualism based on Miami Beach kitsch, some time before Robert Venturi and company suggested designers might have something to learn from Las Vegas. This rebellion has extended to high-style architects and has become the avant-garde now. It is known quite seriously among them and among critics and historians as postmodernism, a semantic incongruity that does to the language what pre-postmodernism did and ante-futurism seems bent on doing to the physical landscape. In any case, the Atlanta Hyatt Re-

gency and many of its offspring concentrate their new sensuality inside with quite delightful results (347). The trademarks of these hotels are glass elevators rising like bird cages on the outside of the service core, through a great courtyard surrounded by balconies which lead to the rooms. In the Atlanta Hyatt Regency, the elevators shoot through a hole in the ceiling to a revolving restaurant on top. Revolving restaurants have become de rigueur for all self-respecting cities in the past twenty years, and they offer a pleasantly kinetic way of drinking and dining, while one watches the city glide slowly by below. In this case, the view only increases awareness of the chaotic conformity of most of present-day Atlanta (348). Not long ago hailed as the symbol of the New South, this city seems to have learned nothing from the mistakes of the Old North. In the TV era, cities, like politicians, are so preoccupied with projecting an "image" that they lose track of what the image is of (349).

However, an interesting archaeological reality has been turned up in Atlanta. In the heyday of the railroad era, a portion of the nineteenth-century city was covered over by giant concrete trestles. Nothing was buried and little was removed from the parts of the city that remained beneath these trestles like the possessions of deceased grandparents in a dark cellar.

346

347

348

350

349

351

A few years ago the nineteenth-century streets were
rediscovered, complete with old storefronts, old kit-
chens, and empty bars, along with hydrants and
lampposts. This remnant of a public world from
which the original public has long vanished needed
little excavation and has now been restored to life
and sociable, slightly swinging, if somewhat damp,
supernostalgic commerce (350). The hefty concrete
trestles overhead buffer it from the progress that has
been overtaking aboveground Atlanta (351).

The irony is that this scenic introversion, which
encapsulates an artificial "natural" environment indoors at street level and a nostalgic street environment below ground, has been the result of Atlanta's
attempt to revitalize its central city to compete with
the suburban shopping centers and to attract conventions. As suggested earlier, the essence of suburbia is
physical openness, but in cities the space gluttony of
automobiles leaves most of the urban outdoors to

them. Portman has developed a pedestrian plaza for the Peachtree Center between the Peachtree Hotel and the Hyatt Regency which in all fairness is a pleasanter environment than that shown (344). But it is really just a jazzed-up version of the empty geometry of the pre-postmodern International School, the main attraction of which is the narcissistic reflection of other buildings (352). Haptic sensuality in design is reserved for the indoor spaces here too. The environmental inversion is not altogether due to the auto, of course; northern winters and southern summers make enclosed street spaces attractive from the point of view of comfort. According to Ada Louise Huxtable, much of the city of Houston, Texas (a place I have never visited), is enclosed and connected by underground tunnels.[7] This is increasingly true of New York also. In the much praised Citicorp building in New York, architect Hugh Stubbins responded to zoning concessions designed by Manhattan planners to induce developers to provide privately supported indoor public spaces (353). These are lively and attractive, but they could be anywhere. The outdoor plaza is interesting, but inside one has no particular sense of being in New York. This building is designed to be energy efficient, but not as efficient as fur coats and gloves.

Interurban Path Systems

Until the invention of the steam engine, rivers and sea-lanes were the highways of the world. They remain important transportation corridors, especially for heavy freight, but they are augmented by—and for personal travel largely superseded by—railroads, automobile highways, and airlines. In all these forms, travel corridors and their terminals are the most distemic places that exist. They are the dendrites of civilization, like the branches and roots of trees, like blood vessels and nerve systems, providing for the life-giving exchanges that make cultural evolution possible. The right to travel is surely the most

civilized right that human beings possess, and those countries which prevent or hinder it unduly are to that extent uncivilized.

The infamous Berlin Wall is one of the most obscene urban structures of all time, precisely because it so visibly abrogates that right (354a,b,c). Traditionally, city walls were designed to restrict access to protect the inhabitants from intruders with hostile intent. To my knowledge, in East Berlin we have a unique contribution of the twentieth century, a wall designed to restrict access *from* a city, to maintain an entire metropolitan population in prison. No photograph can prepare one for the brutal actuality of this wall, which expresses with dreadful clarity

354

a

b

c

the brutality of its intent. That is punctuated by the white cross (lower left in 354c) marking the spot where someone paid the ultimate price for scaling it. The Brandenburg Gate (354a,b), once the entrance to the heart of an historic city, now stands bleak and desolate in a dead space. The effect is to convert an entire townscape into a dungeon.

By contrast, most cities of the world today are choking to death on automobiles spawned by the primal urge to travel. At its best, the private car has provided freedom of movement that transcends all other vehicular systems, a freedom now threatened by dwindling oil resources. But the effect of cars on the central parts of large cities actually has been to reduce freedom of movement, although the illusion of personal freedom to move persists. Planning rhetoric in the United States speaks fatuously of the "love affair of the American with the automobile." Americans are certainly the most dependent on this vehicle for locomotion, but there is no evidence at all that we love cars more than any other people. Private wheels are an obsession for anyone the world over who can dream of possessing them, and if anything Americans are more blasé about their cars simply because we have had more of them longer. The problems of air pollution and energy conservation clearly require that something be done about the use of internal combustion engines to propel individual human bodies over the landscape. But the social, psychological, and political difficulties of getting people to accept alternative forms of transportation will only be aggravated if we consider the desire for the private car as a silly obsession. For almost everybody in an increasingly collectivized world, it remains the last bastion of personal independence. For the crowded inhabitants of apartment buildings and even dense suburbs, it is an important kind of mobile territory. For most blue-collar, white-collar, and professional workers who commute between interactions with family at home and coworkers on the job, the car is often the only place where it is possible to be alone outside of the bathroom. All this must be understood and, if possible, accommodated in the changes that seem at this writing to be inevitable for the developed, and for many developing, countries.

Aesthetically, the automobile and the highway systems on which it depends are at their best in the rural spaces between cities, rather than within them, and we certainly can begin by reducing private cars in central cities to an extent attempted nowhere as yet. An automobile must be able to travel faster than a good bicycle—at least twenty-five miles per hour—to make any sense at all, and yet in many cities one can walk across town faster than one can drive. I will leave further discussion of automobile roads for the next chapter, because here I am mainly concerned with transportation terminals as major nodes and landmarks within cities. It is the nature of the beast that automobile terminals are very diffuse, for urban design purposes destructively so.

In the great railroad era, roughly the century preceding World War II, railroad stations were major monuments and centers of activity in most cities. Like the wharves of the major ports before them, they were places for retail trade and social life. As I have noted, the major shopping street in Zurich is the Bahnhof Strasse, a main avenue connecting the railroad station with the lake and running parallel to the river. The railroad station in Basel, Switzerland, is also a major commercial node and a handsome architectural monument (355). The relation of transport to commerce is underscored by advertising art, the major decoration, which, despite the banality of its subject matter, makes a colorful montage in total effect (356).

Railroad stations and railroad travel in Europe are still very good, not only because mass use of automobiles is somewhat more recent than in America but because distances between urban centers are generally much shorter, and extensive suburbanization has not been planned so completely around the car. New York is one of the very few American cities of the now possibly ending automobile era where commuters use trains in large numbers. Riders of the trains are mostly unaware of crossing Manhattan river boundaries, but burrow into the city through tunnels. For commuters from Westchester and New England, Grand Central Station's star vaulted main concourse is their first view of New York. Grand Central is the only railroad terminal in the United States that I can think of which retains the civilized distemics of the better European stations. The round central information desk, topped by its four-faced clock, is a major indoor landmark, for generations the

355

356

357

place where almost anybody who wants to meet anybody will at one time or another arrange to wait (357). Time is the tyrant that intimidates all travelers on public transport, a psychological drawback that the antiautomobile romanticists of mass transit overlook. But Grand Central is for me and I suspect many other people one of the more permanent symbols of New York. The U.S. Supreme Court recently assured its permanence by upholding its designation as a national landmark. It is a grand, haptic stage for comings and goings which is a pleasure to be in for itself, full of bars where ulcer prone businessmen can unwind with a martini before heading home to the suburbs, of shops where a last-minute gift can be purchased for an almost forgotten anniversary, where Beaux-Arts architecture accepts modern advertising art.

Two subway stops and a transfer away is Pennsylvania Station, once a fine mate to Grand Central (358). Despite a strong protest movement by historic

358

preservationists, its main structure was demolished in the early 1960s to make way for a new Madison Square Garden. At the time I took photo 358, I used to arrive at the station on my way to work as an architect's researcher assigned to the headquarters of a large department store chain which was to have been one of the prime office tenants of the proposed new complex. To salve my conscience, before checking into my office nearby, I would take a turn around the building on the picket line that was protesting the destruction of the station. Eventually I was spotted there by an official of my firm's client. I don't know whether it was due to the client's devotion to the First Amendment or to its contempt for the effectiveness of the protest, but I was not fired, merely asked politely to protest somewhere else. At the time, a great fuss was made about the Doric columns of the McKim, Mead, and White building, but I thought the most splendid part of it was the

359

360

361

steel and glass train shed in the style of the nineteenth-century crystal palaces (359). Photo 360 shows West 33rd Street as it looked in those days with the post office at the extreme right and Penn Station just beyond. Photo 361 shows the same part of the same street as it appears today. The street then was certainly not one of New York's most elegant, but the post office and Penn Station were the best things at the westerly end of it, and the new garden is a sorry substitute for the old station. Its massive sleek drum looks like a Plexiglas oil tank; curved structures of that sort, even when better designed than this one is, tend to break up the continuity of the streetscape. They need space around them and the opportunity to be a focal point on their own. Although there has been some commercial upgrading of the area, it has not become the lively distemic center that such a project as Madison Square Garden should bring forth. There are numerous reminders that skid row is

363

362

364

not far away (362). The eagle at the left of the picture is all that remains of the old station (see 358). Like the World Trade Center the new Madison Square Garden seems to have upset the social and economic ecology of the area around it, and the planning problems must have been suspected early because the intended office tower tenant I worked for changed its mind and moved up near Rockefeller Center.

Intracity travel by train in the United States is not much better, and sometimes worse, than intercity travel. The New York subway stations are in sad contrast to Grand Central and what remains of Penn Station. Most are thug-haunted eyesores and earsores. Official graffiti on the dusty trains does little to liven up the drab loneliness of places where people assemble only for the purpose of getting somewhere else (363). However, San Francisco's new Bay Area Rapid Transit (BART) system is a beauty to behold and a pleasure to ride on (364), although it has been plagued by technical problems and is underused.

Montreal has a handsome new subway, and Washington, D.C., has completed the first part of one (365, 366). European subway systems vary; the one in Paris is well known for being attractive, modern, and efficient, and London's underground, while it is not beautiful, has many stations as well as trains with the comfortable dark wood so typical of England, and the system is remarkably quiet and dependable. Some of the communist countries, which are so uncivilized regarding free travel between nations separated by ideological boundaries, have put considerable emphasis on building subways, possibly because Moscow promoted its exotic subway of the 1930s as a model of socialist achievement. One of the few really elegant contemporary examples of what Czech design talent can do to the urban environment when it is given the opportunity is Prague's new subway (367). The Czech respect for history is also shown in the display in one of the stations of ancient arches discovered in excavating for the tunnels (368).

365

367

366

368

369

370

However, the problem with all subways as far as I am concerned is similar to that of elevators: one is deprived of the sense of moving from here to there through a continuous landscape. One goes from node to node without any awareness of what the nodes connect. This discontinuity is something like that of the television world, a montage of separate scenes and events without clear relationships that give a sense of proportion and scale. Intercity railroad travel, on the other hand, like auto and bus travel, gives one a feeling for the regions in which cities are themselves the nodes.

One advantage of traveling by railroad (or by ship) is that friends and relatives can actually see one another off (369). This used to be true, in an even more exciting way, of the early airports, but in the typical modern air terminal nonpassengers cannot get near the planes. In general, modern air travel, which has so largely replaced railroads and ships for long-range movement, has become an encapsulating experience, a negation of the most important psychological function of travel, that of providing a connected view of the world and its inhabitants. Riding in a

big, wide-bodied DC 10 or 747 jumbo jet is less like going somewhere than like sitting in a cramped auditorium, where a bored audience is plied with reasonably good food and unreasonably bad movies. I have always resented being asked to close my window-shade so that everyone else can see a movie. I was seven years old when Lindbergh flew the *Spirit of St. Louis* to Paris, and I have never gotten over the notion that flying is an adventure, despite all the efforts of airline public relations to make it otherwise. Occasionally, even one of the PR people actually thinks of the *image of flying*, as when one of them hired Alexander Calder to decorate the Braniff planes. In the great show of Calder's work in New York just after his death, he had finally elevated aircraft to the altitude of works of art (370).

In general the environment of modern airports is much worse than that of the planes. It allows one no sense of the outdoors, especially of the sky, which is to the plane as the sea is to the ship. Passengers arrive in a slick, usually crowded, enclosed space that looks very much like the one they departed from an hour, or ten hours, earlier (371a). There is very little

a

b

c

d

except the language of signs to tell us whether we are in New York or London or Madrid. There is endless waiting, sometimes comfortable (b), sometimes not, but always boring since there is so little to be seen of the place we are at. Airport bars, which used to look out on the runways, increasingly are crowded closets where the sole function is to numb boredom and anxiety while the children play on the escalator (c). The only way one knows one has crossed a border is through that ritual gateway, passport control (d).

Of course there are airports where one is fully aware of the comings and goings through the great skyspaces that have so increased distemic opportunities for the world's peoples (372). One of the best designed airports that I know is Dulles International Airport outside of Washington, D.C. That always

inventive architect Eero Saarinen conceived it as a great concrete tent, thrusting us out into the skyscape as a wharf does into the seascape (373,374,375). To keep both the sky and the aircraft visible, Saarinen made the terminal building a freestanding structure, without the usual endless tentacles to the various boarding gates. The planes stay out on the runways, some distance off. Mobile boarding lounges, really large buses, carry the passengers to the planes (376). One would think that this was, twenty years ago, an idea whose time had come, but apparently it hasn't. Off the main concourse of the terminal is a very pleasant restaurant and bar, where one can really enjoy what waiting is necessary in full cognizance of where and for what one is waiting (377).

Despite what seem to me its great virtues, Dulles Airport was underused for a long time. Washington, an hour away by ground transport, is the legislative center of a large and regionally diverse country, and Dulles is not near enough for congressmen who like to hop back home as often as possible to shake hands and find out what their constituents are thinking. So the old National Airport, a few minutes from Capitol Hill and an infernal danger and nuisance to the whole city, has remained the main port of entry. Recently, changes in schedules and landing rights for the Concorde seem to have picked things up at Dulles.

376

377

Cities Designed as Monuments:
National and State Capitals

Thus far I have examined edges and districts, activity nodes, travel terminals, and symbolic landmarks *within* cities, especially as they serve the cosmopolitan community of strangers. Some of these places and the activities that are generated in them are quite local, verging toward the proxemic; others are intercultural and even international, fundamentally distemic. There are certain cities, however, in which the main urban entity is a distemic center and monument for an entire region, state, nation, or, as in the case of the United Nations and the Vatican, a large part of the world. Capital cities are often of this type, especially those which were designed at the

378

379
380

start to *be* capitals and therefore symbolic landmarks.

Capital cities become personifications of the nations they symbolize, beings which act on behalf of their constituencies as if they were actual people. "Paris" and "Bonn" deal with "London" on matters concerning the latter's participation in the Common Market; "Washington" makes overtures to "Peking," which are reciprocated, greatly perturbing "Moscow." These anthropomorphized places appear to act very much like the gods of Greek mythology, beings somehow more powerful than ordinary mortals but essentially human in their behavior. As symbols, they include but also transcend proxemic subgroups and local districts even while frail human ambassadors from these capitals inevitably express special interests and regional loyalties, except on rare occasions.

One such capital is Madrid; it was laid out two centuries before Washington, D.C., but is in some respects a little like it. Madrid has a number of major radial boulevards, intersecting at circles or plazas. In the newer northern part of the city, these are overlaid with a grid, as in Washington. In Madrid, one has the feeling that being a capital is its main function, although it has very lively commercial and cultural centers. An important node has government buildings (378). The king's castle is another governmental node, some distance away (379). Statues of heroes and saints are everywhere, including at

Christmas the most beloved symbol of Christian culture (380), here making its eternal journey over a long urban trail. Very near the palace is the Plaza de España (381), where, tucked behind splendid fountains and monuments, is a quiet symbol both of local culture and the universal human condition with its ironic and eternally frustrated aspirations for truth and justice, those marvelous figments of the human imagination that ripple over a crazy world (382). The figures of Don Quixote and Sancho Panza express something at once proxemically Spanish and internationally distemic (383).

381

382

383

Washington, D.C., is the only city in the traditionally antiurban United States which is accorded the respect most other nations accord their major cities. This remains true despite the current political fashion for viewing with hostility and suspicion the Big Government centered there. As I noted previously, Thomas Jefferson conceived the entire city to be a monument to democracy. Toward that end he chose the architecture of the classical republics of Greece and Rome to symbolize the new nation, but in actuality, Pierre L'Enfant laid out Washington in an essentially baroque plan more nearly associated with the pomp and ceremony of latter-day European emperors. It was a great plan nevertheless, and it remains our most coherently designed city.

Probably no image is as loaded with political symbolism for Americans as that of the U.S. Capitol (384), which appears behind almost every television newscaster in the country when lawmaking is being discussed. The term *Capitol Hill* is used almost as if it were the name of a person who causes things sinister, silly, or beneficent to be done to and for the American people, a schizophrenic being that argues with itself over everything. The Capitol is also a mecca for American tourists. The Capitol steps are a

385

stage for bus loads of high school bands from Tuscaloosa to the Twin Cities (385). On one morning I saw three different bands there in the space of an hour and a half. The cast-iron dome (386) contains within it a frieze depicting the mythical events it symbolizes, like sculptures on a cathedral, and there is even a modest attempt at a native, secular version of the Sistine Chapel (387). At floor level ordinary citizens pay homage to our political saints and martyrs (388).

386

From the West Front a grand transitional space designed by Frederick Law Olmsted, Jr., opens onto a vista of administrative and cultural institutions (389). Directly ahead lies the National Mall, with the obelisk of the Washington Monument at the center and at the far end the Lincoln Memorial. To the right is Pennsylvania Avenue, at an angle to Constitution Avenue and the Mall, forming the Federal Triangle, which is a core of government buildings. On the Mall side are the National Gallery of Art and the new Smithsonian Institution. Pennsylvania Avenue leads past the central business district on the north directly to the White House, the nearest thing Americans have to a public palace. The White House, also a constant image on television newscasts and a favorite focus of protest demonstrations, lies almost, but not quite, on a north–south axis with the Washington Monument. From the base of the Washington Monument, a popular stage for political gatherings, one looks east to the Capitol and west to the Lincoln Memorial. The approach to the latter, on the Memorial Bridge over the Potomac River, is the clearest and most dramatic gateway to an American city I know of (390). Within this classical marble sanctuary is the Daniel Chester French statue of Abraham Lincoln, sadly pondering the state of the union. He gazes with and over armies of tourists across the reflecting pool to the monument and the Capitol, a favorite backdrop for snapshooters (391).

Nevertheless, as the capital of any major world power should be, Washington is a cosmopolitan city as well as a native symbol, although it has its ups and downs in that regard depending on the world outlook of the president in office and the outlook of the world itself. I was fortunate to have lived in Washington as a high school student in the days when, intellectually, it was a little American Athens, during the New Deal of Franklin D. Roosevelt. It was much smaller then, but as Vachel Lindsay says, "Let not our town be large . . . ." At this writing, the *New York Times* is suggesting that it may be rivaling New York as an artistic center. It is now the center of a huge metropolitan area sprawling into adjacent Maryland and Virginia, with all the social, physical, and economic problems of other big cities. But it remains unique in the United States as an urban monument.

388

389

390

391

The combination of a grid overlaid on radial streets joining at major circles forms an array of subnodes, each with a strong identity of one sort or another, and a great many small triangular spaces which make a mosaic of parks, often with statuary (392). In developing his plan for Washington, Major L'Enfant, who as both civil engineer and artist was also our first great urban designer, based his concept on a very careful study of the environment. He very early selected what became Capitol Hill (originally known as Jenkins Hill) as the major site for the capitol, which he described, according to John Reps, as a spot that "stands really as a pedestal waiting for a superstructure." [8] The radial avenues he laid out form a diamond shape pattern more or less parallel to the Potomac and Anacostia rivers. These join at an obtuse angle, creating the original southeastern and southwestern boundaries of the city. The relationship of these rivers to the city is not at all evident today, although the famous Tidal Basin, a parkway, and numerous bridges make the traveler well aware that the Potomac is near at hand.

392

Half a century after L'Enfant designed Washington a *state* capital was laid out in a somewhat similar plan, but one which even more dynamically reflects the original landscape and also provides for a unique social symbolism, contrasting two kinds of distemic institutions. Madison, Wisconsin was designed by an amateur who appears to have been somewhat more interested in land speculation than in aesthetics (L'Enfant eventually got himself fired because, among other things, he was too belligerently concerned with design at the expense of local real estate interests). Wisconsin's Governor James Doty nevertheless came up with one of the most imaginative uses of a unique site to be found on this continent. In the fierce competition that accompanied the location of territorial capitals, Doty had selected an isthmus between two beautiful lakes, but only after taking the precaution of acquiring ownership of the land. On the center of the isthmus is a hill on which he laid

out a square for the capital building (393). The isthmus runs almost exactly northeast and southwest, so that a line drawn down the middle of it intersects the standard township section grid at an angle of forty-five degrees. Doty laid out a major avenue, now called Washington Avenue, along the center line of the isthmus, meeting his capitol square in the middle of its sides. From the corners of the square, streets radiate north, south, east, and west, parallel to the main section lines but at an angle to the square and the street grid laid out around it. Three of these radial streets terminated at the lakeshores, but the westerly one, to become known as State Street, extended along the south shore of Lake Mendota to terminate at the foot of another hill (upper left in 393).

The present capitol was designed early in this century by architect George Browne Post (designer of the New York Stock Exchange) to fit this complex

street system. Four Greek wings face the radial streets, while round, columned porticoes at the intersections of the wings face Washington Avenue and two perpendicular streets leading to the lakes, so that the capitol plan is essentially an octagon within a cross under a soaring dome (394). At the other end of State Street there eventually emerged the University of Wisconsin, crowned by Bascom Hall above a grassy mall facing the capitol (395). Bascom Hall once had a cupola which echoed the capital dome, but that was destroyed by fire. The two major nodes represented two state institutions performing different civic functions, connected by what became a lively commercial street.

394

395

a

Until the 1960s both of these were important landmarks to the people of Wisconsin, who generally were proud of both. One symbolized representative *government* of the common man, the other the *education* of the common man, in a traditionally populist state. But then proxemic neotribalism, the eternal threat that hangs over all distemic relationships and institutions, ran rampant during the student protests against the Viet Nam War. Madison's twin symbols of frontier civilization became the fortifications of enemy groups separated by age and education itself. By the time of President Richard Nixon's Cambodian invasion of 1970, State Street had changed from a cluttered but lively shopping corridor to a virtual no-man's-land, teargassed by police on the "right" and "trashed" by students on the "left." Businesses were boarded up and some began to move out. In a typical tribal response, Wisconsin Middle Americans blamed the troubles on out-of-state students. Both the physical and social unity of Madison were shattered. It became, like the University of California at

Berkeley, a new kind of symbol, a national television symbol of a generation alien to its own culture. Then in midsummer of 1970 a bomb went off in one of the university buildings, killing a researcher, and suddenly, playing at revolution was not fun any more. Madison became somewhat quieter, but the old-time monuments of Middle American culture seemed to have lost their meaning. The public ambience, at least on the university side, was dull and lifeless.

But cultural change, with and without culture shock, occurs fast in our time. A few years later, one of the more flamboyant of the leaders of the student radicals, Paul Soglin, had become a popular and only slightly left-of-center mayor. One of his accomplishments in office was to carry out an old dream of local planners, the development of a pedestrian street mall along State Street. Redesigned by M. Paul Friedburg, State Street is again a genial market corridor, where legislators and students fraternize, apparently amiably enough, along with townspeople and visitors from the hinterland. The new mall helps to reunite the "town and gown" in an unusually well integrated, architecturally and socially diverse, haptically interesting urban composition.

Starting now from Bascom Hall, one looks eastward down a hallway in which the back of a statue of Abraham Lincoln is framed (396a). Lincoln is a symbol of many things to different people, but I think the great hold he has on our imaginations is due more to the fact that he was a great poet than to the fact that he was a president who freed the slaves or saved the Union. In saving the Union, Lincoln saved the basis for the distemic institutions that have been the strongest asset of a nation that is regionally more diverse than it usually likes to think it is and much more diverse than most foreigners think it is. But it is as the symbol of an honest and humane political leader that he appropriately looks out along State Street to the capitol. State Street does not line up exactly with Bascom Hall, and the capital is hidden by a tree as we step through the rectangular door into an arched portico (b). Before us is a marvelous hierarchy of transitional spaces between the administration building, the university, and the city at large. The roundness of the arch is repeated by the round plaza on which Lincoln is seated; whether by design or by accident, the inverted crenellations in the stones of the arch are echoed by the yew shrubs in back of the statue. As we emerge from the portico (c) we are enclosed by a canopy of trees over the mall, with sidewalks on the grassy hill leading down to State Street. As we move to the right we get a glimpse of the capitol dome rising above the urban skyline (d). This kind of partially revealed landscape creates a heightened sense of interest, for which the Kaplans used the term *mystery* or *involvement*.

As we walk down the hill, State Street and the dome of the capitol come into full view (e): But now an undistinguished brick apartment building blocks the capitol; it adds little in the way of mystery, being merely an obstruction, an example of heedless planning that cannot be justified on economic or any other grounds; it would have cost little more than some thought to design that building so that it would not intrude as it does. At the foot of the hill on the left is the Wisconsin Historical Society. Soglin's new pedestrian mall relaxes and unifies the old State Street (f). Local planners have long urged the banning of cars from the entire length of the street, but merchants who still think that shoppers need to tie up old dobbin in front of the store oppose such things, and political reality has left the eastern end of State Street as cluttered with cars and confusion as before. Still, the ambience is lively and the capitol increasingly impressive as one nears it (g). Capitol

Square is covered by a canopy of mature trees, which return a sense of Kaplanesque mystery to the building as one approaches on a broad sidewalk (397). Inside, elegant coffered arches leading to the four wings intersect the rotunda under the dome (398). From a parapet around the great dome, one can look back at the university. But Bascom Hall, an interesting landmark if not a distinguished work of architecture, is now upstaged by a brutalist slab— this time not the emblem of corporate power but of university bureaucracy—which ignored, among other things, the potentialities of advice and talent among its own design faculty and students. But in any case both buildings can be seen now only from above. For the well-being of the educational half of this symbiotic institutional pair, one could wish that the university were as visible from the capitol as the capitol is from the university, as once it was, in fact and in spirit.

397

398

Suburban Distemics: A Workday Community

In this chapter I have focused for the most part on cities because the concentration of diverse populations and human energy there makes distemic relationships most likely to occur and distemic places easy to identify and to photograph, just as proxemic territorial relations are relatively easy to identify in small towns and suburbs. But modern society is highly mobile, both in physical and social terms, and, depending on how the present energy crisis is resolved, it is likely to remain so. A number of social scientists have pointed out that the traditional kinds of communities based on extended family and neighbors relatively rooted in a geographical place are replaced by other sorts of associations based on age, class, profession, and even recreation. Some of these, if they are stable over a long period, can provide a kind of group culture which is not ethnic but which nevertheless fits the proxemic model. Indeed, in the United States, where mobility has been exceptionally high from the beginning, cultural attitudes based on class seem to be far more permanent and pervasive than those based on national origin. Actually, throughout urban history, workplace associations have been sources of cultural identity and can form a kind of community, as in the medieval guilds. Part of the success of Japan as an economic and industrial power has been attributed to the transference to the corporation of the traditional loyalties the Japanese have had toward family and neighborhood. The old garment district in New York had a strong identity as a community which was more specific than the fact that its members were Jewish.

Distemic relationships are not confined to cities. They can occur wherever cooperative social institutions of any sort involve associations between people whose cultural outlooks are substantially different. This can and in varying degrees often does occur in business corporations and government bureaucracies. It is as important for civilized behavior in the spread cities of suburbia as in the big urban centers. At least 30 percent of the American people now shop not on Main Street but in suburban shopping centers, eat out in fast-food chains on the commercial strip or in sophisticated restaurants located in remodeled barns, go to drive-in movies at the edge of cornfields, and work in factories and office buildings located on former farms or wooded hillsides. Some aspects of this will be considered in the next chapter.

I would like to end this chapter with a discussion of a place where artistic and managerial talents of a very high order have combined building architecture, landscape architecture, and planning to achieve a unique landmark, a distinctive but harmoniously integrated district, and a socially diverse and yet symbolically unified community. Although it is set in a rural landscape, as far as I am concerned it is a very urban place, distemic on some dimensions and proxemic on others. It is also ultramodern, made of steel and glass.

Deere and Company is a large corporation which manufactures farm machinery for worldwide markets. Its headquarters and major plant is in Moline, Illinois, a rather dreary industrial city on the Mississippi. When in the great building boom of the 1950s it planned a new headquarters, it could have done as so many corporations did, erect a large skyscraper in the downtown of a major city. The function of a corporate headquarters is largely sales and management, and such headquarters are usually not near their manufacturing facilities but rather in the centers of commerce and finance or, more lately, in the suburbs outside them. Deere and Company chose, for consciously formulated symbolic reasons, to build its new headquarters in the Illinois prairie which had brought the company into being. Here on the edge of an industrial city, not far from its own major plant, salesmen, executives, engineers, lawyers, secretaries, clerks, mechanics, cooks, waitresses, nurses, and gardeners form a workday city in what is really a gorgeous park, a park so beautiful that it is a major tourist attraction (399).

For their architect, Deere and Company had the good sense to hire Eero Saarinen, who designed a building in the steel and glass that was so fashionable at the time. But he did not do it for fashionable reasons, and the steel was not ordinary.

"Farm machinery is not slick shiny metal but forged iron and steel in big forceful functional shapes," Saarinen wrote about his handiwork. "We sought for an appropriate material: economical, maintenance free, bold in character, dark in color."[9] He found it in a new alloy for structural steel which

399

would rust quickly up to a point and then stop, forming an oxidized layer that protected the rest of the steel, like paint. Although the original purpose in developing the steel was utilitarian, Saarinen immediately saw the artistic potential in this new material. The rust is originally a fairly bright orange, but it eventually weathers to a color similar to bronze but with a character of its own. It has such character that, as Saarinen predicted, it has been widely used by architects since.

But rarely so well. The unity of the strong steel frame is elegantly varied through the use of differentiated members for sunscreens, railings, and window muntins, so that despite its forcefulness it has a great delicacy, almost a filigree (400, 401). Curiously, despite the deliberate steeliness, there is a quality in it something like a Japanese pavillion made of wood, and some of this effect can be attributed to the dark

brown color. Nevertheless, the building alone, or in another setting, might not be so memorable. What makes it so powerful is both the unity and the contrast between the forceful steel structure and the soft, flowing landscape around it. In this setting, the pond is to the building as an urban waterfront is to a city center. The grounds were designed by landscape architect Hideo Sasaki and his associates to blend with but not copy the Illinois farmland (402). Symbolic of a productive and harmonious relation of machine to land, the whole unites a diversity of persons, tools, and activities with a particular place, forging meaningful form for members of a corporate community whose working lives are spent making engines of agriculture. The entire composition is legible and coherent; one is not likely to get lost. Yet it promises more than is revealed; it has mystery. One is impelled to proceed inward to find out what

400

401

402

is really going on. Some of what we find is socially structured into more or less private and public areas. Some of what we find is purely symbolic.

The environmental focus of this quintessentially modern place is achieved specifically by the use of sunshades, so that the glass need not be covered by drapes and can thus let the outside in and the inside out at all hours and in all seasons. This reiterates the nature of the company's purpose by framing growing plants and living landform shaped by steel. Along with work activities, the social rituals of daily life in any large corporation—the coffee breaks, conversations in elevator lobbies, and lunches with business associates or with friends in the cafeteria—take place in a setting deliberately intended to express a collective image (403–406). I can only guess at the degree to which the Deere image is actually held by all the people who use or visit this building, but a study by

403

404

405

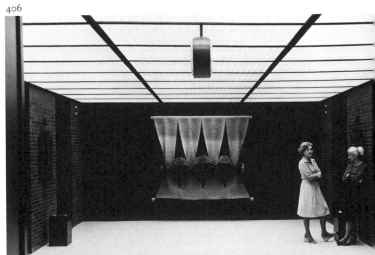

406

E. T. Hall and Mildred Hall, and my own conversations with people there, suggest that it is very high.
The image system contains a measure of historic
myth, a connection with ancestral origins. On the
lower floor, just below the public lobby (407), is a
glass-enclosed exhibition hall displaying, side by side
with giant earth-movers, the first polished steel
plows and other agricultural tools invented by John
Deere (408, 409) and a mural montage of agricultural
memorabilia.

407

408

409

Frank Lloyd Wright said that in order to have great architecture, there must be great clients. In order to have great cities we must have great citizens. In an era when giant national and multinational corporations have taken over the traditional role of popes and emperors as competing patrons of urban design, greatness in a socially artistic sense has unfortunately not been frequent. Saarinen has been justly acclaimed for this great building. Unfortunately and unfairly, Sasaki has not been adequately acclaimed for his contribution to its setting. But the Deere and Company management certainly share the greatness of the building architect and the landscape architect in the conception of this place, which in its entirety is a work of art. It appears to be a consequence of an unusual and admirable preoccupation not merely with the consumer's image of the company's product but with the self-image of the people who do the producing. This was explicitly expressed by William A. Hewitt, who seems to be the guiding genius of the project on the company's side.

Such a *public* outlook is the essential characteristic of distemic environments. The excessive emphasis in the modern world on special interest groups of all kinds *out of context* has led not to uniqueness in a universal order but to conformity in chaos. When man-made and natural form are combined, consciously or unconsciously, with the symbols that make explicit the culture of the people who use and experience a particular geographical space, we say it has a sense of place, the *genius loci*. The sense of place is to the environment what personality is to the person. When a diversity of cultures share a space, environmental forms that unite them create a larger sense of place. This most often evolves slowly over time through the actions of many people, and thus comes to express both individual and collective meanings. Only occasionally do talented people like Saarinen, Sasaki, and Hewitt bring it about all at once. When such designers achieve this, it is not so much because they have the ability to "create" form as to discover it in the elements that are already there.

Of course, it is easiest in our time to rearrange the environment to this extent on rural land owned by a single institution. In towns and cities, so many complex social and physical relations already exist that only the most powerful and arrogant of clients can provide authority for large-scale rearrangements; and when this occurs, more often than not what is lost is greater than what is achieved. In earlier times such power was wielded by princes and priests. Much out of the past that tourists spend time and money to admire was achieved without regard for the lives and property of ordinary persons; for example, in the Paris of Napoleon III by his planner Baron Haussmann. Nevertheless, the environments which the ancient aristocracies constructed so often had meaningful form because their power depended to a great extent on capturing public imaginations through shared symbols, symbols that transcended those of various interests within the population.

Today such power is wielded almost entirely by the bureaucracies of big government and big business. Here too there is often no regard for private lives, even though, at least in the West, property is somewhat better respected. Occasionally, as in the case of Deere and Company, these institutions create coherent environments as symbols of a beneficent power and purpose. When the symbols are recognized as art two things have happened which philosophers have pondered for centuries and which nobody has yet explained. The designers as artists have expressed the particularity of their culture in such a manner that the environment resonates with the feelings of the people who inhabit it. At the same time, in touching the essence of a particular culture in all its uniqueness, they also find something universal that people with widely differing backgrounds and outlooks can respond to. All the great art of history has both expressed its own time and has said something to people of all times. But most such art derived from long-standing tradition. In pluralistic societies of cultural strangers, the environment must somehow at once be meaningful to subgroups, each on their own terms, and yet also have meaning of some sort for all at the same point in time. Unless we can bring about a new emphasis on social and physical contexts, we will continue to obliterate the sense of place, all over the place.

6

Humane Space: Promenades, Parks, and Places for Peace of Mind

In the last chapter I outlined and tried to illustrate what I am calling distemic public life, that type of community which involves people with different cultural outlooks and experiential worlds in the use of a common space. I believe that this differs from the usual concept of cosmopolitan persons and places in that it does not renounce provincialism but rather accommodates it within a larger order. Distemic relationships can occur on a very small regional scale, wherever the residents of conceptually or otherwise fenced-in neighborhoods peacefully and usefully share neutral ground. But these relationships become increasingly important in the national and international landscape.

Ideally, this community of people who do not know one another intimately, and who may not be expected to want to, both underlies and overrides native culture without threatening or obliterating it. Despite the importance of local identity to human security, human happiness, and certain creative aspects of human behavior, we are in fact one species. Although culture is almost entirely a human phenomenon, its origins lie in our social inclinations as mammals. We are at our most *human*, our most *civilized*, when we are able to combine our personal and cultural uniquenesses in collective and cooperative enterprises which are often quite impersonal. In any case, we have created for ourselves a global habitat which will not enable us to survive as a species without such cooperation.

At this writing, the more dangerous aspects of neotribalism which have been turning many of the world's cities into guerrilla battlegrounds now threaten the most fundamental mechanism for international society with a new fad for assaulting embassies and diplomats. But tribalism is not merely a local phenomenon; it also appears in the highest echelons of government and corporate bureaucracies in all countries, diminishing our collective ability to preserve the planetary home which inexorably we all share. We do not have to share each other's myths and symbols, sacred or profane, for the needed collective action, but we need to be able to deal with each other on levels that transcend them. We do not have to love each other for this purpose, but the mechanisms that provide for it often have surprisingly cheerful results. Why else would the tourist industry be such an important economic asset to so many countries?

Some years ago William H. Whyte began a study of human behavior in the public spaces of New York City. His work, which he called the Street Life Project, has spawned a number of similar research efforts by his students and others. These studies use time-lapse photography and direct observation to determine what people actually do as opposed to what theorists presuppose them to do. They have considerably improved Fifth Avenue and a number of other places by providing places to stop, sit, and congregate. One of Whyte's first discoveries ran counter to some favorite myths of pop sociology. His cameras clearly revealed a surprising fact: people seemed to be enjoying themselves on city streets. They could actually be detected laughing and smiling! While they often (but not always) travel in pairs or small groups and appear to be friends, they are surrounded by, actually immersed in, crowds of strangers.

The best public places of cities may be "impersonal" in the neighborhood sense without being cold or alienating in the broader social sense. On the contrary, freedom from social pressure and release from the boredom of the familiar and near, however dear, can be exhilarating precisely because one is surrounded by strangers who are not threatening, who may even be cordial, who can be companionable without being in any emotional sense demanding. Probably many an individual has felt less lonely alone in a crowded park than at home in a hostile family. My own feeling is that only in urbane public spaces, on any level of scale, and in their physical opposite, quiet, natural landscapes, can an individual feel fully at one with the human race. In this final chapter I will take a look at both of these opposite kinds of spaces in terms of their socially unifying functions.

Promenades

One of the most delightful pedestrian malls I know is the Ramblas in Barcelona, laid out by the Spanish architect, Antonio Gaudí. Gaudí is best known for his Temple of the Holy Family (Templo de la Sagrada Familia), which was an attempt to achieve a Gothic emotional effect by the use of contemporary forms (410). In the Ramblas Gaudí created a truly modern place by leaving the original Gothic intact. Located in one of the world's most cosmopolitan cities, it is a distemic space surrounded and suffused by the proxemics of Spanish culture, which is largely Catholic but also very Mediterranean. As noted in chapter 2, the Mediterranean cultures put a high value on public street life, which they regard as being quite separate, physically and psychologically, from private life.

Stretching from the waterfront twenty blocks or more through the old city, the Ramblas is a great avenue for travel on foot, with an attractively paved area at least fifty feet wide lined with overarching trees and punctuated by kiosks. On each side, narrow vehicular service roads separate the main pedestrian way from ample sidewalks in front of stores, restaurants, and offices. At siesta time the stores close, but even on a rainy December afternoon the Ramblas will be full of pedestrians (411). When the shops open again at six o'clock, the scene becomes

411 412

even livelier, and at Christmastime the trees are outlined in lights (412).

The siesta in this case is an example of the way in which local proxemic cultures provide uniqueness to distemic places. One obviously does not have to be a Spaniard to love the Ramblas. Anyone from anywhere can enjoy its milieu, and people from every-

where do. For those in the north who are used to quitting work at five, having cocktails at six, and eating at seven, doing business all evening and going out to dinner at midnight takes a little getting used to. But not much. Photos 413, taken at three in the afternoon, and 414, taken at the same spot around nine o'clock in the evening of the same day, suggest

413 414

415   416

how tradition shapes time as well as space. The
scene is one of the narrow, twisting streets of the
Gothic Town (Barrio Gótico) to the east of the
Ramblas.

Here, as elsewhere in the true *polis*, commercial
activities share space with other social functions,
religious, political, and intellectual. The focal point
of the Gothic Town is the old cathedral (415). The
plaza in front of this cathedral faces a chic shopping
street (416). In the medieval side streets there is
delightful sensual intensity in the density of local
consumer goodies offered by the proprietors of
"mom and pop" stores (417). At the same time the
distemic tourist trade can, with the international
tender of a plastic card, avail itself of a Crucifixion
sans cross in combination with a Spanish cannon and
an English hunting scene (418).

417   418

A more localized, latter-day equivalent of the Ramblas in Barcelona is the Esplanade of Brooklyn Heights in New York (419). Brooklyn Heights, located on a bluff overlooking lower Manhattan from across the East River, was largely farmland a century and a half ago. In 1814 commuting was made possible by the steam-powered Fulton Ferry, named for the man who was popularly considered to be the inventor of the steamboat. The wealthy bankers, brokers, shippers, and merchants who had offices in the Wall Street area found they could now live in the country on the Brooklyn side and get to work more easily than from the fashionable neighborhoods in northern Manhattan. Unlike the suburbanites who later spread onto Long Island and into Westchester and New Jersey, these captains of industry could view their financial command posts across the river from town houses along the bluffs. Because of this and probably also because it was so well bounded by the riverfront and two major thoroughfares, Brooklyn Heights became a very elite neighborhood in the nineteenth century, its streets lined with brownstone town houses on 25-foot × 100-foot lots and punctuated by mews on the London model.

Among those who lived on the bluffs was Washington Roebling, son of the great engineer who conceived the Brooklyn Bridge and himself the heroic engineer who built it. He lived at 110 Columbia Heights with his wife, Emily, his acknowledged helpmate in the project. Their house looked out on the work site, and there, after he became ill with caisson disease, they could keep their eyes on the bridge; she was able to relay his instructions for its construction.[1] However, the opening of the bridge in 1883 and subsequent extensions of the Manhattan subway through tunnels under the river led to the explosive development of Brooklyn. Brooklyn Heights ceased to be the fashionably residential enclave it had been. The town houses and mansions were cut up into rooming houses, and for half a century the area was a little-noticed part of Brooklyn—although people like Lewis Mumford lived there. In 1950, at the beginning of the great highway building boom that has consigned so many such places to final urban oblivion, the Brooklyn Queens Expressway was planned to follow the river below the bluffs. But in this case an imaginative solution

419

420

led to the resurrection of Brooklyn Heights as one of the most attractive places in all of greater New York. A member of the City Planning Commission, Fred Tuemmler, cantilevered two levels of expressway traffic above a feeder road serving the docks below, and over it all projected a pedestrian promenade (420).

The Esplanade became a dramatic linear park with spectacular views of the now towering skyline of Manhattan (421) (see also 258 and 259), of the harbor, the river, and New York's most beloved landmarks,

421

including the Statue of Liberty (422), the Empire State Building, and the famous bridge itself (423). Its attractiveness and accessibility drew attention to the community around it. In the fifties and sixties young professionals began fixing up the old town houses, and now the gentrification of the area is not only complete but extending to nearby areas of Brooklyn.

422

423

The Esplanade is a marvelously distemic place not only in the social sense but also in a scenic and symbolic sense. It combines historic architectural elegance and traditional landscape plantings, street furniture and pavings with the industrial and technological forms and activities of a great modern cityscape. Ships of all kinds move up and down the river and dock at the containerized piers below. Helicopters whirr overhead, shuttling passengers in from Kennedy and La Guardia airports, but the heavy traffic on the expressway, out of sight under the park, is well muffled by the massive concrete cantilever, so that one hears only a gentle swish, not unlike ocean breakers, and under most weather con-

424

ditions breezes from the harbor carry the auto fumes somewhere else. This place combines the best of many urban worlds and minimizes the worst of them. Because the Esplanade is so well used at all hours it is miraculously free of crime for that region. On the other hand, it is one of the clearest expressions of the proxemic–distemic hierarchy that I can offer. The old town houses and mansions are set off from the public space of the Esplanade by fences, hedges, and private transition zones (424), but their windows exercise psychological surveillance and make the whole "defensible" in Newman's sense. Behind them is a hierarchy of mews and courtyards, with major streets providing vistas of the Esplanade at regular intervals.

At the center of the hierarchy is Montague Street. It was once the main approach to the Wall Street ferry and is now the major commercial street of the neighborhood, with restaurants, stores, banks, professional offices, the local newspaper, and the Brooklyn Planning Office, mostly in the two lower levels of converted brownstone town houses, with apartments above (425, 426).

As in the Ramblas, retail commercial activities are adjuncts of a path system which is an attraction in itself. In combination they produce a complex setting for sociability that leads to a kind of theater that goes back to the agoras of antiquity. Market streets have served this purpose in cultures throughout the world

425

426

427

428

(427). The street in old Jerusalem shown in 428 has
been a shopping street since before the birth of
Christ. The curtailment of free-market activities in
most communist countries has led to a certain bleakness in the urban environment and repression of the
social one, as is so often noted by travelers. Nevertheless, even in those countries where there is a
tradition of promenading in public it remains
strong, while the bazaar goes underground in the
furtive free enterprise of the black market. The citizens of Prague, for example, turn out on any holiday
in any season to stroll on the Charles Bridge, which
has been closed to automobile traffic (429).

429

Pedestrian Street Malls

In most cities of the world, but especially in the United States, automobile traffic has seriously interfered with the sociability of commercial streets and potential promenades. On the other hand, during the last decade a goal that planners and urban designers had been seeking for the previous twenty years, the outdoor shopping street closed to vehicular traffic, has suddenly come into vogue. Having participated in a number of failed proposals of that sort in the 1960s, I was considerably surprised to find, on a cross-country trip in 1977 to obtain photographs for this book, one small and medium city after another, from Madison, Wisconsin (396f), to Idaho Falls, Idaho, dressed up for business with a pedestrian street mall, usually accompanied by some degree of historic preservation. I had last seen Dubuque, Iowa, twelve years earlier, as a gray, forgotten river town lacerated with truck routes and memorable only for a high, rickety bridge that defied gravity with a left turn in midair. The bridge still defies gravity, but I was amazed to find the formerly gloomy courthouse brightly repaired and surrounded by a new park and

430

pedestrian shopping mall. The steeple of the dismembered town hall was mounted on a new pedestal and it now provides a delightfully silly landmark (430).

Most of these attempts to revitalize the central business districts of old towns and cities have been carried out in the face of stiff competition from the suburban regional shopping centers and have been possible only with considerable government funding. The new streets seem to do best not with large chains and widely advertised mass merchandise but with boutiques and trendy, formerly counterculture fashions. But all new cultures begin as countercultures. If the energy crisis and the inflation of suburban real estate bring about an urban implosion, as seems likely, the urbane commercial promenade, so important in the past, may be the wave of the future. The former governor of Massachusetts, Michael Dukakis, staked his political fortunes on a state planning policy directed toward the regeneration of existing urban centers and an alternative to more suburbanization. His political fortunes took a tumble, but probably not for this reason. In any case, his planning director, Frank Keefe, and his staff developed comprehensive proposals in this direction that have become models for the nation, including the first national *urban* park in U.S. history, now being planned for the old mill city of Lowell.

Rockefeller Center

If our cities are once again to include humane cosmopolitan centers as well as healthy neighborhoods, some lessons can be learned from one of the oldest, most famous, and most successful downtown revitalizations of this century, New York's Rockefeller Center. In a city where office buildings, like automobiles, get out of style and out of order about the time they are paid for, Rockefeller Center has remained a prestigious business address for nearly half a century. At the same time it is one of the most popular focal points in midtown Manhattan, drawing to it the population of the entire area for both business and pleasure at all hours. It not only has continued to be commercially up-to-date itself but has also generated new fashionability around it.

Architect Alan Balfour has written a fascinating

history of this center. His explanation for part of its success is that it was originally conceived as a new home for the Metropolitan Opera House and that, while for economic and political reasons it did not turn out that way, the essential theatricality of the original concept remained. In his preface to *Rockefeller Center* Balfour states that "when all the pieces came together, they presented a remarkable picture of architecture's power as both stage and play, a theatre in which we are all compelled to perform."[2]

Balfour's definition of architecture is admirably broad; it fits the greatest architecture of most places and times, but sadly little of our own. Most importantly, it fits the *spaces defined by buildings*, not merely the individual building. While a great many people were involved in the evolution of Rockefeller Center, only some of whom were architects, the most influential mind from a design point of view was, according to Balfour, Raymond Hood. Hood was a master of the mid-modern style that has come to be known as Art Deco, of which Rockefeller Center may be the world's finest example. However, it is not the architecture of the buildings but the magnificently articulated outdoor *space* that makes it such a marvelous experience to be in. The buildings of course help to shape this space, which is a complex of many spaces. Overall they follow the general height-to-width ratios discussed in chapter 2 in connection with residential streets. In terms of look-alike buildings, also considered there, Hood's gray limestone facades with their classic setbacks are remarkably alike, without of course being identical. They provide the visual unity which is such an important aspect of this place. The variety comes partly from a subtle play of forms but mainly from all the plants, objects, and activities that have been added to attract and keep people in the place.

No photograph can convey the real sense of such a space, which is utterly three-dimensional and which, like all such spaces, involves the fourth dimension of movement, of time. My photos can only suggest a few of its dimensions. As in the walls of buildings and in the fences that bind neighbors and neighborhoods, here too it is the openings that matter most. But, unlike the openings in private walls, which must be controlled by the territory holders, these are public and must remain open and accessible. Al-

though Rockefeller Center is privately owned and maintained, it is in this sense one of the most truly public places in the city. The major access is from Fifth Avenue, along a double promenade in which there is a linear fountain with plantings (431). The strong vertical lines of Hood's RCA building carry the eye both inward and upward, but the bold black and gold decorations and the flags that surround the central plaza also hold the eye down. Even in the two-dimensional photograph, one is very aware that there is a *space* there, not just a building.

One feels very strongly the *involvement* the Kaplans talk about, referred to earlier, because more, much more, information is promised than is actually revealed at this point. It must be virtually impossible, at least for a stranger, to pass down Fifth Avenue without looking into this space, as the young lady in 431 is doing. The main plaza contains a sunken area below pedestrian terraces (432a) and fashionable shops (b) surrounded by flags of the nations, which reinforce the distemic publicness of it all (c). Paul Manship's somewhat arthritic statue of *Prometheus* still manages to leap out in gold against the dark stone wall of the sunken court (d), with a

431

cascading fountain behind it, and provides a very strong visual focus to what is the major activity center. In the summertime this sunken court is an outdoor restaurant (d); in the winter it is a skating rink surrounded by interior restaurants off the underground concourse (433). Here we have enclosed space that does not turn its back on the outside, even in the cold.

The drama of Rockefeller Center is only heightened by the comparatively boring spaces of the other corporate centers around it. Some of the plazas facing directly onto Sixth Avenue are, or seem, larger than Rockefeller Center plaza, a good illustration of the maxim that more can be less (434). Water is almost always an attraction to human beings, but this is an easy way out for the designer. Except for the pool in 434, the space and the buildings that confine without defining it are visually inert.

433

Such places are often called sterile, and the sterility derives from the fact that they are so horribly obvious. There is never any drama when one knows exactly what is to come next, when there is near certainty that what is around the corner is a replica of what is here. Rockefeller Center is not like any other place on earth; the essential characteristics of most of the plazas across Sixth Avenue can be found in the Prudential Center in Boston or Constitution Plaza in Hartford, Connecticut. Such places all over the metropolitan map can be lively centers when other business draws people to them, but otherwise they are expensive, empty holes (435). They lack theatricality, which is to say they were not designed for human action and interaction.

434

435

Street Theater

Theater is probably the oldest form of human art and also the oldest form of public sociability. The rituals and tales around the campfires of hunter—gatherer societies reenacted the emotional and technical activities of the day and thus educated young and old about the science of life as it was known. One of the most venerable theaters of the Western world, the theater at Athens (436), brought the whole populace together for enjoyment and for relearning of the lessons, moral, political, and practical, of that world. With an estimated 25,000 free citizens, classical Athens was a small city by our standards, but it was the most cosmopolitan place on earth for its own time. In our time, theater, like everything else, has become specialized and fragmented and too often the proxemic territory of a conceptual elite. But until the invention of the motion picture and television, even the most esoteric theater was a *public* art. The audience of a play, opera, or concert is a true community of strangers; if the performance is successful, the audience will for a brief moment be an emotionally intimate community as well. With the advent of television, drama has been reduced to the dimensions of a living room. So-called live theater has now attempted to emulate the close-up view of humanity which the motion picture presents so well. "Intimate," small theaters and theaters-in-the-round have become the vogue. There is a kind of drama that works well on that scale, of course, but it is no substitute for the grand epic stage when it comes to coalescing a large, diverse society.

Civilized social engagement requires a certain detachment fostered by the formal, somewhat arbitrary conventions discussed earlier in regard to social

use of distemic space. Engagement on an intimate level can as easily turn into fisticuffs as into love-making. In his now classic study, *The Social Order of the Slum*, sociologist Gerald Suttles observes that gang fights often originate *within* rather than between ethnic groups.[3]

Rockefeller Center has an indoor theater which has probably drawn as wide a popular audience as any stage of recent times, Radio City Music Hall. Recently it went out of business but was resurrected and still seems to be able to draw a wide Middle American audience. The more elite Center for the Performing Arts, which Rockefeller Center was originally intended to be, eventually emerged farther uptown as Lincoln Center. It has its merits as a public place but it suffers from the problems of most single-use centers, one of which Jane Jacobs drew attention to about the time Lincoln Center was begun, that of being very dull when the single use is not in operation (437).[4] Even when the Metropolitan Opera is in action there, Lincoln Center as an outdoor place to go to for its own sake cannot compete with Rockefeller Center on the same pre-Christmas evening (438, 439).

440

a

b

c

d

Traditional rituals, religious and secular, which are so important in maintaining both the local village culture and the larger culture of complex nations and which in ancient times were the very core of theatrical art, are today more often found in the public streets and plazas and shopping centers of modern towns and cities than on the formal stage. At the terminal of the Ramblas in Barcelona's waterfront, on the day of Epiphany, a tourist who does not speak Spanish may find what he thinks is a political event (440a). But as dark descends on the plaza and an expectant crowd gathers, a stentorian voice announces, "Caspar, Balthasar, and Melchior have come to Barcelona!" (b). They come by sea, of course, which is the sensible way to come to Barcelona (c), and ride up the Ramblas in a convoy of glorious floats to the cathedral square (d). This drama of the winter solstice is reenacted in many different ways throughout the Christian world, as are its counterparts in the Jewish, Moslem, and Buddhist worlds. In the United States the show tends to be a somewhat tinny mass production with the power to enchant mostly the very youngest segments of the population, but is occasionally performed with style and artistry and some sense of community, as at Rockefeller Center (439).

The annual Easter parade on Fifth Avenue is not a staged production at all, but a show where only the audience are actors. On the predictably cold and rainy day, New Yorkers assert their faith in the rebirth of spring by strolling in flowery hats and other finery. But in St. Augustine, Florida, Easter has a special meaning as a commemoration of the founding of this oldest city in the United States. Crowds assemble at the plaza of the restored old town (441) hours ahead of time, awaiting the arrival of floats from all over the region (442a). The pageant is led by an elegant lady in Spanish attire riding a white horse (b) and a float on a local theme (c), followed by the full complement of a typical American parade (442d–f, 443).

441

a

b

c

d

e

f

A uniquely American festival is the Fourth of July. Some readers of my generation may share with me regret for the lost spontaneity of the day when children were free to blow their fingers off with firecrackers. At dusk every father in town could meet all the other fathers in town in a glorious star war with rockets and Roman candles for the benefit of the youngsters that had survived the day. Today's suburban versions are less lethal, but they seem somewhat tepid by comparison. The fire department usually plays Daddy to the whole community, and

Photo by Ted Dully, *The Boston Globe*

445

the rest of us are reduced to being passive spectators, as so often happens in the modern world. But in Boston, the fireworks conducted over the Charles River Basin by the late Arthur Fiedler and his Pops Orchestra represented a really theatrical event (444). Fiedler is irreplaceable, but the event continues without loss of splendor, celebrating our own historic national liberation at a time when that is the new achievement or the as yet unachieved goal of so many neighborhoods in the global village.

The traditional street theater of this country nevertheless also reaffirms local identities. The town of Wall, South Dakota (445), celebrated the seventy-fifth anniversary of its founding in 1977. A seventy-fifth birthday represents a state of urban infancy that older nations will surely find astounding, but it was a big time for the people of Wall. The town's major industry and reason for existence is the Wall Drug Store, which got its start by offering free ice water to travelers on the dry, hot prairie (446a). This institution has now become a major emporium with its own kind of theatricality, complete with drugstore Indians and drugstore cowboys (b). When we stopped for our free ice water, we happened to stumble into preparations for the anniversary, the featured attraction of which, appropriately enough for a farming community, was a parade of tractors (c). The smaller a community is, the more spontaneous such festivities are likely to be, and the more likely it is that the line between actors and audience

b

will be vague and variable (d, e). This one clearly verges toward the proxemic end of the proxemic–distemic continuum, but the tourist business drawn by Wall Drug holds up the distemic side. Nobody challenged our presence as strangers. Some people thought I was a photographer for a regional newspaper. The *commedia dell'arte* includes such history as a place three-quarters of a century old is likely to know (f), along with localized manifestations of characters from the mass media (447).

But the curious thing is that the tales of our recently wild and still not altogether domesticated West have been transmitted by electronic bards worldwide and have replaced local mythology in the neighborhood movie houses of the global village. American cowboy films attract audiences from Tokyo to Turin, and their idealization of rugged individualism seems to be as attractive in socialist countries as in capitalist ones. An actor once described to me walking into a movie house in Cairo

d

e

7

f

b

c
d

and seeing himself speak Egyptian, not a word of which he understood. Blue jeans, the basic costume of cowboy characters, have become the uniform of international youth in most of the Western world and parts of the rest of it. Recently it was reported that there was a major smuggling ring bringing them into Yugoslavia across the Danube.

The physical and social mobility of people in the United States and increasingly in other countries continually stirs the proxemic−distemic mix. In the hills of western Massachusetts, in the town of Cummington, there are concerts in the summertime at the local fairgrounds (448a,b,c,d). The music is mostly what the record labels call bluegrass, although the

grass isn't very blue in the Berkshires. The ambience is as pleasantly small town as you can get. The audience seems to be made up mostly of people from the region nearby, although some university students manage to find their way up there. But in fact I was told that one of the men warming up behind the scenes in 448e hailed from New Jersey. To the north of Cummington, in another small town called Charlemont, music not very precisely described as "classical" attracts a somewhat different audience (449). This audience tends to be proxemic by social class and distemic by place of origin. It contains a higher proportion of personal strangers than the one in Cummington, but I would say the pervasive sense of a cordial community of interest is about equal in both cases.

Town Squares and Commons

The unique fusion of people and places found in such communities as those described above is of course being overlaid by the mass culture of the drive-in chains and highway strips so frequently deplored in the proxemic communities of the intelligentsia. But in their own way the fast-food shops are highly sociable places, (450) and their very uniformity is reassuring to many people in a world of too rapid change. They tend to confirm a kind of national identity. I recall in the early days of the Viet Nam War driving through what seemed to me a desert of chrome, neon, and plastic near the naval base in Norfolk, Virginia, while a nasal voice on my car radio sang to the plunking of a guitar: "Maw, this is

450

what ahm fahtin' faw." It probably was. I can also recall thinking, while in the jungles of the South Pacific during World War II, how good it would feel to be back in such an environment. We all may regret the passing of some aspects of our consumer civilization if the energy shortage takes it all away from us.

However, the problem for the moment is to salvage the symbols of local and regional individuality. This requires preserving, and if necessary restoring, the physical appearance and social purpose of the town square, wherever the town may be and whether the town is a freestanding community, a suburb, or a city neighborhood. Its role is as old as civilization, and we can't do without it. We find it in the ruins of Pompeii (451a) as well as in the tropical towns of the Caribbean (b,c), where the church, the market, and the gazebo for public events play the same essential role that they do in the town common of Petersham, Massachusetts (d).

The lovely old squares of European towns (e) have been a model for American architects and landscape architects who have struggled for decades, with little success, to achieve something like them here. But many American cities have a rough equivalent, like the Courthouse Square in Springfield, Massachusetts (f). In the small industrial city of Jamestown, New York, the plaza outside a new city hall is the stage for ethnic festivities (452). The major immigrant influxes of the nineteenth century to that city were first Swedish and then Italian. Old conflicts have long vanished in a genuine version of the American melting pot, but the two groups maintain a romantic identity with their ancestral roots even though in fact there is little cultural difference between them. One year the festivities are Swedish, the next year they are Italian.

452

a

b

c

d

e

f

453

455

456

454

The New England town common or village green can be a highly proxemic space for isolated smaller communities, as in Petersham (451d), but in Amherst, Massachusetts, the same kind of space is a distemic transition zone between two academic institutions and between a partly transient population and the permanent resident community. It is adjacent to—actually a spatial extension of—the venerable Amherst College campus (453, 454). That exceptionally beautiful campus is, visually speaking, the focal point of the town. It once was also the social and economic focal point, but in the last two decades the Ivy League subcommunity has been upstaged by its younger, bigger, and more ungainly plebeian neighbor on the north side of town, the University of Massachusetts (455, 456). That small-group, territorial identity persists even where it is least appropriate, in the conceptual world of academia, may be suggested by what seems to me a remarkable lack of personal interaction between members of the faculties of these two educational institutions, even though they are less than a mile apart. However, representatives of both schools routinely join forces at public meetings on public issues. The students are, as students are likely to be, somewhat more egalitarian, encouraged by institutional policy which allows pupils at five schools in the region to take courses in any of the others. But even the students tell me there is relatively little socializing among the various college populations. On the other hand, in its distemic role the common does bring all the subcommunities, including the surrounding agricultural population, together for political action, for a carnival (457), or for a farmers' market.

457

In 1973, Amherst claimed to be the first town in the country to vote to raise the United Nations flag alongside the United States flag. Despite the social "fences" that stand between its proxemic subgroups, the town as a whole is primarily an intellectual community, it is almost entirely dependent for its economic base on the "education industry," and it expresses to a substantial extent the more or less liberal values of such a community. At the flag-raising ceremony a local group performed folk dances of various nations (458). But in the nearby town of Hadley, settled at about the same time as Amherst and sharing many of its New England physical characteristics, there is a significantly different population, with a much greater proportion of farmers and working-class people, and a correspondingly more conservative, home-centered outlook. At the time of the UN flag ceremony, the barns of Hadley were plastered with billboards demanding, "Get U.S. out of the United Nations."

458

The great problem for political decision-makers, and for the planners and designers who are commissioned to create, preserve, or restore such spaces, is that their usefulness and acceptability are so influenced by the varied outlooks and subjective attitudes of the people who use them. In traditional societies, the technical skills, insights, and talents of the designers simply intensify the collective consciousness.

In pluralistic societies like our own, the designer, to the extent that he or she is an artist, must draw on personal experience which may or may not correspond to the experience of those designed for. The type of public architecture that is mainly an expression of the ego of the designer has lately gotten a bad name, but the alternative often advanced, that of gathering objective "data" and determining the statistical average of the public pulse, leads to designs which are considerably worse because they are devoid of all affective experience. The designer, like an honest judge, should be prepared to disqualify himself when he suspects that his point of view is too far out of phase with that of his clients. Economically, this may be asking him to commit suicide. But even more problematical for the designer is how to determine in advance when one can influence the environment for the better, when for the worse, and when not at all. I would like to underscore this point with another personal experience.

A New England common I know intimately is one of two social nodes in the town of Castine, Maine (459). I attended the grammar school shown in the center of the picture and a high school out of sight to the right. I ate peanut butter sandwiches at lunchtime beneath the statue at the center. The social events that focus on that space, which we called the green, were and still are subject to the seasonal population changes that were discussed in chapter 4 in connection with Nantucket and other such places. In my time the winter population was about five hundred; the summer population was about two thousand. The latter consisted then and consists now mostly of upper-middle-class business people and a contingent of artist and literary types, some of them very distinguished. Among the most distinguished was the poet Robert Lowell, who later lived in the house at the left of 459. His occasional domicile there is relevant to this discussion because he wrote a poem about that green and its environs called "Fourth of July in Maine."[5] Talent like Lowell's never lies, but it never tells the whole truth or nothing but the truth either. When I first read that poem I both admired and hated it. I admired it because it conjured up so accurately a social and physical environment I knew

459

460

well; I hated it because what was recalled fit my own associations with the place so incompletely. I hated the poem not for what was in it but for what it ignored.

I particularly resented Lowell's reference to the statue as "a dandyish Union Soldier." To me that figure was and still is what a monument ought to be, an idealization of things worth remembering because they happened to so many people, with the details that are best forgotten left out. It may be the job of some poets to tell us things about our ancestors that we would rather not hear, but as far as I am concerned the job of statues is to help us make it worthwhile to be a descendant, worthwhile being alive at all. I saw, and can still see, through the granite eyes of that weatherproof Union soldier, looking over us, out across that small harbor and the hills of neighboring Brooksville, a world without end, a world worth defending because it is the only world there is.

More accurately, of course, it is the only world there is from a distemic and rational point of view. How many different worlds there are from a personal and proxemic perspective is underscored by the fact that a poet whose ethnic origins and social experience are relatively similar to my own can present a view of the same place that is so contrary. But of course it was not the same cognitive place and the experience was not that similar. Lowell's poem and, so far as I know, his residence in that town were set in what he described as "high New England summer." My most vivid images of it are more like photo 460. The poems of Gordon Bok describe much better the community I knew, when the Lowells and Cabots of Castine had left the town to us and the sea and the cod, when they had, like Bok's northern goose, "wandered off to warmer bay and sound."[6] Lowell's poem instantly invoked my territorial imperative and, much to my surprise, made a provincial chauvinist out of me.

The work of poets, playwrights, novelists, painters, photographers, and composers can draw on personal experience without infringing the rights of others because the others can choose whether or not to look or listen. In the art of the public environment this is not the case, and the frustrations that result from cognitive dissonance among both designers and the public are illustrated by the sequel to my story. Shortly before the time Lowell was contemplating the little patriots parading in Castine in the context of the world of the Viet Nam War, I received an unusual commission. The distinguished sculptress Anna Hyatt Huntington had donated a large statue she had made to a small foundation dedicated to promoting the works of women. The statue was of the young Abraham Lincoln on horseback reading a book (a symbol of self-education which might be much more appropriate to school yards today than that Union soldier). Her gift was conditional on the selection of a suitable place for it. I was elected to find such a place.

Mark Hatfield, then governor of Oregon, was known as a Lincoln buff, and he had indicated that he would very much like to have the statue join the pantheon of heroes outside his capitol in Salem. But American statues tend to cluster in the aesthetically fenced-off neighborhoods of historic districts, civic centers, and corporate plazas, leaving the rest of the urban landscape to become uglier and duller than ever. I suggested that the gift of the statue be used to dress up some otherwise poorly adorned place instead. With the help of some people in the art department at the University of Oregon, I discovered a newly incorporated municipality just named Lincoln City, which had consolidated five other

towns along the coastal highway U.S. 101, a collection of commercial strips serving vacationers to the spectacular Oregon coast. Toward the northerly end of the strip, at a junction with the highway from Portland, a large field had previously been donated to the public as a park. There was not much in it except some picnic tables and a radio transmitting tower (461).

It seemed to me, and to representatives of the new city with whom I talked, to be an appropriate spot for the statue of young Mr. Lincoln. The Chamber of Commerce organized itself with considerable enthusiasm and raised the money to get the sculpture out there and install it in that field. As is generally the case in our object-oriented culture, they were thinking of the symbolic value of the *thing*, the statue. As an environmental designer, I was preoccupied by the possibilities that the statue would become a focus and catalyst for a *place*. My frame of reference was the Castine green and others like it in the resort communities of coastal Maine. My assignment included designing a base for the statue, which, with the approval of the artist, I made low and accessible so that children could play on and around it. I also volunteered a sketch plan for the park, in the hope that that would stimulate the development of a social and aesthetic node for the new city on that otherwise scruffy highway which was its main street.

Through the years I heard reports from people who had been there that the park was not used much, that the grass was uncut, that my small plaza around the statue had been vandalized. I began to feel guilty that I had not let Governor Hatfield have it for the state capitol, and I still do. Twelve years later I visited Lincoln City again (462). In the little

461

462

463

b

c

d

park, the grass was mowed and the figure looked nice from some points of view (463a). I was pleased to see children playing on it as planned (b). But the base had indeed been vandalized (c). Nothing much had been done to the park. Lincoln City obviously had its mind on other matters. I wandered over to the strip and into a restaurant which had been owned by one of those who worked hard to get the statue there. In the restaurant was the sort of park that apparently more nearly fits the cognitive worlds of those who come to places like Lincoln City and of those who cater to them (d). That cognitive world did not include places like the Castine green. There was something to be learned for me in this particular Las Vegas, but by that time I had already learned it—I guess. Form follows social function, not the other way around, at least in the short run.

I returned to the field where the statue was. A group of surveyors were setting up their transit. When I asked them what they were doing, one said, "We're looking for a park." They told me that they were employed by a firm in Portland hired to pre-

pare a landscape plan for it. Somewhat cheered, I drove south along the strip to city hall. There wasn't much activity there, and when I introduced myself to the man who seemed to be in charge, he offered no information. But maybe that park will be a real town center yet.

464

City Parks

The park in Lincoln City may well be developed further because so-called urban beautification of this sort, as noted, is much more fashionable now than it was ten years ago and at this writing is still being funded despite a taxpayers' rebellion. Less than a hundred miles east of Lincoln City is Portland. Portland has undergone extensive downtown redevelopment and historic preservation. It includes a spectacularly beautiful park by landscape architect Lawrence Halprin, the focus of which is a now famous man-made waterfall (464). Halprin planned his waterfall to be walked in and climbed on. Another seven hundred miles to the east, nature provided a waterfall, and man put a park and then a city around it. One comes precipitously onto Idaho Falls where Route 20 crosses under Interstate 15. The familiar commercial strip leaps up out of the open range (465). But here the very center of the city is the falls (466). The park (located on both banks of the river) has a temple of the Latter-Day Saints for a striking landmark (467). Some of the motels have the good sense to face onto this park and to feature it in their promotions.

465

466

467

Of all urban spaces, parks are perhaps the most congenial and the most civilized. A park almost by definition is a public place, but parks can be public on the proxemic scale and be largely the territory of a neighborhood, like the town common in Petersham (451d) or the Castine green (459). Small parks in large cities and parts of large parks can be the part-time turf for various neighborhood groups, and they have special value for the elderly who seek human sociability without overdemanding involvement (468, 469). For urban residents of all ages and classes, small and large parks offer contact with nature, animal, vegetable, and mineral. They provide the opportunity to have a good time just being alive in an approximation of our original environment of earth and sky, plants, and water, with space to run in or simply to reflect in (470, 471). A young man can practice Zen and the art of motorcycle maintenance (472)[7] and city children can observe the living things which country children have all around them (473).

468

469

470

472

471

473

A city park can be the most distemic kind of space of all, uniting human beings in a community of strangers based on the fact that we are indeed one species dependent on the ecosystem of our common earth. One can measure the social health of cities by the physical health of their parks. Sadly, many parks are territories of a destructive kind, dangerous places too often controlled by individuals or groups at war with themselves and the rest of the human race.

I am always reassured that New York City is alive when I can get a look at Central Park, although it is not as well as could be wished. One cannot go into many parts of that park at night. I can remember when it was safe for anyone in all parts at all hours. I was fortunate to have lived near it for a time when I was a child, and I learned to know its endlessly varied landscape on roller skates, which is a good way to know a place like that. I think Central Park shaped my view of what an American city should and could be. Frederick Law Olmsted, in the act of designing that park, founded the profession of landscape architecture, actually giving it its name. Olmsted was also our first modern city and regional planner. He established a model not only for city parks but for the best type of suburb, combining the amenities of natural open space with ready access to the amenities of the city.

At the time Olmsted was put in charge of the construction of Central Park—just before the outbreak of the Civil War—the built-up part of New York City stopped to the south of it. Harlem to the north was an upper-class suburb. Julius Gy. Fabos, Gordon T. Milde, and Michael Weinmayr, in a book summarizing his long career a century later, described the site as "swampy, brush-filled, littered with the debris of evicted squatters, crossed by dirt rights of way, and infested with goats."[8] Today, from the top of mid-city skyscrapers, it looks like a giant walled garden (474), literally a garden belonging to all the people of the city and prized by many as are few other spaces in a culture not noted for its care of public property.

Most rural or wild areas deteriorate rapidly, both aesthetically and ecologically, with intensive human use. The genius of Central Park is that it absorbs masses of people in a way that not only does not diminish its "natural" qualities but actually enhances them, although there is real concern that its ecological health is not being maintained. It has environments for all tastes, moods, and seasons. On any good weekend people engaged in the ancient sport of people-watching line the benches shoulder to shoulder along the linear pedestrian way on the Fifth Avenue side. The long, looping road that weaves

a

around the park, originally designed for carriages
but now accommodating cars as well as any park can,
has for more than ten years been limited to bicycles
on weekends. From Central Park West one can enter
along a tree-shrouded, winding path (475) and settle
down in the autumn sunshine for reading or contemplation (476). The serpentine pathways and stairways
wind up and down and around gracefully shaped
landforms and rock outcroppings, into places which

b

c

are virtually forests (477a) In a system later
adopted for the modern auto parkway and expressway, intersecting vehicular roads are separated
by overpasses or underpasses. Pedestrian paths are
separated from vehicular roads (b,c), a principle later incorporated in New Town planning theory.
The paths lead to clearings where a father and
small son can engage in landscape painting (d). One

d

478

can listen to an orchestra in a band shell (478), an informal wind ensemble under a plane tree, or a rock group taking up the whole sidewalk without complaint from passersby. Such is the distemic sociability of this place that a stranger lady with a shopping bag comes down the sidewalk, stops in the middle of the group without a by-your-leave, does a bit of a dance (479), and goes on her way to the sound of applause. There are also large, open playing fields for active sports. The generally naturalistic design of the park, influenced by the English Romantic gardens, is brilliantly balanced by the more formal mall and the Victorian Bethesda Fountain, a major node and landmark (480), but the lake beyond is almost Japanese in quality.

479

480

481

482

Olmsted clearly recognized that the brick and stone walls of the city would grow up around his park, and he planned to screen them out with trees, a practical idea before the invention of the elevator and the rise of the skyscraper. But as far as I am concerned, the most entrancing aspect of the park today is that Manhattan's dramatic skyline now looms over it, reminding us of where we are and making its sylvan virtues all the more delightful in contrast (481). Olmsted did not even plan on the extensive zoo that is such a lively node on the Fifth Avenue side. But urban people need contact with animal as well as vegetable nature, and the nearly universal attraction of animals for children suggests that this association is probably innate. In any event, nothing unites the generations like a zoo (482).

The foregoing description may seem unduly optimistic and romantic to numerous people who are closely involved with managing Central Park and to others who have been greatly worried in recent years about its ecological and social health. But this is how it has appeared to me coming in from out of town on numerous occasions. The wonder of Central Park is not that there are problems but that things are as good as they are, considering the budgetary, managerial, and political difficulties facing New York City.

Nancy Linday, a member of Whyte's Street Life Project, wrote an article for the magazine *Landscape Architecture* which should be required reading for all students of park management. Among other things, this article supports my thesis that social behavior in distemic places must be controlled by more impersonal and authoritative means than behavior in proxemic, or neighborhood, public places. The mall and the Bethesda fountain (480) have long been popular gathering places. Linday notes that Olmsted and Calvert Vaux, his architect collaborator, planned them for "poor and rich to come together . . . and enjoy what they find in it in more complete sympathy than they enjoy anything else together."[9] But in the early 1970s gangs began to divide the area into turfs of their own; Hispanic young people took over the fountain and the plaza, while white patrons stayed behind portable barriers at a nearby cafe. For a while the mall "had become a haven for relaxed activity, a sort of city-country fair, while the Fountain was falling apart."[10] But by 1977 the lawns were badly eroded, and the crafts people had abandoned their space to drug traders and other criminals.

Part of the problem, according to Linday, was due to understaffed and inept management and inadequate cooperation between Parks Department officials and the Police Department. But the other part of the problem is the difference in the use of public space between Hispanic and northern European cultures. She observes:

> The Hispanic plaza is a center for activity, and the early evening paseo an established tradition. The northern European park is a pastoral retreat, with peaceful contemplation of nature as its intended use. The clash between intense activity, dancing and Latin music, and quiet open air dining is based on these opposing cultural conceptions of park plaza use.[11]

As suggested, Central Park as a whole is remarkable in accommodating these differences without leading to clash. But, as Linday recommends, careful and thoughtful planning is necessary to organize the use of spaces so that the activities do not conflict on the one hand and destroy the environment of the park on the other. She also notes that it is essential for us to distinguish between cultural differences and criminal activity, which ultimately drives out all activities but those of the criminals.

As for legibility, mystery, and involvement, all of these Kaplan and Lynch elements can be found in Central Park. Its beautifully orchestrated series of intimate and open nodes, varied and meaningful landmarks, and its softly or strongly defined activity districts are linked by a network of dendritic path systems that follow grassy or rocky landforms. Spaces are to architecture—especially to landscape architecture—what chords are to music. Paths are to the designed environment what melody is to music. In Central Park we have the work of a visual, haptic Beethoven. Here also the curvilinear forms of nature are a counterpoint to the strong but permeable rectangular edge formed by the surrounding city. It is an accessible enclosure on a grand scale (483). Will this great piece of urban art be preserved for posterity?

483

484

Frederick Law Olmsted designed a vast number of parks in many North American cities. His "Emerald Necklace," which is the core of the park system of Boston, is first of all a path system, linking nodes of various kinds and sizes. By means of complex hydraulic engineering, he converted the polluted mud flats south of the then newly filled Back Bay from an environmental liability to an ecological and aesthetic asset. The Emerald Necklace connects the preexisting Boston Common and Public Garden, where the statue of Edward Everett Hale contemplates what was once a waterfront (484), with Commonwealth Avenue and what he designed to be Fenway Park, Jamaica Pond, the Arnold Arboretum, and Franklin Park in a continuous riverway for vehicles and pedestrians. It results in an irregular crescent west and south of the city proper. In a different way it is as splendid as Central Park, but it would require another book to do justice to Olmsted's work.

The Community of Man and Nature

Olmsted, like many of the leading intellectuals of his time, was influenced by the Romantic landscape ideal of England, as well as by the Transcendentalists at home, but his work and thought really did not follow the spirit of the Romantic movement. Although Romanticism professed a concern with pure nature undefiled by human artifice, it was concerned mainly with mood and illusion, and the Romantic gardens of the eighteenth and nineteenth centuries were in fact highly artificial. The Romantic movement was a reaction both to the social pretentions of court society and to the ugliness and squalor of emerging industrial cities, as in Blake's vision of "dark satanic mills . . . in England's green and pleasant land." Olmsted squarely faced the industrial world as it was developing around him. As Albert Fein has noted, he realized that the dominant fact of that world was the "strong tendency of people to flock together in towns." His main efforts were concentrated on humanizing towns by reintroducing nature to them. On the other hand, he joined forces with people like John Muir, founder of the Sierra Club, in the wilderness preservation movement which led to the establishment of the National Park System, and to equivalent preservations of natural areas on the part of state agencies.

The contemporary wilderness preservation movement is an extention of the Romantic movement in that it represents an idealization of nature. But, in keeping with the twentieth-century outlook—especially the American outlook, which puts "science" well ahead of "aesthetics"—it has a much more realistic and scientific basis than its predecessors among the Romanticists and Transcendentalists. In fact, the natural science underpinnings obscure the equally important social realities behind the modern view of nature. The idealization of "wild" nature as superior to "human" nature goes back to Rousseau but not much farther. Primitive societies can hardly afford to

idealize nature; their attitude toward it is a mixture of reverence and fear. Agricultural societies show somewhat more confidence in nature. But until the end of the Renaissance, most cultures looked toward human settlements for security and well-being and more often than not viewed the untamed wilderness as threatening. This has been true in the East as well as the West, as vividly demonstrated by the cultural geographer Yi-Fu Tuan in his book *Topophilia*.

The idealization of anything depends on there being a considerable distance between the viewer and that which is idealized. The cities of the industrial era have not merely become too often unhealthful and ugly, but their citizens are increasingly dependent on large numbers of other human beings in comparison with agricultural and handcraft communities. Few of us meet our survival needs by acting directly on the nonhuman environment. The cooperative, interlocking systems of modern technology require that other people constantly mediate between us and the rest of nature. Many scientists have suggested that we nevertheless have an innate attraction for natural environments and growing things. Plant and animal forms have served as decorative motifs throughout human history and continue to have artistic appeal and mystical significance even in industrial cultures. Louis Sullivan applied them to his skyscrapers and made them an important part of his design philosophy (485).[12] Rudolf Steiner incorporated them into his Goetheanum (486). But I think

485

486

the special appeal of the idea of wilderness for modern urban man is a consequence of its social neutrality. Unless we are farmers or fishermen, sailors or airplane pilots, nature demands little of us personally. Our survival depends not on influencing it directly but on influencing the behavior of a long chain of other human beings who eventually are expected to "do something" about whatever it is that is needed from the environment.

Primary in the concept of the wilderness experience is solitude, "getting away from it all," *it* being competition with other people, the "rat race." (Calhoun's studies of real rats show that they too need space to get away from each other.) Current political rhetoric, especially among academic youth, constantly calls for more involvement or interaction. The truth is that many of us have too much involvement with each other. This is especially true of imaginative people, scientists, statesmen, and philosophers as well as artists, who start the cultural innovations that are required for adaptive behavior in an environment of dense, demanding humanity. Individuals vary widely in their need for social involvement. Some seem to need a great deal, but we can assume that any normal person wants to be alone once in a while. For those who can go a long way with a little social activity, natural environments are a means to come to terms not only with the cosmos but also with other human beings, by putting social relationships in a larger perspective.

It seems to me no coincidence that "earth day," which heralded the popular recognition of relationships that natural scientists had been pointing out for a century, took place in the spring of 1970. That was a short time after our species had landed on the moon. The prosthetic eyes of the cameras carried by the astronauts gave the rest of us the first glimpse of our earth as a small orb in infinite space and thus completed a revolution in human consciousness that began with Copernicus and Galileo. This consciousness has been slowly eroding the Judeo-Christian hubris which gave man the illusion of dominance over all living things. The view of our small planet alone in space does not encourage human beings to feel dominion over anything, except perhaps their own behavior, and even that must now be understood in natural terms. It is ironical but appropriate

that it took the ultimate technological feat of our era to bring about such humility. But it was foreshadowed by that pioneer of air travel, Charles Lindbergh, who said:

> Lying under an acacia tree with the sounds of dawn around me, I realized more clearly facts that man should never overlook: that the construction of an airplane, for instance, is simple when compared to the evolutionary achievement of a bird; that airplanes depend on an advanced civilization, and that where civilization is most advanced, few birds exist. I realized that if I had to choose, I would rather have birds than airplanes.[13]

I can agree with Lindbergh's choice, but not with such a definition of civilization. (Obviously, neither did he.) This book is an attempt to redefine civilization to include both airplanes and birds. To the same journalist, Alden Whitman, to whom Charles Lindbergh made the above statement, Anne Morrow Lindbergh said about the early days of their marriage, when Lindbergh was still a hero, "In order to be alone, we had to fly. We just lived in the plane, really."[14]

The great, natural national parks differ from Olmstedian urban parks in that their central purpose is not merely to bring people sociably in contact with nature but to allow them to be alone with and in it without recourse to personal airplanes. At least for some people, solitude is not antisocial but a prerequisite for sane companionship. Henry Thoreau may have extolled the advantages of living alone in what was once the wilderness of Walden Pond, but he took the trouble to write a book about it. That kind of labor is not necessary for communicating only with nature. Thoreau said he could earn a year's living from that wilderness in six weeks of work. One can assume that he spent much of the other forty-six weeks associating via imagined or written words with his fellow human beings.

The difficult problem faced by the National Park Service—and by its counterparts and supporters in state governments and private organizations—is to make the wilderness experience available to large numbers of people. There are so many people and there is so little wilderness that it is becoming almost an impossibility. But the National Park Service has come close, so far, to achieving the impossible. Kathryn Rushing quotes an early National Parks Association report: "The stillest crowded place in America . . . is the rim of the Grand Canyon."[15] Fortunately, one natural social factor which has assisted in solving the problem is that people differ in their desire for solitude. Most people using natural and rural parks tend to follow the clustering impulses discussed earlier in this book. The main activity nodes will be crowded with families, vehicles, and tents, but the more adventuresome can, even on the busiest holidays, usually find secluded trails farther out. Park Service planners and designers have been very adroit in providing for both in such a way that conflicts are minimized. They have been minimized but not prevented, and the problem of protecting the rights of those who want to contemplate nature while recognizing the rights of those who want to act in or on it becomes worse every year.

I can recall the first time I stood on the rim of the Grand Canyon and was struck with the immense stillness referred to in the quotation above. I had the feeling I was looking both backward and forward into eternity, that time and motion were suspended. Returning recently, I anticipated reexperiencing that stillness. The infinity of time and space was there, but stillness in the near ground was smashed by beer-swizzling picnickers and romping children. On the same spot on the rim where I had stood before (487), I held my camera ready for the right moment to catch the shifting shadows of a storm sweeping over the ridges beyond (488). As I waited a man directed a small boy to stand a few feet away, focused a long lens on the child so that everything beyond would be a pink blur, and said, "Now try to look natural." He reminded me of the joke about trying *not* to think of an elephant. I later told this story to an artist friend, A. C. Scott, who obliged me with the scene in 489.

488

489

A.C. Scott

Look Natural Kiddo!

490

491

On the other hand, when later we drove into Yosemite from the eastern Tioga Pass Entrance, early in the morning, we could almost feel that we had the whole world to ourselves (490). Most of the tourists come in from the west and head for Yosemite Village. Ansel Adams has made this landscape so familiar and so famous that I am inhibited from displaying many of my own poor attempts to record it, except for one more shot, right off the main road, which suggests how well the Park Service has indeed bequeathed us places for cosmic quietude (491).

In the Redwoods National Park we were again immersed in living stillness among man-sized ferns and trees that were growing when Columbus discovered America (492, 493). The few people we met on the trail walked with the hushed reverence of people entering a cathedral, acknowledging the brotherhood of strangers with a brief smile or a nod. But when we returned to the parking lot, two juveniles in a large car had their radio wide open to routine rock, splintering the silence.

494

495

At the time, a great political controversy raged over plans to extend the park. Logging companies concerned with profits and loggers concerned with jobs were pitted against conservationists. North on 101, the subject of the controversy was in plain view just over the park boundary (494), where these great lords of the forest were being harvested to make fences for suburban patios (495). A current advertisement for one of the large forest products companies shows a picture of Boy Scouts walking under the tall redwoods. The message under it boasts of what the company does with trees, turning them into "consumer goods for example. Playing cards . . . matches. Cotton swabs . . . paper towels, tissues, napkins. Paper plates." If proxemic proclivities can lead to dangerous gemeinschaft, obviously there is also such a thing as destructive distemics. The culture of consumerism often seems to combine the worst of both.

But there are also parks where great natural events can provide an almost urban kind of theater without diminishing the naturalness of the surroundings. Such a place is the Old Faithful geyser at Yellowstone National Park (496a−d). Here, a man-made structure, the Old Faithful Inn, also fits the landscape, looking somewhat like a Norwegian stave church (497). It was built in 1904 (when people arrived on horses) by a young architect who used only native materials, and although it is considerably marred by the inevitable parking lots it is an enchantingly appropriate place to enjoy that particular setting in sociability, the sort of a place where strangers easily become friends (498). Through the windows of not very soundproof rooms one can watch the geysers mark the hours from dusk to dawn. But most of Yellowstone is a scenic wilderness, where one can watch elk sunning themselves like cows in a pasture; one may also run the risk of greeting a grizzly bear. As in Yosemite, there are trails for those willing to venture off on foot in order to be alone with the cosmos. Unlike the "multiple use" preserves of the Forest Service, here the birth and death cycles of nature are allowed to run their own course. A tree trunk is etched in worm hieroglyphics. When it falls it lies where it fell until the earth reclaims it.

At Wind Cave National Park in South Dakota buffalo herds roam wild. It takes a while to locate

a

b

496

c

497

498

d

them. Wardens and other visitors report them now here, now there. We pursued rumor all one afternoon, forcing our small car over twisting park roads and grassy hills, eventually catching up with the buffalos in Custer State Park (499). The sight of these regal beasts, which the Indians had hunted for centuries and which the white man nearly brought to extinction in a few decades, recalls the mythic American sense of freedom, freedom to roam.

Auto Pathways

Both the success and the ever-present threat of failure of the National Park System and the best of the state parks are a consequence of the freedom of movement offered to masses of people by the automobile. The car has brought so many people to the parks that the people, and especially their cars, threaten to overwhelm and obliterate the thing they seek (500). The negative impact of auto travel on both city and countryside is widely recognized, especially among intellectuals. I suspect, however, that in addition to its very real liabilities, the overwhelming popularity of the car has fueled intellectual scorn for it. And as with so many things in life, it is possible that we must lose it before we come to appreciate all that it has meant to us in a positive sense.

Irritation with the worst features of our worst highways tends now to obscure the best features of the best ones. Taken as a whole, the interstate highway system and the supporting network of state and country roads have linked the diverse regions of this nation into a physical community in a way that no other mechanism could have done. Travel by car offers a sense of the connections between places and events, a sense that is denied us both by the high-flying jet airplane and by essentially spaceless tele-communication systems. These provide only a montage. Foot travel and bicycle travel, which we will most certainly have to use more from now on than we have in past decades, can give us a better sense of the details of the *local* landscape than the car (501). But there is no way to get the sense of both the totality and the diversity of a large region at that speed. Earlier the railroads had linked the coasts cognitively, as well as in other ways, making it possible for the traveler to comprehend the intervening continent within a time frame that allows it to be all of a piece. It seems to me entirely possible that the image of the landscape they provided made plausible the concept of a union of states which before the Civil War had remained a squabbling collection of

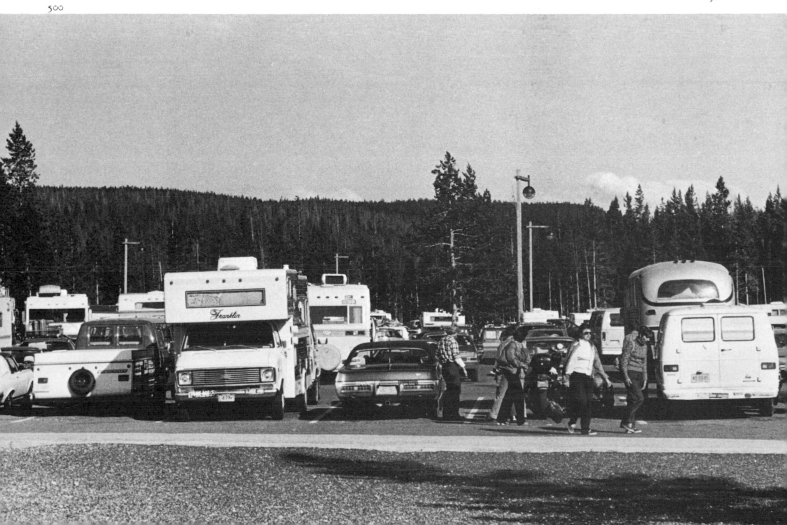

localities. But the railroads restricted the choices of travelers to prearranged timetables and predetermined corridors. While they often presented grand scenery, they tended to run through the dirty backyards of cities; in fact they often converted their rights-of-way to urban backyards if they were not so to begin with.

The automobile has given the individual a choice from a great hierarchy of routes to be followed on a schedule of his own choosing. The common tendency of all living beings to follow the familiar route to anything and anywhere unless forced by circumstance to alter habit (Newton's First Law of Motion) has kept many modern motorists as slavishly confined to expressways as travelers once were to rails. But the options are there for those who want them. The interstate highway system gives us a better sense of the natural and rural landscape than the railroad, but it has undermined our sense of the urban landscape. One can drive across the entire continent from

Boston, Massachusetts, to Seattle, Washington, on Interstate 90 and hardly see a good-sized city except for Chicago. Possibly this fact has tended to confirm our antiurban myths and encourage our increasing and long overdue concern with the natural environment. On the other hand, the sense of movement through a large landscape is the greatest aesthetic gift of the modern auto and highway system, especially when the road alignment is designed to enhance the sense of movement. Landscape architect Lawrence Halprin has called this the "choreography of the freeway." He was undoubtedly influenced in the use of this word by his dancer wife. It is most appropriate because it suggests the *art* of movement in a context where such things are not usually considered.[16]

Christopher Tunnard and Boris Pushkarev in *Man-Made America* note that from an aesthetic point of view the best American highway designs appeared in the 1930s around New York City and that the two main characteristics of a modern expressway, the separation of intersections by overpasses and opposing lanes of traffic separated by a median, both precede the automobile.[17] The broad median is a feature of numerous carriage-era boulevards like Commonwealth Avenue in Boston, and, as noted, Olmsted provided grade separation of intersections in Central Park. According to Tunnard and Pushkarev, the first limited access road in the United States was the Bronx River Parkway, planned in 1906, when there were only 105,000 cars in the whole country. Farther north of New York, following the east side of the Hudson River Valley, is the Taconic State Parkway, which Tunnard and Pushkarev called "the most beautiful and dramatic freeway in the United States to date."[18] The design, credited by them to Charles J. Baker of the New York State Department of Public Works, reflects the Olmsted tradition of working with the natural landscape and of using landforms and plants which are already there or which are at least indigenous. In this respect, the Taconic is unlike the Connecticut and Westchester parkways, which were artificially planted and somewhat more arbitrarily aligned.

The exceptionally graceful spiral curves of the Taconic Parkway (502a) flow over the landscape in an endlessly varied series of openings and closings,
now over a ridge (b), then through a cut revealing a valley and hills beyond (c), along a gently sloping hillside, and over another crest (d), with continually changing views of the Hudson Valley between the Berkshire and the Catskill mountains (e,f). As the parkway threads its way southward, the environment becomes more enclosed (g), but the spiral holds it all together in a harmonious composition. Near the terminal at Peekskill is Fahnestock Memorial Park (h). Small, natural parks like this one would be inaccessible for one-day trips for residents of most large cities without the automobile and roads to get them there.

Such parkways are in marked contrast to many expressways, the northern end of the New Jersey Turnpike, for example, which are scenes of mechanical madness. Highways like this both create and reveal the surrealistic landscape of our oil dependent civilization (503a–d). But on all kinds of highways, the psychological benefits of the private car mentioned in chapter 5—a portable territory and freedom of choice in an increasingly crowded and regimented world—keep people rolling along regardless of cost. I am told that in Hungary people will spend 50 percent of their income on a car. Part of the appeal is probably a primordial and innate love of movement for its own sake, which has been characteristic of our species through time. American Indians, who have

a

b

c

d

resisted so much of the white man's industrial culture, love to race over the landscape in trucks as they once did on horses.

For the motorist who really loves to drive, the selection of routes can be orchestrated to provide symphonic range of movement experiences. The height-to-width ratios discussed in chapter 2 in connection with residential streets also apply to highway path systems. The rather enclosed, small-scale landscape of New England is best sensed on two-lane roads, like that shown in 504. In the Far West the sense of space is overpowering, so much so that the car at any speed on any road seems to be drifting (505). But one suddenly senses one's own power in the kinesthesia of foot on brake and accelerator, hands on wheel and shift lever as one climbs off the plains into the mountains (506a–f). Vachel Lindsay described the appeal of the car more than sixty years ago in his "Santa-Fé Trail":

a

b

d

c

e

Butting through the delicate mists of the morning,
It comes like lightning, goes past roaring.
It will hail all the windmills, taunting, ringing,
Dodge the cyclones,
Count the milestones,
On through the ranges the prairie-dog tills—
Scooting past the cattle on a thousand hills . . .[19]

f

510

512

But he also spoke of the contrasting need for quiet, close contemplation of the landscape. As "the United States goes by," the narrator of the poem sits on a milestone and watches the sky, musing:

> They are hunting the goals they understand.—
> San-Francisco and the brown sea-sand.
> My goal is the mystery the beggars win.
> I am caught in the web the night winds spin.
> The edge of the wheat ridge speaks to me.
> I talk with the leaves of the mulberry tree [507].[70]

When we are in a car, the United States does not just go by, as it does when we're riding in a train or bus; we can choose where it goes relative to our own goals, and we can stop. If we want, we can stop in Kansas and listen, as Lindsay did, to the edge of the wheat ridge (508). We can pick flowers in the Ozarks (509). We can explore the mysteries of the earthscape, examining the white bones of an animal or the rusty bones of a machine (510–512).

HUMANE SPACE: PLACES FOR PEACE OF MIND   275

513

b

c

State highway departments provide roadside picnic areas; some are noisy, crowded, and dirty, next to the road; others are surprisingly secluded and serene (513a). One can stop in small towns which time seems to have left behind, like a village in the mountains of Idaho (b). We stopped in Goldfield, Nevada, where the only gold was in an antique shop, and that appeared to be the only shop. In the only restaurant (c), air conditioning was aided by a South Sea island painted on velvet (d). The temperature outside was 110° Fahrenheit. There were two people at the only bar, a young girl serving drinks and an old man drinking them. Outside, the United States roared by, headed for Las Vegas.

The most monotonous thing about modern highway travel is not the boring character of even the worst highways but of the highway services. Chain motels and fast-food joints clutter the expressway interchanges with the same logos and the same structures, whether it is Indianapolis or Idaho Falls. Service plazas on the Illinois Turnpike at least accept their relationship to the car by putting restaurants on bridges over the highway. The worst visual impact is in arid landscapes, so spectacular in their natural state, so easily scarred by the detritus of civilization without the healing tissue of plant life (514, 515). Most motels ignore as far as possible the relationship between human beings and the environment they come to see (516).

514

515

516

But if you are a resourceful traveler willing to explore the byroads or lucky enough to have good advice, there are places to stay where you can experience the surroundings. One is a former ranch in the Big Horn Mountains of Wyoming, at which you can have a drink or a meal near a stream (517) and take a walk to the top of a hill at sundown to see what you came to see (518, 519). Another is a motel in Lincoln City, Oregon, which, whatever may be said of its urban design, does pay attention to its shore (520).

517

518   519

520

A frustrating impediment and blight on the landscape for many passenger car travelers are those privately owned mobile accommodations, the pickup campers, travel trailers, and motor homes that clog the narrow park roads and bring the commercial strip right into the wilderness. Many are as large as long-haul trucks, but few are as expertly driven. Yet they are the pride of their owners' hearts, and they are really home for a great population of not yet older citizens who have retired from whatever jobs earned them the price of these expensive turtle shells. They form a real proxemic community based on age, class, and mobility. The social life of some of the people who live in vehicles like these was empathetically described twenty years ago by John Steinbeck in *Travels with Charley*, and he portrays vividly their advantages to the owner. But these are outweighed in my opinion by their disadvantages to the non-owner.

521

The energy crisis may solve the problem of such vehicles for the likes of us and more importantly for beleaguered Park Service officials (521). But I think people will freeze and starve before giving up the mobility provided by private cars. I think the automobile has encouraged a kind of respect for nature even while spoiling it (522). Contrary to the ethnocentric nonsense often heard in the United States, worship of the auto is not limited to Americans. Other cultures even worship it in spirit as well as in body, as vividly suggested by R. W. Wilkie's photograph of a Bolivian priest blessing the truck of an owner, and the symbolic trucks of would-be owners, in a festival of the Virgin (523).

522

523

Photo by R. W. Wilkie

To repeat, the right to travel is the most basic right of any society that can call itself a civilization. Freedom is only as real as the means to achieve it, and for achieving this freedom no technical gadget is superior to the private car. What we should do, if we prize the right, is twofold. We should limit the use of cars to spaces where cars make sense, and that is outside of large cities. Who has calculated the amount of energy consumed by idling engines just on Park Avenue, New York (524)? This is not freedom, it is insanity, especially when we also need the freedom to breathe clean air. The other thing we must do, while improving mass transit, is to develop a sensible car for use where population mass is insufficient for buses or trains. Such a car would, among other things, be driven by an electric motor-generator which could act as a brake while recharging lightweight batteries, and thus not only save fuel but also eliminate airborne carcinogenic asbestos fibers issuing from brake and clutch linings.

The mechanics of car design are not directly relevant to the subject of this book, but the effect of the oil crisis on our lives and landscapes is. Especially since World War II, a political preoccupation of civilized people everywhere has been social justice. Social justice requires an adequate supply, worldwide, of both the necessities and amenities of life. Basic needs are universal, but what are considered to be amenities, as we have seen, vary greatly with age, class, and ethnic culture. We are now witnessing a desperate search for oil and other resources to support an evergrowing need for basics and everrising expectations for amenities in an overpopulated world. If this continues to lead first-, second-, and third-world countries to combine distemic technology with headhunter proxemics, our species may or may not survive, but civilization, at least in the short term, surely will not.

Now, as we approach a new historic watershed, contemplating changes in the nature of the human landscape that not even the most farsighted can foresee, we must somehow devise ways of arranging fences, neighborhoods, and the spaces between them so that the social mammal in us all can find a habitat in which to feel secure. But at the same time we must organize them to permit human culture to continue to evolve on our essentially fenceless and defenseless planet.

524

Epilogue

The energy problem which looms so ubiquitously over all the older human problems today may be the salvation of both our cities and the wilderness if we can use more effectively that most basic kind of energy, human energy. Curiously, the kind of landscape which is in most danger today is the kind that depends most on human energy, the agricultural landscape, and this in a time of mounting worldwide hunger combined with increasing worldwide unemployment. This is especially ironic in the United States, a country whose basic myths derive from the Jeffersonian ideals of an agricultural society. It has been possible in our time to preserve wilderness because, in general, wilderness is not most desired for development. Agricultural land is.

Furthermore, agricultural practice has changed from human labor aided by machines to machine production in large, rural food factories. These changes have been thoughtfully analyzed in the writings of J. B. Jackson, among others. Waiting for my car to be serviced in Idaho Falls, I leafed through the literature provided by the garage for its customers. It consisted entirely of agribusiness journals, and I was amazed at the difference between these publications and the literature of the New England and Wisconsin extension services which I knew. The articles were about how to contract for large-scale aircraft spraying, the engineering problems of interstate irrigation systems, and so forth. Contour plowing and moving spray irrigation have already altered the landscape patterns of the Midwest and Far West, creating fantastic planting designs best seen from the air. This tapestry has been beautifully illustrated in the photographs of Georg Gerster in his book *Grand Design: The Earth from Above.* But from the ground, not all the changes are so attractive.

With a world food shortage as threatening as a world fuel shortage, much more attention should be paid to preserving good land for crops. But aesthetically, also, the agricultural environment is as worthy of heritage preservation as the wilderness or the historic parts of old cities, presenting as it does the environment of man and nature in collaboration. The ranchland of Wyoming (525) is no less beautiful inherently than the semiwilderness of Yosemite; the latter is more precious simply because it is rarer. Indians herding horses in New Mexico (526) and

525

526

bales of hay in South Dakota (527) both can speak to us as the ridge of the wheatfield spoke to Vachel Lindsay from the roadside sixty years ago, even though in a somewhat different dialect. Despite industrialization, regional differences remain, shaped as human habitats have always been shaped, by landform and climate. A cornfield in Wisconsin (528) is not the same as a cornfield in Massachusetts (529).

527

528

529

530

531

The upstate New York milkshed (530) has small resemblance to the struggling New England farm (531). Where the problem in the West is to save trees, the problem in New England is to save meadows (532).

532

533

The Harvard Forest Museum at Petersham, Massachusetts, documents in vivid dioramas the changes that have taken place in the New England landscape since colonial days. First, the virgin forest was cleared in small patches for farms, then the hills were virtually denuded of trees; and now they are largely filled with second-growth woodland in which one can find old pasture walls and cellar holes. Even in my own childhood the view from the road was one of grassy meadows full of black-eyed Susans and Indian paintbrushes, dotted with small houses and small barns, merely punctuated by woodlands. Today you can barely see the landscape for the trees, many of which are no older than I am. There are now only two really productive agricultural areas in all of New England. One is the Aroostook potato country of northern Maine, already in ecological and economic trouble. The other is the tobacco landscape of the Connecticut valley (533), ecologically still healthy but steadily encroached upon by the bulldozer. Here the fertile floodplain every year is being dug up and paved over for commercial and residential development. Not only is an invaluable land bank being robbed, but an aesthetic landscape unique in the world is about to go the way of the passenger pigeon. The last economically viable shade tobacco company is reportedly barely hanging on. When it goes, this landscape, as it now is, will be gone (534a–d, 535a–d).

a

b

c

d

535

a

b

c

d

Eternal change is of course the essence of nature. Man cannot stop change, but he has the god-given gift to direct it by making conscious choices no other creature can make. We can now, as we always could, choose wisely and well or stupidly and destructively. We can plan, as we seem hell-bent on doing, that the changes will be a continuation of the blight of the present, a travesty on the past, and a curse on the future. Or we can think out and feel things out so that change can reinforce the continuity of life. This book started with the small-scale, personal, proxemic landscape. There are many voices urging, on the basis of sound reasoning, that we return at least in part to the small-scale. Among the better known are those of E. F. Schumacher asserting that "small is beautiful" and of Amory Lovins arguing that *small*, if coordinated in the right kind of larger systems, is efficient, safe, adaptive, and productive.

As this is being written, planning students at the University of Massachusetts have explored the implications for the western part of the state of Lovins's "soft energy path." They have compared that with the present so-called hard path based on fossil fuels and nuclear power. In their study the soft path has not turned out to be as soft a path to trod as some enthusiasts would like to believe, but that is not surprising and certainly would not surprise Lovins. What emerged was a landscape of mountains dotted with windmills, forests cut and managed to produce fuel, and a mosaic of cottage industries. The students appeared to be somewhat frightened by the scenario they had conjured up. The windmills would spoil the skyline. Private woodlots would have to be managed, and that, they felt, would lead to local conflict. In any case, trees would have to be cut and that might spoil the "natural" environment.

Far too many planners seem preoccupied with controls, with negatives, with preventing people from doing what should not be done. They are less inclined to think in terms of new possibilities. Of course conflict could develop and very well may, but there is no certainty of that. Schumacher's theories and the ideas of many others, including those elaborated earlier in this volume, suggest that local community control could foster territorial unity instead and draw forth new human energies. The forests could be clear-cut and the hillsides made hideous,

managed for quantitative output without regard to aesthetics. On the other hand, landscape architects could collaborate with the owners of small properties to assure not only a continuing supply of a renewable resource, but the restoration of the more open landscape that once characterized New England. Windmills might mar the horizon, but they can be designed to enhance it also. Who would say that the Dutch landscape is spoiled by windmills? On the plain of Lassithi in east central Crete, ten thousand windmills cover an area of a few square miles, averaging about one for every two-and-a-half acres (536a), creating a spectacular scene. They are in continuous use for irrigation. On the mountain ridges above the plain there are beautiful stone tower windmills which formerly milled grain (536b). Either type could generate electricity or do other kinds of work. Except here and there, the stony soil of New England never made for really good farming, which is why so many New Englanders settled the West. But a soft technology could derive fuel from the fermentation of plants which might be marginal for food but useful for producing ethanol or methane gas. New England would not look the same as it does now, but it could well look beautiful in a new way and become economically healthy once again. Old stone fences could be uncovered to delineate new relations among neighbors.

But an ecologically, aesthetically, and socially healthy change of this magnitude requires the one resource the human race has always been most careless of, human imagination. Thinking, which is the conversion of imagination into actuality, is very hard work. Most technology, itself the product of thought, has been directed to saving everybody the trouble of thinking. Thought is the last thing anyone is willing to pay for, but all energy starts there. One reason thought has gained a bad name is that the myths of our culture have so largely separated it from feeling. It takes work to keep in phase the disparate parts of MacLean's "triune" brain. Doing that kind of work is my own definition of art. That kind of work and that kind of resource require that we keep some space open purely for contemplation.

Feeling is always personal, and I have not hesitated to introduce personal experiences in my effort to think my way through the writing of this book. I

a

b

would like to end it with a final example of my own experience of a place which has miraculously remained open for those who not only seek peace with their neighbors but with themselves, who seek peace of mind. Gian-Carlo Menotti, who has spent his life filling the world with beautiful sounds, says that he likes to live in Scotland because he loves silence: "Silence is very expensive in most countries, especially in Italy, where you have to be a millionaire to afford it. But in Scotland silence is very cheap. . . . Nobody knows me there. They call me Mr. McNotti and they leave me alone."

Somewhere three centuries or more back, I have—or am alleged to have—Scottish ancestors. The stories my mother used to tell about them made them stand out among the others that contributed to my lineage. I was most intrigued with what I thought the Scottish landscape looked like. I had a particularly romantic image of Loch Lomond and of high roads and low roads, no doubt because of the song by that name. A few years ago I finished some business in Aberdeen early and found myself with a car and two free days on my hands. I decided to explore the highlands, to find the headwaters of the streams that feed Loch Lomond, and to try to follow them to the lake. Usually, high anticipations lead to disappointment, since the imagination can easily outstrip any reality. But in this case the opposite was true; I was totally unprepared for the beauty of the landscape. The feeling of the great open highlands, covered with heather and broom, and with only an occasional cottage and a few sheep here and there, was that of being in untrammeled nature. But in fact it was once forest which had been cut for pasture and then overgrazed, and its present beauty is, from some points of view, the result of an ecological disaster. There are plans to reforest parts of it, plans which I hope are not too successful. That greathearted Scotsman Ian McHarg, who has had much to say on these matters, writes movingly in his *Design with Nature* of his childhood poised between the industrial ugliness and human degradation of Glasgow on one side and the Scottish countryside on the other. Images fostered by McHarg also accompanied me as I drove through the highlands and found a waterfall on a stony mountainside which, if I read my map correctly, led to a river that fed the lake. By jogging in and out on back roads, I maintained glimpses of it as it became a cascading stream and then broadened out into Loch Lomond. I expected to find Loch Lomond a tourist trap, resembling Niagara Falls, surrounded by motels and chain restaurants. Instead I found a rainbow, ending squarely in the middle of the lake. The only structure in sight was a telephone booth. I called my wife in England and said, "Guess where I am?" Not having my childhood images, she was not as impressed as I might have wished. From the door of the telephone booth I could see Loch Lomond with Ben Lomond rising beyond, much as it must have looked in Robert Burns's day. There it was, soft in the gloaming, only eighteen miles from the slums of Glasgow (537).

Notes

Chapter 1. Home Space: Fences and Neighbors

1 Carl G. Jung, *Memories, Dreams and Reflections* (London: Fontana Library Series, 1969). For an exceptionally good summary and elaboration, see Clare Cooper, "The House as Symbol of the Self," in *Designing for Human Behavior*, ed. J. Lang et al. (Stroudsburg, Pa.: Dowden, Hutchinson and Ross, 1974).

2 Kent C. Bloomer and Charles W. Moore, *Body, Memory, and Architecture* (New Haven and London: Yale University Press, 1977), p. 1.

3 Irwin Altman, *The Environment and Social Behavior* (Monterey, Cal.: Brooks Cole, 1975), pp. 5–31.

4 David Mallet, "I Knew This Place," © Cherry Lane Music Co. (Blue Hills Falls, Me.: Neworld Records 1975). Also in Gordon Bok, Ann Mayo Muir, and Ed Trickett, *The Ways of Man* (Sharon, Ct.: Folk-Legacy Records, 1978).

5 Paul Leyhausen, "The Communal Organization of Solitary Mammals," *Symposium* 14 (1965): 249–63; repr. in Harold M. Proshansky et al., eds., *Environmental Psychology* (New York: Holt, Rinehart & Winston, 1970). See also Leyhausen, "Dominance and Territoriality as Complemented in Mammalian Social Structure," in *Behavior and Environments*, ed. A. H. Esser (New York: Plenum Press, 1971), pp. 22–33.

6 U.S. Law Enforcement Assistance Administration, "Emotional Impact of Burglary as Serious as Robbery, Study Finds," *LEAA Newsletter* 7, no. 4 (1978): 5–6.

7 Oscar Newman, *Defensible Space* (New York: Macmillan Co., 1972).

8 The relation of neighboring to street pattern is especially well described in John B. Lansing et al., *Planned Residential Environments* (Ann Arbor: University of Michigan, 1970). Interestingly, this study was done for a highway department.

9 Ervin H. Zube, ed., *Landscapes: Selected Writings of J. B. Jackson* (Amherst: University of Massachusetts Press, 1970), p. 70.

10 The concept of *haptic* is well developed for design purposes in Bloomer and Moore, *Body, Memory, and Architecture*, chap. 4. The source of the word is in J. J. Gibson, *The Perception of the Visual World* (Boston: Houghton Mifflin, 1950), pp. 97–98.

11 For a further discussion of the meaning of yards to North Americans, see J. B. Jackson, "Ghosts at the Door," *Landscape* 1, no. 1 (1951): 3–4, and Roger L. Welsch, "Front Door, Back Door," *Natural History* 88, no. 6 (1979):76–82. For a more comprehensive anthropological view of front–back relationships, see Amos Rapoport, *Human Aspects of Urban Form* (New York: Pergamon Press, 1977).

Chapter 2. Street Space: To Go Through or to Go To

1 Amos Rapoport, *House Form and Culture* (Englewood

Cliffs, N.J.: Prentice-Hall, 1969), p. 70.

2 For an extended analysis of the use of street spaces by various cultures, see Rapoport, *House Form and Culture*, and *Human Aspects of Urban Form*. Also Beck et al., in A. H. Esser and B. B. Greenbie, eds., *Design for Communality and Privacy* (New York: Plenum Press, 1978), pp. 225–51. See also Erving Goffman, *Relations in Public, Microstudies of the Public Order* (New York: Basic Books, 1971), and Gerald D. Suttles, *The Social Order of the Slum: Ethnicity and Territory in the Inner City* (Chicago: University of Chicago Press, 1968). For cultural variations in the use of interpersonal space, see Edward T. Hall, *The Hidden Dimension* (New York: Doubleday, 1966).

3 For more on aligning buildings with each other, as compared to aligning them with the landform or street, see Christopher Tunnard and Boris Pushkarev, *Man-Made America: Chaos or Control?* (New Haven: Yale University Press, 1963), pt. 2, chap. 3.

4 For a chilling analysis of life in Pruitt-Igoe, see Lee Rainwater, "Fear and the House-as-Haven in the Lower Class," *Journal of the American Institute of Planners* 32:1 (1966): 23–31. Also Yancy in Stephen Kaplan and Rachel Kaplan, eds., *Humanscape: Environments for People* (North Scituate, Mass.: Duxbury Press, 1978), pp. 293–307.

Chapter 3. Village Space: Fences and Neighborhoods

1 For a fresh discussion of small towns, see Denman in Kaplan and Kaplan, eds., *Humanscape*, pp. 274–79.

2 There has been a great deal of discussion of myths in the anthropological literature, but perhaps the most comprehensive consideration of the relation of mythology to the perception of space and place is Yi-Fu Tuan, *Topophilia: A Study of Environmental Perception, Attitudes, and Values* (Englewood Cliffs, N.J.: Prentice-Hall, 1974).

3 On information overload in cities, see Stanley Milgram, "The Experience of Living in Cities," *Science*, 13 March 1970, pp. 1461–64, 1468. Excerpts printed in Kaplan and Kaplan, eds., *Humanscape*. Amos Rapoport has used this as a key concept throughout in the *Human Aspects of Urban Form*.

4 To my knowledge, Erikson first presented the concept of "pseudo-species" in E. H. Erikson, "Ontogeny of Ritualization," in *Psychoanalysis—A General Psychology: Essays in Honor of Heinz Hartmann*, ed. Rudolph M. Lowenstein et al. (New York: International Universities Press, 1966), pp. 601–21, but followed it up in *Dimensions of a New Identity: The 1973 Jefferson Lectures in the Humanities* (New York: W. W. Norton, 1974).

5 Suttles, *The Social Order of the Slum*. This is perhaps one of the most precise studies of the social geography of low-income urban neighborhoods.

6 On the sociology of the suburbs, see also Herbert J.

Gans, "Planning and Social Life: Friendship and Neighbor Relations in Suburban Communities," *Journal of the American Institute of Planners* 27:2 (1961): 134–40, and *The Levittowners* (New York: Random House, 1967). On openness as a cultural norm, see also Rapoport, *Human Aspects of Urban Form*, Jackson, "Ghosts at the Door," and Zube, ed., *Landscapes: Selected Writings of J. B. Jackson*.

7 The definition of the "community of limited liability" is well developed by Suttles, *The Social Order of the Slum*, who credits the original concept to Morris Janowitz.

8 Steven V. Roberts, "Old Fashioned at 27," *New York Times Magazine*, 6 December 1970, p. 45.

9 The Springfield Study with Tuthill and Brown is described in more detail with maps in Barrie B. Greenbie, *Design for Diversity* (Amsterdam: Elsevier Scientific Publishing Co., 1976), pp. 167–77.

10 On patterns of use in parks, see Derk DeJonge, "Applied Hodology," *Landscape* (Winter 1967–68): 10–11.

11 On the conflicting religious outlooks of the Taos Indians, see Winthrop Griffith, "The Taos Indians Have a Small Generation Gap," *New York Times Magazine*, 21 February 1971, p. 28.

12 Hall, *The Hidden Dimension*, pp. 144–53.

13 The gentrification of Boston is well discussed in *Young Professionals and City Neighborhoods* (Boston: Parkman Center for Urban Affairs, 1977).

Chapter 4. Distemic Space: The Community of Strangers

1 All of the references to MacLean in the bibliography deal with this theory. One of the most concise statements of the theory is Paul D. MacLean, "The Brain's Generation Gap: Some Human Implications," *Zygon/Journal of Religion and Science* 8, no. 2 (1973b): 113–27. For an extremely readable summary, see Anne H. Rosenfeld, *The Archaeology of Affect* (Washington, D.C.: U.S. Department of Health, Education and Welfare, U.S. Government Printing Office, 1976). Various ramifications of MacLean's theory have been explored by Arthur Koestler, *The Ghost in the Machine* (London: Hutchinson and Co., 1967) and, more recently, by Carl Sagan, *The Dragons of Eden* (New York: Random House, 1977).

2 Calhoun's theory of "conceptual space" is best presented in John B. Calhoun, "Space and Strategy of Life," in *Behavior and Environment*, ed. A. H. Esser, pp. 339–87.

3 The term *proxemics* was first presented and defined in Hall, *The Hidden Dimension*, p. 1. It was further elaborated in Edward T. Hall, "Proxemics," *Current Anthropology* 9, nos. 2–3 (1968): 83–108. In Edward T. Hall, *The Handbook of Proxemic Research* (Washington, D.C.: Society for the Anthropology of Visual Communication, 1974) the etymology of the word was explained as a combination of "proximal," or near, with the suffix

"-emic," used by anthropologists to describe a system viewed from the inside, especially a human culture viewed from its own point of perspective. The opposite is "-etic," which refers to viewing a system from the outside. In *The Handbook of Proxemic Research* Hall actually uses the word *proxetic* to refer to close, interpersonal, spatial behavior as viewed from the outside. I have combined "distal" with "-emic," not only to pair it with "proxemic" but to suggest that human spatial relationships which involve both greater social distance and larger scale also constitute a unique system which must be viewed from the inside. This requires more detailed observation and more holistic insights than the "-etic" generalizations on which so much urban and regional planning is based. For examples of such observation, see William H. Whyte, "The Best Street Life in the World," *New York Magazine* 7, no. 28 (1974): 26–33; Nancy Linday, "Drawing Socio-Economic Lines in Central Park: An Analysis of New York's Cultural Clashes," *Landscape Architecture* (November 1977): 515–19; Goffman, *Relations in Public*; Barrie B. Greenbie, *An Ethological Profile of Jamestown, N.Y.* (Jamestown, N.Y.: Department of Development, and Amherst: University of Massachusetts Extension Service, 1976); and Barrie B. Greenbie, "An Ethological Profile of a Small No-Growth Industrial City," in *The Behavioral Basis of Design*, Book 1, Selected Papers, EDRA-7, edited by Peter Suedfeld and James A. Russell (Stroudsburg, Pa.: Dowden, Hutchinson, and Ross, 1976). The basis for my proxemic–distemic equation is developed in considerably more detail in Greenbie, *Design for Diversity*. A summary and elaboration of this theory can be found in Barrie B. Greenbie, "A Model for Accommodating the Human Need for Small Scale Communities Within the Context of Global Cooperative Systems," *Urban Ecology* 3 (1978): 137–53.

An early exploration of the proxemic side of the equation, which antedates my use of Hall's term, will be found in Barrie B. Greenbie, "Social Territory, Community Health, and Urban Planning," *Journal of the American Institute of Planners* 40, no. 2 (1974): 74–82. The latter is reprinted in Kaplan and Kaplan, eds., *Humanscape*.

4 For numerical dimensions relating to personal relationships, see Hall, *The Hidden Dimension*, chap. 10. For numerical dimensions of the larger landscape, see Kevin Lynch, *Site Planning* (Cambridge, Mass.: MIT Press, 1962).

5 August Heckscher, *The Public Happiness* (New York: Atheneum, 1962). See also J. B. Jackson, *The Necessity for Ruins and Other Topics* (Amherst: University of Massachusetts Press, 1980), pp. 67–75.

6 The Kaplans have developed their ideas over a number of years in a rich and voluminous series of papers, many of which can be found in the Proceedings of the Environmental Design Research Association, published by Dowden, Hutchinson, and Ross. Of all the work in environmental psychology with which I am familiar, theirs is the most responsive to human behavior in experiential terms and makes most allowance for evolutionary development. The concept of *involvement* is well presented in their *Humanscape*, pp. 84–90. It evolved from (and in their minds has superseded) the term *mystery*, which Stephen Kaplan used earlier and which can be found in Ervin Zube et al., *Landscape Assessment: Values, Perceptions, and Resources* (Stroudsburg, Pa.: Dowden, Hutchinson, and Ross, 1975), pp. 92–101. My students and I like *mystery* and have held on to it. It seems to me that *mystery* is characteristic of the environment and *involvement* is the consequent effect of mystery on us.

Chapter 5. Urban Space: The Marketplace of Goods and Symbols

1 For the genesis of the redevelopment of Boston and further details, see Boston Redevelopment Authority, *1965–1975 General Plan for the City of Boston and the Regional Core* (Boston: The Agency, 1964) and Walter M. Whitehill, *Boston: A Topographical History*, 2d ed. (Cambridge, Mass.: Harvard University Press, 1968).

2 Richard Allen Chase, "The Social Ecology of the Museum Learning Environment: Implications for Environmental Design and Management," in *Design for Communality and Privacy*, ed. A. H. Esser and B. B. Greenbie (New York: Plenum Press, 1978), pp. 278–309.

3 Lewis Mumford, *The Highway and the City* (New York: Harcourt, Brace and World, 1953), pp. 45–46.

4 Ibid., p. 49.

5 Vachel Lindsay, "On the Building of Springfield," in *Collected Poems* (New York: Macmillan, 1926), p. 74.

6 Robert Ardrey, *The Territorial Imperative* (New York: Atheneum, 1966), pp. 183–88.

7 For the description of Houston, see Ada Louise Huxtable, "Deep in the Heart of Nowhere," *New York Times*, 15 February 1976, p. 36.

8 John W. Reps, *The Making of Urban America* (Princeton, N.J.: Princeton University Press, 1965), p. 250.

9 Aline B. Saarinen, ed., *Saarinen on His Work* (New Haven: Yale University Press, 1962), p. 76.

Chapter 6. Humane Space: Promenades, Parks, and Places for Peace of Mind

1 For an enthralling history of the building of the Brooklyn Bridge, see David McCullough, *The Great Bridge: The Epic Story of the Building of the Brooklyn Bridge* (New York: Simon and Schuster, 1972).

2 Alan Balfour, *Rockefeller Center: Architecture as Theatre* (New York: McGraw-Hill, 1978), p. vii.

3 Suttles, *The Social Order of the Slum*.

4 Jane Jacobs, *The Death and Life of Great American Cities* (New York: Random House, 1961).

5 The poem referred to is in Robert Lowell, *Near the Ocean* (New York: Farrar, Straus & Giroux, 1967), pp. 27–34.

6 Gordon Bok is known mostly as a Maine folksinger, but he writes many of his own songs, and at their best they are, as far as I am concerned, true poetry. He captures the dogged human landscape of the Maine coast that is hidden by the condescending folksiness of so much writing about this much-written-about place. The reference to the northern goose is from his *Turning Toward the Morning* (Sharon, Ct., Folk Legacy Records, FSI-56, 1975), which is nice but not the best. The best is *Peter Kagan and the Wind* (Folk Legacy Records, FSI-44, 1972).

7 Robert M. Pirsig, *Zen and the Art of Motorcycle Maintenance* (New York: Bantam Books, 1976).

8 Julius Gy. Fabos, Gordon T. Milde, and Michael Weinmayr, *Frederick Law Olmsted, Sr.: Founder of Landscape Architecture in America* (Amherst: University of Massachusetts Press, 1968), p. 20.

9 Linday, "Drawing Socio-Economic Lines in Central Park," p. 515.

10 Ibid., p. 517.

11 Ibid., p. 518.

12 Although Louis Sullivan is the father of the skyscraper, since he was the first to use steel frames as a substitute for masonry bearing walls, his philosophy of design was much closer to the modern environmentalists' attitude to nature than that of typical architects of skyscrapers today. See not only Louis H. Sullivan, *The Autobiography of an Idea* (New York: Dover, 1956) but also John Szarkowski, *The Idea of Louis Sullivan* (Minneapolis: University of Minnesota Press, 1956).

13 Alden Whitman, "Life with Lindy," *New York Times Magazine*, 8 May 1977, pp. 16–17.

14 Ibid.

15 Kathryn K. Rushing, "NPCA: Sixty Years of Idealism and Hard Work," *National Parks and Conservation Magazine* (May 1979): 8.

16 Lawrence Halprin, *Freeways* (New York: Reinhold, 1966).

17 Tunnard and Pushkarev, *Man-Made America*, p. 160.

18 Ibid., p. 167.

19 Lindsay, *Collected Poems*, p. 153.

20 Ibid., p. 158.

Bibliography

Altman, Irwin. *The Environment and Social Behavior.* Monterey, Cal.: Brooks Cole, 1975.

Appleton, Jay. *The Experience of Landscape.* New York: John Wiley and Sons, 1975.

Ardrey, Robert. *The Territorial Imperative.* New York: Atheneum, 1966.

————. *The Social Contract.* New York: Atheneum, 1970.

Balfour, Alan. *Rockefeller Center: Architecture as Theatre.* New York: McGraw-Hill, 1978.

Berger, Bennett H. *Working-Class Suburb.* Berkeley: University of California Press, 1960.

Bernstein, Leonard. *The Unanswered Questions: Six Talks at Harvard.* The Charles Eliot Norton Lectures. Cambridge, Mass.: Harvard University Press, 1976.

Bloomer, Kent C., and Moore, Charles W. *Body, Memory, and Architecture.* New Haven and London: Yale University Press, 1977.

Boston Redevelopment Authority. *1965–1975 General Plan for the City of Boston and the Regional Core.* Boston: The Agency, 1964.

————. *South End, District and Proposed 1978–1980 Neighborhood Improvement Program.* Boston: The Agency, 1977.

Calhoun, John B. "Design for Mammalian Living." *Architectural Association Quarterly* 1, no. 3 (1968):1–12.

————. "Space and Strategy of Life." In *Behavior and Environment,* edited by A. H. Esser, pp. 329–87. New York: Plenum Press, 1971.

Chase, Richard Allen. "The Social Ecology of the Museum Learning Environment: Implications for Environmental Design and Management." In *Design for Communality and Privacy,* edited by A. H. Esser and B. B. Greenbie, pp. 278–309. New York: Plenum Press, 1978.

Chermayeff, Serge, and Alexander, Christopher. *Community and Privacy.* New York: Doubleday, 1963.

Clark, Kenneth. *Civilization.* New York: Harper and Row, 1969.

Condor, Josiah. *Landscape Gardening in Japan.* New York: Dover, 1964.

Cooper, Clare. "The House as Symbol of the Self." In *Designing for Human Behavior,* edited by J. Lang, S. Burnette, W. Moleski, and D. Vachon, pp. 130–46. Stroudsburg, Pa.: Dowden, Hutchinson, and Ross, 1974.

Cullen, Gordon. *Townscape.* New York: Reinhold, 1961.

Darling, Frank F. *Man and Nature in the National Parks.* Washington, D.C.: The Conservation Foundation, 1967.

Davidoff, Paul, Gold, Linda, and Gold, Neil Newton. "Suburban Action: Advocate Planning for an Open Society." *Journal of the American Institute of Planners* 36, no. 1 (1970): 12–21.

DeJonge, Derk. "Applied Hodology." *Landscape* (Winter, 1967–68): 10–11.

Downs, Anthony. *Opening Up the Suburbs: An Urban Strategy for America.* New Haven and London: Yale University Press, 1973.

Erikson, E. H. "Ontogeny of Ritualization." In *Psycho-*

analysis—*A General Psychology: Essays in Honor of Heinz Hartmann*, edited by Rudolph M. Lowenstein et al., pp. 601–21. New York: International Universities Press, Inc., 1966.

————. *Dimensions of a New Identity: The 1973 Jefferson Lectures in the Humanities*. New York: W. W. Norton, 1974.

Esser, A. H., et al. "Territoriality of Patients on a Research Ward." Recent Advances in Biological Psychiatry, edited by J. Wortis, vol. 7. New York: Plenum Press, 1965. Also in *Environmental Psychology*, edited by H. M. Proshansky et al., pp. 208–14. New York: Holt, Rinehart & Winston, 1970.

————. "Dominance Hierarchy and Clinical Course of Psychiatrically Hospitalized Boys." *Child Development* 39, no. 1 (1968): 147–57.

————, ed. *Behavior and Environment*. New York: Plenum Press, 1971.

————. "Cottage Fourteen: Dominance and Territoriality in a Group of Institutionalized Boys." *Small Group Behavior* 4, no. 2 (1973): 13–46.

————, and Greenbie, B. B., eds. *Design for Communality and Privacy*. New York: Plenum Press, 1978.

Eysenck, H. J. *The Inequality of Man*. London: Temple Smith, 1973.

Fabos, Julius Gy., Milde, Gordon T., and Weinmayr, Michael. *Frederick Law Olmsted, Sr.: Founder of Landscape Architecture in America*. Amherst: University of Massachusetts Press, 1968.

Fein, Albert. *Landscape Into Cityscape: Frederick Law Olmsted's Plans for a Greater New York City*. Ithaca, N.Y.: Cornell University Press, 1967.

Fischer, Fred. *Der Wohnraum*. Zurich: Verlag fur Architektur im Artemis Verlag, 1965. Translated as *The Living Space*. Mimeographed. 1971.

Fleetwood, Blake. "The New Elite and an Urban Renaissance." *New York Times Magazine*, 14 January 1979, sec. 6, pp. 16–22, 26, 33, 35.

Fried, Marc. "Grieving for a Lost Home." In *The Urban Condition*, edited by L. J. Duhl, pp. 151–71. New York: Basic Books, 1963.

Gans, Herbert J. "Planning and Social Life: Friendship and Neighbor Relations in Suburban Communities." *Journal of the American Institute of Planners* 27, no. 2 (1961): 134–40.

————. *The Urban Villagers*. New York: Macmillan Co., 1962.

————. *The Levittowners*. New York: Random House, 1967.

Gerster, Georg. *Grand Design: The Earth from Above*. New York: Paddington Press, 1976.

Gibson, James J. *The Perception of the Visual World*. Boston: Houghton Mifflin, 1950.

————. *The Senses Considered as Perceptual Systems*. Boston: Houghton Mifflin, 1966.

Glazer, Nathan, and Moynihan, Daniel. *Beyond the Melting Pot*. Cambridge, Mass.: MIT Press, 1963.

————, eds. *Ethnicity, Theory and Experience*. Cambridge, Mass.: Harvard University Press, 1975.

Goffman, Erving. *Relations in Public, Microstudies of the Public Order*. New York: Basic Books, 1971.

Goldberger, Paul. *The City Observed*. New York: Random House, 1979

Gordon, Milton M. *Assimilation in American Life: The Role of Race, Religion, and National Origins*. New York: Oxford University Press, 1964.

Greeley, Andrew M. *Why Can't They Be Like Us?* New York: E. P. Dutton and Co., 1971.

Greenbie, Barrie B. "New House or New Neighborhood? A survey of Priorities Among Home Owners in Madison, Wisconsin." *Land Economics* 45, no. 3 (1969): 359–64.

————. "What Can We Learn from Other Animals? Behavioral Biology and the Ecology of Cities." *Journal of the American Institute of Planners* 37, no. 3 (1971): 162–68.

————. "Social Territory, Community Health, and Urban Planning." *Journal of the American Institute of Planners* 40, no. 2 (1974): 74–82.

————. "An Ethological Profile of a Small No-Growth Industrial City." In *The Behavioral Basis of Design*, Book 1 Selected Papers. EDRA-7. Edited by Peter Suedfeld and James A. Russell. Stroudsburg, Pa.: Dowden, Hutchinson, and Ross, 1976.

————. *Design for Diversity: Planning for Natural Man in the Neo-Technic Environment: An Ethological Approach*. Amsterdam: Elsevier Scientific Publishing Co., 1976.

————. "A Model for Accommodating the Human Need for Small Scale Communities Within the Context of Global Cooperative Systems." *Urban Ecology* 3 (1978): 137–53.

Griffith, Winthrop. "The Toas Indians have a Small Generation Gap." *New York Times Magazine*, 21 February 1971, p. 28.

Hall, Edward T. *The Hidden Dimension*. New York: Doubleday, 1966.

————. "Proxemics." *Current Anthropology* 9, nos. 2–3 (1968):83–108.

————. *The Handbook of Proxemic Research*. Washington, D.C.: Society for the Anthropology of Visual Communication, 1974.

Hall, Edward T and Hall, Mildred. *The Fourth Dimension in Architecture: The Impact of Building on Man's Behavior*. Santa Fe, N.M.: The Sunstone Press, 1975.

Halprin, Lawrence. *Freeways*. New York: Reinhold, 1966.

Howard, Sir Ebenezer. *Garden Cities of Tomorrow*. London: Faber & Faber, 1946. (First published in 1898 as *Tomorrow: A Peaceful Path to Real Reform*.)

Heckscher, August, *The Public Happiness*. New York: Atheneum, 1962.

Huxley, Julian. *Religion Without Revelation*. New York: Harper and Bros., 1927. Reprinted, New York: New American Library, 1959.

Huxtable, Ada Louise. "The Blooming of Downtown Brooklyn." *New York Times*, 30 March 1975, p. 32.

———. "Deep in the Heart of Nowhere." *New York Times*, 15 February 1976, p. 36.

———. "Architecture for a Fast-Food Culture." *New York Times Magazine*, 12 February 1978.

Jacobs, Jane. *The Death and Life of Great American Cities*. New York: Random House, 1961.

Jackson, J. B. "Ghosts at the Door." *Landscape* 1, no. 1 (1951):3–4. Excerpts printed in *Humanscape*, edited by S. Kaplan and R. Kaplan, pp. 175–78, 271–73. North Scituate, Mass.: Duxbury, 1951.

———. *The Necessity for Ruins and Other Topics*. Amherst: University of Massachusetts Press, 1980.

Jellicoe, Geoffrey, and Jellicoe, Susan. *The Landscape of Man*. New York: Viking Press, 1975.

Jung, Carl G. *The Undiscovered Self*. Translated by R. F. C. Hull. Boston: Little, Brown, 1958.

———. *Man and His Symbols*. New York: Dell Publishing Co., 1964.

Kaplan, Stephen, and Kaplan, Rachel. eds. *Humanscape: Environments for People*. North Scituate, Mass.: Duxbury, 1978.

Koestler, Arthur. *The Ghost in the Machine*. London: Hutchinson and Co., 1967.

Kramer, Hilton. "Beyond the Avant-Garde." *New York Times Magazine*, 4 November 1979.

Langton, Jane. *Dark Nantucket Noon*. New York: Harper and Row, 1975.

Lansing, John B., Marans, Robert W., and Lehaner, Robert B. *Planned Residential Environments*. Ann Arbor: University of Michigan Press, 1970.

LeMasters, E. E. *Blue-Collar Aristocrats: Life-Styles at a Working-Class Tavern*. Madison, Wis.: University of Wisconsin Press, 1975.

Leyhausen, Paul. "The Communal Organization of Solitary Mammals." *Symposium* (Zoological Society, London) 14 (1965): 249–63. Reprinted in *Environmental Psychology*, edited by H. M. Proshansky et al., pp. 183–94. New York: Holt, Rinehart & Winston, 1970.

———. "Dominance and Territoriality as Complemented in Mammalian Social Structure." In *Behavior and Environments*, edited by A. H. Esser, pp. 22–33. New York: Plenum Press, 1971.

Linday, Nancy. "Drawing Socio-Economic Lines in Central Park: An Analysis of New York's Cultural Clashes." *Landscape Architecture* (November 1977): 515–19.

Lipman, Jean. *Calder's Universe*. New York: The Viking Press, 1976.

Lomnitz, Larissa Adler. *Networks and Marginality: Life in a Mexican Shantytown*. New York: Academic Press, 1977.

Lorenz, Konrad Z. *On Aggression*. New York: Harcourt, Brace & World, 1966.

Lovins, Armory B. *Soft Energy Paths*. New York: Harper and Row, 1977.

Lynch, Kevin. *The Image of the City*. Cambridge, Mass.: MIT Press, 1960.

———. *Site Planning*. Cambridge, Mass.: MIT Press, 1962.

———. *What Time Is This Place?* Cambridge, Mass.: MIT Press, 1972.

MacLean, Paul D. "Contrasting Functions of Limbic and Neocortical Systems of the Brain and Their Relevance to Psychophysiological Aspects of Medicine." *The American Journal of Medicine* 25, no. 4 (1958): 611–26.

———. "The Brain in Relation to Empathy and Medical Education." *The Journal of Nervous and Mental Disease* 144 (1967): 374–82.

———, Boag, T. J., and Campbell, D. *A Triune Concept of the Brain and Behavior*. Toronto: University of Toronto Press, 1973.

———. "The Brain's Generation Gap: Some Human Implications." *Zygon/Journal of Religion and Science* 8, no. 2 (1973): 113–27.

———. "Special Award Lecture: New Findings on Brain Function and Sociosexual Behavior." In *Contemporary Sexual Behavior: Critical Issues in the 1970s*, edited by Joseph Zubin and John Money. Baltimore: Johns Hopkins University Press, 1973.

———. *The Triune Brain Evolving*. New York: Plenum Press, forthcoming.

Martin, John. "The Landscape Garden in France." Unpublished paper, Amherst, University of Massachusetts.

Maslow, A. H. *The Farther Reaches of Human Nature*. New York: The Viking Press, 1971.

McCullough, David. *The Great Bridge: The Epic Story of the Building of the Brooklyn Bridge*. New York: Simon and Schuster, 1972.

McHarg, Ian L. *Design with Nature*. Garden City, N.Y.: The Natural History Press, 1969.

McLuhan, H. Marshall. *War and Peace in the Global Village: an inventory of some of the current spastic situations that could be eliminated by more feed-forward*; coordinated by Jerome Agel. New York: McGraw Hill Co., 1968.

Michelson, William. *Man and his Urban Environment: A Sociological Approach*. Reading, Mass.: Addison-Wesley, 1970.

Milgram, Stanley. "The Experience of Living in Cities." *Science*, 13 March 1970, pp. 167, 1461–64, 1468. Excerpts printed in *Humanscape*, edited by S. Kaplan and R. Kaplan, pp. 225–32. North Scituate, Mass.: Duxbury, 1978.

Mumford, Lewis. *The Highway and the City*. New York: Harcourt, Brace and World, 1953.

———. *The Brown Decades*. New York: Dover Publications, 1955.

———. *City in History*. New York: Harcourt, Brace and World, 1961.

Newman, Oscar. *Defensible Space*. New York: Macmillan Co., 1972.

———. "Community of Interest." *Human Nature*, January

1979, pp. 56–64.

Novak, Michael. *The Rise of the Unmeltable Ethnics.* New York: Macmillan Co., 1971.

Parkman Center for Urban Affairs. *Young Professionals and City Neighborhoods.* Boston: Parkman Center for Urban Affairs, 1977.

Patterson, Orlando. *Ethnic Chauvinism: The Reactionary Impulse.* New York: Stein and Day, 1977.

Popko, Edward S. *Transitions: A Photographic Documentary of Squatter Settlements.* Stroudsburg, Pa.: Dowden, Hutchinson, and Ross, 1978.

Proctor, Mary, and Matuszeski, Bill. *Gritty Cities.* Philadelphia: Temple University Press, 1978.

Rainwater, Lee. "Fear and the House-as-Haven in the Lower Class." *Journal of the American Institute of Planners* 32, no. 1 (1966): 23–31.

Rapoport, Amos. *House Form and Culture.* Englewood Cliffs, N.J.: Prentice-Hall, 1969.

———, and Hawkes, Ron. "The Perception of Urban Complexity." *Journal of the American Institute of Planners* 36, no. 2 (1970): 106–11.

———. *Human Aspects of Urban Form.* New York: Pergamon Press, 1977.

Reps, John W. *The Making of Urban America.* Princeton, N.J.: Princeton University Press, 1965.

Rosenfeld, Anne H. *The Archaeology of Affect.* U.S. Department of Health, Education and Welfare. Washington, D.C.: U.S. Government Printing Office, 1976.

Rushing, Kathryn K. "NPCA: Sixty Years of Idealism and Hard Work." *National Parks and Conservation Magazine* (May 1979), pp. 6–12.

Saarinen, Aline B., ed. *Saarinen on His Work.* New Haven: Yale University Press, 1962.

Sagan, Carl. *The Dragons of Eden.* New York: Random House, 1977.

Schumacher, E. F. *Small is Beautiful: Economics As if People Mattered.* New York: Harper and Row, 1973.

Sennett, Richard. *The Fall of Public Man.* New York: Alfred A. Knopf, 1974.

Sullivan, Louis H. *The Autobiography of an Idea.* New York: Dover, 1956.

Suttles, Gerald D. *The Social Order of the Slum: Ethnicity and Territory in the Inner City.* Chicago: University of Chicago Press, 1968.

———. *The Social Construction of Communities.* Chicago: University of Chicago Press, 1972.

Szarkowski, John. *The Idea of Louis Sullivan.* Minneapolis: University of Minnesota Press, 1956.

Tönnies, Ferdinand. *Fundamental Concepts of Sociology* (Gemeinschaft und Gesellschaft). Translated by Charles P. Loomis. New York: American Book Company, 1940.

Trefethen, James B. *The American Landscape: 1776–1976, Two Centuries of Change.* Washington, D.C.: Wildlife Management Institute, 1976.

Tuan, Yi-Fu. *Topophilia: A Study of Environmental Perception, Attitudes, and Values.* Englewood Cliffs, N.J.: Prentice-Hall, 1974.

———. "Rootedness vs. Sense of Place." *Landscape* 24, no. 1 (1980): 3–8.

Tunnard, Christopher, and Reed, Henry H. *American Skyline: The Growth and Form of Our Cities and Towns.* Boston: Houghton Mifflin, 1955.

———, and Pushkarev, Boris. *Man-Made America: Chaos or Control?* New Haven: Yale University Press, 1963.

———. *A World With a View.* New Haven and London: Yale University Press, 1978.

Venturi, Robert; Brown, Denise Scott; and Izenour, Steven. *Learning From Las Vegas.* Cambridge, Mass.: MIT Press, 1972.

Webber, Melvin M. "Order in Diversity: Community Without Propinquity." In *Cities and Space*, edited by Lowdon Wingo, pp. 23–54. Baltimore: Resources for the Future, Inc., 1963.

Welsch, Roger L. "Front Door, Back Door." *Natural History* 88, no. 6 (1979): 76–82.

Whitehill, Walter M. *Boston: A Topographical History.* 2d ed. Cambridge, Mass.: Harvard University Press, 1968.

Whyte, William H. "The Best Street Life in the World." *New York Magazine* 7, no. 28 (1974): 26–33.

Wilkie, Richard W. "The Process Method vs. The Hypothesis Method: A Non Linear Example of Peasant Spatial Perception and Behavior." In *Proceedings of the 1972 Meeting of the International Geographical Commission on Quantitative Geography*, edited by Maurice Yeates, pp. 1–31. Montreal: McGill-Queens University Press, 1974.

———. "Toward a Behavioral Model of Peasant Migration: An Argentine Case Study of Spatial Behavior by Social Class Level." In *Population Dynamics of Latin America*, edited by Robert N. Thomas, pp. 83–114. Muncie, Ind.: Ball State University Press, 1972.

Wilson, Edward O. *Sociobiology: The New Synthesis.* Cambridge, Mass.: Harvard University Press, 1975.

Zube, Ervin H., Brush, Robert O., and Fabos, Julius Gy. *Landscape Assessment: Values, Perceptions, and Resources.* Stroudsburg, Pa.: Dowden, Hutchinson, and Ross, 1975.

Zube, Ervin H., ed. *Landscapes: Selected Writings of J. B. Jackson.* Amherst: University of Massachusetts Press, 1970.

List of
Places Illustrated

Note: *Photographs may also be located by subject in the index.*

Facing page 1   Pelham, Mass.

Chapter 1

1–2	Emily Dickinson House, Amherst, Mass.
3	Former Conkey House, Amherst (now restored)
4	Amherst
5	Amsterdam
6	Lincoln, Mass.
7	Kalmar, Sweden
8	Kalmar, Sweden
9	Kent, Conn.
10	Amherst
11	Nantucket, Mass.
12a	Easton, Conn.
12b	Madrid
12c	University of Virginia, Charlottesville
12d	Santa Fe, N.M.
12e	New York City
12f	Castine, Maine
12g	Beverly, Mass.
12h	Rome
12i	Brooklyn Heights, N.Y.
12j	Nantucket, Mass.
12k	Tom Sawyer's fence, Hannibal, Mo.
13	Amherst
14	Sandwich, Mass.
15	Holyoke, Mass.
16	Levittown, Long Island, N.Y. Anonymous photo ca. 1947.
17	Levittown, Long Island, N.Y., 1976
18–19	Anse Galet, St. Lucia, West Indies
20	Amherst
21	Parthenon, Athens
22	Holyoke
23	Natchez, Miss.
24	Bradley House, Madison, Wis.
25–26	Amherst
27	Stanton Hall, Natchez
28	Natchez
29	Santa Fe, N.M.
30	Amherst
31	Holyoke
32	House by Frank Lloyd Wright, Madison, Wis.
33	Amherst
34	Jamestown, N.Y.
35	Holyoke
36	Germany
37	Anse Galet, St. Lucia, West Indies
38	Kensington, London, England
39	Madison, Wis.
40	Kent, Conn.

41	New York City
42	Amherst
43	North Hadley, Mass.
44	Vancouver, B.C.
45	Holyoke
46a–m	Amherst
47a–d	Amherst
48	Amherst
49	Amherst
50a–d	Madison, Wis.
51	Amherst, 1973
52	Japanese velvet tapestry
53	Amherst, 1976
54	Yard, Amherst
55	Amherst

Chapter 2

56	Ostia, Italy
57	Hanover Street, Boston
58	Castine, Maine
59	Amherst, Mass.
60	Old Jewish Ghetto, Rome
61	North End, Boston
62	Madison, Wis.
63	Castine
64	Castine
65	Castine
66	Castine
67	Greek Revival House, Amherst
68	Nantucket, Mass.
69–70	Amherst
71	Nantucket
72	Bernardston, Mass.
73	Anse Galet, St. Lucia, West Indies
74	Scotland
75	South England
76	South End, Boston
77	New Bedford, Mass.
78	Tapiola, Finland
79	Amherst
80	Amherst
81	Madison, Wis.
82	Main Street, Stanley, Idaho
83	Near Stanley
84	Midwest farmscape showing section lines. Photo courtesy U.S. Soil Conservation Service
85	The Back Bay from John Hancock Tower, Boston
86	Central business district from John Hancock Tower, Boston
87	View from Telegraph Hill, San Francisco
88	Pioneer Valley, Mass.
89	Holyoke, Mass.
90a–d	Springfield, Mass.

91	Yarmouth, Maine
92	Madison, Wis.
93	Sunderland, Mass.
94	Holyoke, Mass.
95–96	Springfield, Mass.
97	Ostia, Italy
98	Brooklyn Heights, N.Y.
99a	Ramsay Garden, Edinburgh, Scotland
99b	Louisburg Square, Beacon Hill, Boston
99c	Public square in old city, Amsterdam
99d	Nineteenth-century city, Amsterdam
100	Cuzco, Peru. Photo by R. W. Wilkie
101	New York City
102	New York City
103	View of upper east nineties, New York City
104	New Haven, Conn.
105	Mouse habitat, Calhoun Laboratory, U.S. National Institute of Mental Health, Bethesda, Md.
106	Glasgow, Scotland
107	The Hague
108	The Hague
109	Amsterdam
110	Old Belgrade from bridge on the Danube, Yugoslavia
111	New Belgrade from bridge on the Danube
112	Old Belgrade
113	New Belgrade
114	Belgrade
115	Belgrade
116	Habitat, Montreal. Photo courtesy Moshe Safdie Associates, Architects
117	East Jerusalem
118	Taos Pueblo, New Mexico
119	Lewis Wharf condominiums, Boston
120	Belgrade
121a–e	French Quarter, New Orleans
122–23	Garden District, New Orleans
124	Garden District, New Orleans
125a–d	Garden District, New Orleans
126	Garden District, New Orleans
127	French Quarter, New Orleans
128–30	Lafayette Cemetery, Garden District, New Orleans

Chapter 3

131a–l	Bayonne, New Jersey
132a–l	South End, Springfield, Mass.
133	Cliff dwelling ruins, Mesa Verde, Colorado
134	Church of San Geronimo, Taos Pueblo, N.M.
135	Copacabana, Bolivia. Photo by R. W. Wilkie
136	Favelas, Rio de Janeiro. Photo by R. W. Wilkie

137	Planned squatter housing, Mexico City	188	Community Center, South End, Boston
138–39	Amsterdam suburb	189	South End, Boston
140	West wall, old city, Jerusalem	190	South End, Boston
141	Armenian Quarter, old city, Jerusalem	191	Union Park, South End, Boston
142	Moslem Quarter, from Christian Quarter, old city, Jerusalem	192	Columbia Point, Boston. Photo ©Alex MacLean, Landslides
143	Israeli landscape	193	Sunderland, Mass.
144	East Jerusalem	194	France
145	Tel Aviv	195	Allegheny Drive, Madison, Wis.
146	Tel Aviv		
147	Jaffa waterfront, Israel	Page 106	Fifth Avenue at 42nd Street, New York City
148	A street in Jaffa		
149	Kibbutz residence, Israel	Chapter 5	
150	Tel Aviv		
151	Kirdi farmsteads, Cameroon, Africa. Photo by Dr. Georg Gerster	196	Statue of Paul Revere, North End, Boston
152	Entrance to Chinatown, San Francisco	197	Boston Common from the John Hancock Tower
153	Chinatown, Boston	198	Boston Public Garden
154	Central Boston. Photo ©Alex MacLean, Landslides	199	Washington Street, Boston
		200–01	Boston Common at Tremont Street
155	North End, Boston. Photo ©Alex MacLean, Landslides	202	Boston Common from Charles Street
156	Old North Church from Revere Park, Boston	203	The State House from Beacon Street, Boston
157	Haymarket, Boston	204	The State House from Park Street, Boston
158	Entrance to North End, Boston	205	Old State House, Boston
159	St. Leonard's Church, Boston	206	Granary Burying Ground, Boston
160	Copps Hill Burying Ground, Boston	207	Construction at Huntington Avenue, Boston
161	Bunker Hill from North End, Boston	208	Rescue by minuteman, Boston
162	Old North Church from Copps Hill, Boston	209	Approach to escalator, Prudential Tower, Boston
163–64	North End playground, Boston	210	View south from John Hancock Tower, Boston
165–66	Revere Park, Boston	211–12	Prudential Center, Boston
167	Lewis Wharf, Boston	213	Christian Science Center from the top of the Prudential Tower
168	Waterfront Park, Boston		
169	Haymarket, Boston	214a–e, 215	Christian Science Center, Boston
170	Quincy Market, Boston	216	Boylston Street, Boston
171a–d	South Boston	217	Copley Square from the top of the Prudential Tower, Boston (telephoto lens)
172	Beacon Street, Boston		
173	State House, Boston	218	Copley Square from the top of the John Hancock Tower
174	Contemporary West End, from Beacon Hill, Boston	219	Copley Square from southwest, Boston
175	Beacon Hill, Boston	220	Copley Square from the Boston Public Library
176	Mt. Vernon Street, Beacon Hill, Boston		
177	Louisburg Square, Boston	221	Copley Square from Boylston and Dartmouth streets
178	The Back Bay, Boston		
179	Commonwealth Avenue, Boston	222	Trinity Church, Boston
180	Railroad boundary, Boston	223	Reflection of Trinity Church in John Hancock Building
181	Turnpike boundary, Boston		
182	Tremont Street, South End, Boston	224	John Hancock Tower, 1973, with windows missing
183	Syrian Quarter, South End, Boston		
184	Chinese Quarter, South End, Boston	225	Copley Square from Trinity Church
185	South End, Boston	226	Courtyard of Boston Public Library
186	South End, Boston	227	Government Center from Tremont Street, Boston
187	Puerto Rican Community Development, South End, Boston	228	Fountain, Government Center, looking

	south, Boston
229	Boston City Hall
230	Sears Crescent, Government Center, Boston
231	Tremont Street entrance, Government Center, Boston
232	Faneuil Hall between City Hall and Sears Crescent, Boston
233	U.S. Custom House from Government Center, Boston
234	Sixty State Street under construction, Boston
235	U.S. Custom House from Haymarket, Boston
236	U.S. Custom House, Boston
237	Faneuil Hall, ca. 1974, Boston
238	Faneuil Hall, 1979, Boston
239	Quincy Market, Boston
240	Salem at Cross Street, North End, Boston
241	Quincy Market, Boston
242	Statue before Faneuil Hall, Sixty State Street behind, Boston
243	Snapshot of Boston from boat, 1934
244	Boston from Logan Airport, 1979
245	Charles River Basin from Prudential Tower, Boston
246	Charles River from Cambridge, Mass.
247	Lighthouse, Nantucket Harbor, Mass.
248	Lower Main Street, Nantucket
249	Oil tanks, wharf area, Nantucket
250	Main Street, Nantucket
251	Wharf, Nantucket
252	Golden Gate Bridge, San Francisco
253	Ferry Terminal and Oakland Bay Bridge, San Francisco
254	Union Square, San Francisco
255a–d	Mime, Union Square, San Francisco
256	Statue of Liberty, New York Harbor
257	Staten Island Ferry, New York
258	Lower Manhattan from Brooklyn Heights, N.Y., 1963
259	Lower Manhattan from Brooklyn Heights, N.Y., 1976
260	East River from the top of the World Trade Center, New York City
261	FDR Drive at Williamsburg Bridge, New York City
262–63	Walkway, Brooklyn Bridge, New York
264	New York Harbor from Brooklyn Bridge
265	Empire State Building from RCA Building, New York City
266	Memorial to James Gordon Bennett, Herald Square, New York City
267	Statue of Horace Greeley, Greeley Square, New York City
268	Statue of George M. Cohan, Times Square, New York City
269	Sculpture Garden, Museum of Modern Art, New York City
270	Painting by Chuck Close, Museum of Modern Art, New York City
271–72	Art Museum, Basel, Switzerland
273	Museum of Natural History, New York City
274	Museum of Science, Boston
275	Ford Foundation Building, New York City
276	United Nations Plaza, New York City
277	Manhattan skyline from Roosevelt Island, East River
278	United Nations Secretariat, New York City
279	Harbor esplanade, Rotterdam, The Netherlands
280–81	War Memorial, Rotterdam
282	Peace Memorial, Rotterdam
283	The Lijnbaan, Rotterdam
284–87	Amsterdam
288	Hoorn Harbor, The Netherlands
289	Bronze figures, Hoorn Harbor
290	Stockholm, from the top of the tower at Scandia Park
291	Old Town Hall, Stockholm
292	Old Town Square, Stockholm
293	City hall plaza, Stockholm
294	Fountain from city hall, Stockholm
295	Stockholm
296	Park, downtown·Stockholm
297	Farmers' market, Stockholm
298	Stockholm
299a–d	Vällingby, Sweden
300	Farsta, Sweden
301	Harbor, Oslo
302	City Hall, Oslo
303	Statue of FDR, Oslo
304	Civil War Memorial, Vicksburg, Miss.
305	Downtown redevelopment, Vicksburg
306	Waterfront, Vicksburg
307	Riverfront Park, Natchez, Miss.
308	Gateway Arch, St. Louis
309a–d	Gateway Arch, St. Louis
310	View east over Illinois from Gateway Arch, St. Louis
311	Gateway Arch and Old Courthouse, St. Louis
312	Old Courthouse framed by Gateway Arch, St. Louis
313	Gateway Arch from Interstate Highway 70
314	Prague, from Petrin Park
315a–d	Charles Bridge to Mala Strana (Little City), Prague
316	Astronomical clock, Old Town Hall, Prague
317	Campa, old mills, Prague
318	Old city wall, Prague

319	Stalin era apartments, Prague
320	Contemporary apartments, Prague
321	Florence, Italy
322	Tower of Palazzo Vecchio from Uffizi Arch, Florence
323	Michelangelo's *David* (copy) before Palazzo Vecchio, Florence
324	Cathedral and campanile, Florence
325	Bridge ruin near Tiberina Island, Rome
326	Ruins of the Roman Forum
327	St. Peter's Square, Rome
328–30	Colonnade, St. Peter's Square, Rome
331	Vatican wall
332	Vatican gateway
333	Limmat River from Lindenhof, Zurich
334	Limmat River from Quai Bridge, Zurich
335	View of Fraumünster Church from Limmat Quai, Zurich
336	Sculpture in main shopping district, Zurich
337	Zurich
338	General Guisan Quai, Zurich
339–40	Enfield Mall, Enfield, Conn.
341–43	Main shopping center, Columbia, Md.
344	Peachtree Plaza Hotel from Spring Street, Atlanta
345	Main Lobby, Peachtree Plaza Hotel, Atlanta
346	The Hyatt Regency Hotel, Atlanta
347	Lobby from above, Hyatt Regency Hotel, Atlanta
348	Atlanta from revolving restaurant, Hyatt Regency Hotel, Atlanta
349	Building adjacent to Hyatt Regency Hotel, Atlanta
350	Underground Atlanta
351	Demolished building and Peachtree Hotel tower, Atlanta
352	Peachtree Center, Atlanta
353	Citicorp Building, interior plaza, New York City
354a–c	The Berlin Wall
355	Railroad station, Basel, Switzerland
356	Train sheds, Basel railroad station
357	Information desk, Grand Central Station, New York City
358	Pennsylvania Station, New York City, 1963
359	Train shed, Pennsylvania Station, New York City
360	West 33rd Street, New York City, 1963
361	West 33rd Street, New York City, 1978
362	Madison Square Garden Center, New York City
363	New York subway
364	BART subway, San Francisco
365	Subway entrance, the Mall, Washington, D.C.
366	Washington subway
367–68	Prague subway
369	Railroad station platform, Basel, Switzerland
370	Alexander Calder exhibition, Whitney Museum, New York City, 1977
371a–c	Kennedy International Airport, New York
371d	Passport control, Heathrow Airport, London
372	Airport, Barbados
373–77	Dulles International Airport, Washington D.C.
378	Government Building, Madrid
379	Palacio Real, Madrid
380	Christmas symbol on Calle de Alcalá, Madrid
381	Plaza de España, Madrid
382	Don Quixote and Sancho Panza, Plaza de España, Madrid
383	Artist in Plaza de España, Madrid
384	U.S. Capitol, Washington, D.C.
385	Capitol steps, Washington
386	Capitol dome, Washington
387	Interior of Capitol dome, Washington
388	Head of Lincoln, Capitol rotunda, Washington
389	View from West Front of Capitol, Washington
390	Lincoln Memorial from Memorial Bridge, Washington
391	Snapshooter at Lincoln Memorial, Washington
392	Dupont Circle, Washington
393	Lithograph of Madison. Courtesy State Historical Society of Wisconsin
394	Capitol from State Street, Madison
395	Bascom Hall, University of Wisconsin, Madison
396a–d	Bascom Hall, University of Wisconsin
396e–g	State Street, Madison
397	Capitol Square, Madison
398	Capitol rotunda, Madison
399–409	Deere & Company, Administrative Center, Moline, Ill.

Chapter 6

410	Temple of the Holy Family, Barcelona, Spain
411	Ramblas, Barcelona, afternoon
412	Ramblas, Barcelona, evening
413	Street in Barrio Gótico, Barcelona, afternoon
414	Street in Barrio Gótico, Barcelona, evening
415	Cathedral, Barcelona

416	Cathedral Square, Barcelona	455	University of Massachusetts, Amherst
417	Ramblas, Barcelona	456	View of Amherst from the top of the Campus Center, University of Massachusetts
418	Barcelona		
419	Brooklyn Heights Esplanade, Brooklyn, N.Y.	457	Spring fair, Amherst common
		458	Folk dancing, Amherst common
420	Cantilevered expressway under Esplanade, Brooklyn Heights	459	The Green, Castine, Maine
		460	Castine harbor, winter
421	Esplanade, Brooklyn Heights	461	Park, Lincoln City, Ore., 1965
422	New York Harbor from Esplanade, Brooklyn Heights	462	Route 101, Lincoln City
		463a–c	Park, Lincoln City, 1977
423	Esplanade, Brooklyn Heights	463d	Restaurant garden, Lincoln City
424	Esplanade, Brooklyn Heights	464	Waterfall, Civic Center, Portland, Ore.
425	Montague Street, Brooklyn Heights	465	Route 20, Idaho Falls, Idaho
426	Brooklyn Heights	466–67	Idaho Falls
427	Market, Castries, St. Lucia, West Indies	468	Veterans' Park, Holyoke, Mass.
428	Jerusalem, old city	469	Plaza de España, Madrid
429	Charles Bridge, Prague	470	Park, Mexico City
430	Clock tower and courthouse, Dubuque, Iowa	471–72	Look Park, Northampton, Mass.
		473	Private pond, New Salem, Mass.
431	Rockefeller Center from 5th Avenue, New York City	474	Central Park from top of the RCA Building, New York City
432a–d	Rockefeller Center, New York City	475	Entrance to park from Lower Central Park West
433	Rockefeller Center, New York City		
434	Plaza on Sixth Avenue, New York City	476	Park walk near Central Park West
435	Constitution Plaza, Hartford, Conn.	477a–d	Central Park, New York City
436	Ruins of the theater at Athens	478	Bandshell, Central Park
437	Lincoln Center for the Performing Arts, New York City	479	Sidewalk musicians, Central Park
		480	Bethesda Terrace and Fountain, Central Park
438	Lincoln Center, Christmas season, 1979		
439	Rockefeller Center, Christmas season, 1979	481	View to southeast over Bird Sanctuary, Central Park
		482	Central Park Zoo
440a–d	Epiphany pageant, Barcelona, Spain	483	Central Park, night, from St. Moritz Hotel
441	Plaza, St. Augustine, Fla.	484	Statue of Edward Everett Hale, Boston Public Garden
442a–f, 443	Easter parade, St. Augustine		
444	Esplanade fireworks, Boston. Photo by Ted Dully, *The Boston Globe*	485	Carson Pirie Scott department store, Chicago
445	Wall, S.D.	486	Chimney, Goetheanum, near Basel, Switzerland
446a	State highway rest stop, S.D.		
446b	Wall Drug Store	487–88	South Rim, Grand Canyon, Arizona
446c–f, 447	Anniversary parade, Wall	489	Cartoon of Grand Canyon by A. C. Scott
448a–e	Country music festival, Cummington, Mass.	490–91	Tioga Pass, Yosemite National Park, Cal.
		492–93	Redwood National Park, Cal.
449	Outdoor concert, Charlemont, Mass.	494–95	Highway 101 north of Redwood National Park
450	Fast-food restaurant, Enfield, Conn.		
451a	Ruins of Pompeii	496a–d	Old Faithful, Yellowstone National Park
451b	Town Square, Soufrière, St. Lucia, West Indies	497–98	Old Faithful Inn, Yellowstone National Park
451c	Town Square, Castries, St. Lucia, West Indies	499	Buffalos, Custer State Park, S.D.
		500	Parking lot, Yellowstone National Park
451d	Town common, Petersham, Mass.	501	Station Road, Amherst, Mass.
451e	Square, French town	502a–g	Taconic State Parkway, New York
451f	Courthouse Square, Springfield, Mass.	502h	Fahnestock Memorial Park, New York
452	City Hall plaza, Jamestown, N.Y.	503a–d	New Jersey Turnpike
453	Amherst common from Amherst College, Amherst, Mass.	504	Country road, western Massachusetts
		505	Highway 160, Colorado
454	Town common, Amherst		

506a–f	Rocky Mountain highways
507	Interstate 70, Kansas
508	Kansas wheatfield
509	Mark Twain National Forest, Mo.
510–11	Idaho landscape
512	Wyoming ranch
513a	Roadside picnic area, Idaho
513b	Yellow Pine, Idaho
513c–d	Goldfield, Nev.
514	Arizona gas station
515	Arizona landscape
516	View from motel window, Taos, N.M.
517–19	Motel, Wyoming
520	View from motel window, Lincoln City, Ore.
521	Shopping center display of recreational vehicles
522	Taconic Parkway overlook, New York
523	Festival of the Virgin of Copacabana, Bolivia. Photo by R. W. Wilkie
524	Park Avenue, New York City, from Pan Am Building

Epilogue

525	Wyoming landscape
526	Horse roundup, Taos, N.M.
527	South Dakota hayfield
528	Wisconsin cornfield
529	Cornfield, Amherst, Mass.
530	Upstate New York
531	Farmyard, Amherst
532	Hayfield, Amherst
533	Pioneer (Connecticut River) Valley, Mass.
534a–d	Shade tobacco farms, Pioneer Valley, Mass.
535a	Tobacco farms and University of Massachusetts from Mt. Holyoke summit
535b	View of the University of Massachusetts from Route 9, Hadley
535c	Subdivision on farmland, Sunderland, Mass.
535d	Apartment complex on farmland, Amherst, Mass.
536a–b	Windmills on the plain of Lassithi, Crete
537	Loch Lomond, Scotland

Subject
and
Photograph
Index

Note: Page numbers are in roman; photograph numbers are in *italic.*

Aberdeen, Scotland, 290
Academia, territories in, 102, 111
Accessibility of distemic places, 119
Acculturation, 82
Acropolis, 14, 82
Adams, Ansel, 264
Adaptability of humans, 65
Addams, Charles, 3
Adolescents, 74
Advertisement for forest products, 266
Aesthetics, 8, 127, 168, 190, 260
Africa, Cameroon, Kirdi farmsteads, 88; *151*
Agora, 226
Agribusiness, 281
Agricultural revolution, 111−12
Agriculture, 214, 260
Air pollution, 190
Air travel, 116, 143, 189, 195−99, 225, 261, 269; *244,
    371−77*
Alienation, 113
Altman, Irwin, 4
Ambiguity, 119
Amherst College, Amherst, Mass., 244−45; *453*
Amherst, Mass., 244−45; *1, 2, 4, 10, 13, 20, 25, 26, 30,
    33, 42, 46−49, 51, 53, 55, 59, 69, 70, 79, 80, 453−58*
Amsterdam, The Netherlands, 4, 56, 60, 84, 135, 162; *5,
    99c−d, 109, 138, 139, 284−87*
Anacostia River, 207
Ancestor worship, 122
Anonymity of city life, 116
Anthropologists, x, 71, 86, 109, 112, 118
Anthropomorphism of cities, 200
Antiurbanism in United States, 203
Apartment buildings, 6, 22, 24−28, 31−32, 55−66, 166,
    177; *42, 46, 47, 94−121, 125, 166, 177*
Arabs, 86−87
Arboreal ancestors of humans, 12, 64
Archipelago, Stockholm, Sweden, 164; *290*
Architects, 2, 22, 32, 46, 119, 124, 145, 174, 178, 184, 242
Architecture, 120, 137, 153, 174, 193, 213, 218, 229, 258;
    International School, 150, 157−58, 162−63, 166, 186
Ardrey, Robert, x, 65, 114, 179−80; *Social Contract, The,*
    114
Argentina, 118
Armenian quarter, Jerusalem, 85; *141*
Arnold Arboretum, Boston, Mass., 259
Arno River, Italy, 177
Aroostock County, Me., 285
Art, 32, 112, 156−57, 159−61, 195, 218, 232; *270, 370*
Art deco, 165
Artists, 178, 246, 261
Art of movement, 270
Asia, 148
Astronauts, 9, 261
Athens, 14, 82, 117, 178, 232; *21, 232*
Atlanta, Ga., 185−88; *344−52*

Atrium, 56
Australian aborigines, 114
Authority, 7, 74, 218
Automobiles, 17, 120, 146, 165, 184, 187, 189–90, 268–80; *500, 505d, 507, 521–23*

Back Bay, Boston, Mass., 51, 98, 123–24, 132–33; *85, 178, 179*
Baker, Charles J., 271
Balconies, 18, 22, 28, 65; *32, 41, 65, 104, 120*
Balfour, Alan, 228–29
Barcelona, Spain, 220–23, 234; *411–18, 440*
Barns, tobacco, 22, 285–87; *43, 533–35*
Bascom Hall, University of Wisconsin, Madison, 209, 211; *395, 396a–d*
Basel, Switzerland, 182; *355*
Bauhaus, 49, 129
Bayonne, N.J., 75–78, 89, 96; *131a–l*
Beacon Hill, Boston, Mass., 56, 96–97, 123, 125; *172–77*
Behavior, 72–73, 89, 109–15, 117, 213, 219, 261, 257–58. *See also* Social behavior
Beirut, Lebanon, 116
Belfast, Ireland, 116
Belgrade, Yugoslavia, 61–62; *110–13, 120*
Ben Lomond, Scotland, 290
Bennett, James Gordon, 154; *266*
Berger, Bennet, 74
Bergman, Ingmar, 120
Berkshires, 241, 270; *448, 449*
Berlin Wall, 189–90; *354a–c*
Bernini, 180
Bethesda Fountain, Central Park, New York, N.Y., 256–57; *480*
Bicentennial, U.S., 92, 128; *208*
Big Horn Mountains, Wyo., 278; *517–19*
Black separatism, 118
Blacks in South End, Boston, Mass., 99
Blake, William, 259
Bloomer, Kent C., 2, 5, 9, 16
Bluegrass music, 240–41; *448a–d*
Blue jeans, 240
Blue Lake, Taos, N.M., 82
Body language, 37; *56*
Bok, Gordon, 247, 247n
Bolivia, 279; *523*
Boston, Mass., 51, 56, 64, 89, 90–103, 121–45, 148, 150 237, 259, 270; *57, 85, 86, 119, 153–92, 196–246, 444, 484*
Boundaries: city, 121; ideological, 194; national, 85–86, 196; neighborhoods, 72, 73, 77, 90, 98–99, 102, 120; personal, 2; social, 59, 70, 75, 102, 104, 111, 117; suburbs, 74, 103; territorial, x; United Nations, 120; water, 90, 152, 164, 174; *154, 155, 256, 257, 260, 261, 290*
Boylston Street, Boston, Mass., 132, 136; *216*
Bradley House, Madison, Wis., 14; *24*

Brain, x–xi, 120, 178; triune, 109–11
Brandenburg Gate, Berlin, Germany, 190; *354a–b*
Breuer, Marcel, 161
Bridges: Brooklyn, 153, 223–24; *262–64, 419, 423;* Charles, Prague, 175, 227; *315a–d, 429;* Dubuque, Iowa, 228; Golden Gate, 148; *252;* New York, 152; Verrazano-Narrows, 153
Bronx River Parkway, 271
Brooklyn Bridge. *See* Bridges
Brooklyn, development of, 223
Brooklyn Heights, 223–26; *98, 419–26*
Brooklyn-Queens Expressway, 223; *420*
Brooksville, Me., 247
Brotherhood, 108, 111
Brown, Marilyn, 78
Brunelleschi, 178
Buildings: alignment, 53; as projections of body, 2; curtain wall, 153; flat-topped, 150; openings, 3; relation to land, 49
Bulfinch, Charles, 96, 124–25
Bunker Hill Monument, Boston, Mass., 93; *161*
Bureaucracies, 212, 213, 218, 219
Burns, Robert, 290
Busing, 117

Calder, Alexander, 195; *370*
Calhoun, John B., 59, 105, 111, 261
Cambodia, invasion of, 210
Cambridge, Mass., 103, 144
Cambridge Seven, 129
Canals, 162, 177, 179; *284–87, 317*
Cantons, Swiss, 182
Cape Cod, Mass., 9, 146; *14*
Capital cities, 125, 200–12
Capitals, financial, 150
Capitol Hill, Washington, D.C., 199
Capitol: Madison, Wis., 208–12; *393, 394, 396e–g, 397, 398;* Washington, D.C., 203; *384–89*
Caribbean, 242; *17–19, 37, 73, 372, 551b, c*
Carter, Jimmy, 102
Cartesian design principles, 3, 36, 43
Castine, Me., 246, 251; *58, 63–65, 459, 460*
Castles, 174, 200; *379*
Cathedrals, 174, 178, 180, 220, 222; *314, 324, 327–31 410, 415*
Catskills, 271
Cemetery, Lafayette, New Orleans, La., 68; *128–30*
Central business districts, 124, 171, 184, 228
Central Park, New York, N.Y., 253–58, 270; *474–83*
Cerebral cortex, 117
Chagall, Marc, 182
Chain restaurants, 213, 277, 290
Chain stores, 184
Change, 72, 117–18, 288
Charlemont, Mass., 241; *449*

Charles Bridge, Prague, Czechoslovakia, 175, 227; *315a–d, 429*

Charles IV of Bohemia, 174–77

Charles River, Boston, Mass., 93, 97, 144, 237; *245, 246, 443*

Chase, Richard Allen, 157

Chicago, Ill., 270

Childhood, influence, 2, 32, 65, 74, 112

Child-raising, 118

Children in high-rise, 59

Chinatowns, 89, 101; *152, 153*

Chinese, South End of Boston, 99

"Choreography of the freeway," 270

Christian quarter, Jerusalem, 85; *142*

Christian Science World Headquarters, Boston, Mass., 129–32, 137; *212, 213, 214a–d, 215*

Christmas, 182, 234; *440a–d*

Churches, 129–35, 137, 161, 174, 182, 242, 266; *212–14, 217–23, 311, 335*

Churchill, Winston, 73

Church spires, 96, 146; *171, 193, 247, 248*

Cinematography, 120

Citicorp building, New York, N.Y., 188; *353*

Cities, 112–13, 150, 165, 177, 180, 195, 270; choking on automobiles, 190; evolution of, 112; function of, 109; as personifications, 200; seaport, 150–68

Citizen participation, Stockholm, Sweden, 166

City: opposing views of, 108; design by transportation, 153; people, 146; as song, 128, 136; *209*; relation to neighborhood, 108

City hall: Boston, Mass., 137; *227, 229, 232–34*; Oslo, Norway, 168; *301, 302*; Stockholm, Sweden, 165; *293, 294*

City Planning Commission, New York, N.Y., 223

Cityscape, 225

City states, 177

Civic centers, 248

Civic functions, 209

Civicness of Dutch, 161

Civilization, 109, 177, 189, 194, 251, 261, 270, 280

Civilized life, 9

Civil War, 170, 171, 253, 269

Clichés, 145, 156

Cliff dwellings, Mesa Verde, Col., 81; *133*

Clock, astronomical, Prague, Czechoslovakia, 175; *316*

Clustering, 2, 99, 262

Cognition, 63, 72

Cohan, George M., 155; *268*

Collectivism, 190

Columbia, Md., 141, 184–85

Columbia Point, Boston, Mass., 102; *192*

Columbus, statue of, 120; *132d, e*

Commerce, 77, 121, 137, 154, 159, 165, 222, 226–27

Commercial activities: relation to public space, 222

Commercial centers, 159

Commercial strips, 213, 248–49; *462–463d*

Commons, New England, 132, 241–49; *197, 200–02, 451d, 453, 454, 457–59*

Commonwealth Avenue, Boston, Mass., 259, 270

Common will in gemeinschaft, 113

Communal society of Rousseau, 114

Communication: visual vs. verbal, x–xi; with nature, 261

Communism, 72, 174–77, 227

Communist housing, 61–62; *319, 320*

Communist subways, 194

Communities, handcraft, 260

Communities, resort, 146–48

Community, 7, 84, 21, 62, 63, 70, 96, 102, 104; based on geography, 213; city as, 108; of common interest, 84, 108, 156, 177, 213–18, 241, 245, 279; corporate, 214; definition of, 71–72; development, 6; distemic, 177, 219; of limited liability, 74, 84, 88; of man as abstract conception, 108, 111; of chosen people, 108; of man and nature, 259–68; space in housing, 55; *94*; of strangers, 114, 121, 177, 232, 253; whaling, 146–47

Conceptually fenced neighborhoods, 119

Conceptual resources of low-income people, 84

Conceptual space, 111

Conceptual territory, 84, 155

Condominiums, 21, 54, 94, 166; *40*

Conflict, 32, 84, 112, 157, 288

Conformity, 46–47, 74, 118

Consciousness, 112, 245

Conservationists, 266

Constitution Plaza, Hartford, Conn., 231; *435*

Constitution, U.S., 73

Construction, appeal of, 127; *207*

Constructivism, 160; *282*

Consumerism, 242, 266

Contemplation, 288

Continental Congress, 158

Contracts, origins of, 113–14

Control of behavior. *See* Social behavior, control of

Convention hotels, 185–88; *344–49*

Copenhagen, Denmark, 165

Copernicus, 261

Copley Square, Boston, 132–36, 139

Copps Hill Burying Ground, Boston, Mass., 93; *160*

Cornfields, 282; *528, 529*

Corporate headquarters, 213

Corridors, 36, 55, 64, 210

Courtyards, 24, 56, 58, 65, 136, 155, 165; *95, 96, 101, 121b–d, 226, 269, 293*

Courthouse: Dubuque, Ia., 228; *430*; Saint Louis, Mo., 171; *312*; Square, Springfield, Mass., 242; *451f*

Crete, Plain of Lassithi, 228; *536a, b*

Crime, 6, 7, 116, 226, 258

Cross, Wilbur, 71

Crowding, rats and mice, 111

Crystal palaces, 192–93

Culture: differences, 35, 65, 72, 73, 120, 158, 218, 258; art unifies, 156; boutique, 146; centers, 103; change,

211; cosmopolitan, 182; enriched by trade, 114; evolution of, 109–10; group, 213, of hinterland, 150; house-oriented, 97; mass, 241, 266; middle-class, 88; object-oriented, 248; particularity in universality, 218; population size, 178; regional, 150; Scandinavian, 165; rituals, 234

Cummington, Mass., 240–41; *448a–e*

Curtain wall buildings, 153

Custer State Park, South Dakota, 268; *499*

Darwin, Charles, x, 109

David, by Michelangelo, 178; *323*

Deere and Company, 213–18; *399–409*

Defensible space, 7, 31, 56, 78, 116, 226

Definitions: distemic, 112–17, 219; haptic, 8–9; proxemic, 112–17

Dendrites, 189

Department stores, 184

Depression, Great, 71

Design, 28, 32, 33, 35, 75, 135, 137, 139, 165, 246, 260, 281; automobile, 280; highway, 270; shopping centers, 184; urban, 3, 137, 148, 153, 174

Design for Diversity, x, 109

Designers, 32–33, 70, 71, 127, 184, 245, 246, 248, 262

Diaspora, 87

Dickinson, Emily, house 3; *1, 2*

Dissonance, cognitive, 248

Distemics: defined, 112–17, 112*n*, 219; control of behavior, 114–15, 247–50; destructive, 266; places, integrated, 117–18; of corporations, 213–18; space surrounded by proxemic, 220–21; underly and override culture, 219; 112–267, passim

Diversity: 7, 35, 112, 113, 114, 127, 213; architectural, 49, 211; domain of individual, 116; ethnic, 75; of neighborhood, 73, 113

Domes, capital: Madison, Wis., *394, 395, 396e–g, 397, 398*; Washington, D.C., 203; *386, 387*

Dominance: hierarchies, 6; of man over nature, 261

Don Quixote and Sancho Panza, 201; *381–83*

Dorchester, Mass., 99, 102–03, 145

Doty, Governor James, 208

Drama, ix, 42, 58, 127, 128, 157, 165. *See also* Theater

Dubuque, Ia., 228; *430*

Dukakis, Michael, 228

Dulles International Airport, Virginia, 196–99; *373–77*

Duplex houses, 20–21; *39*

Dutch. *See* Holland

Earth day, 261

East River, New York, N.Y., 153, 157, 223; *260, 261*

Ecology, 24, 32, 102, 109–10, 113, 193, 290, 253–54, 257–58, 281–90

Eden, 114

Edges, 12, 81, 119, 121, 144, 200

Edinburgh, 56; *99a*

Education, 118, 156, 157, 248

Egalitarians, 8, 114, 166

Elderly, 55, 251, 279

Elevators, 58, 64, 153, 257

Eliot, Charles, 144

Ellis Island, 150, 158

Embarcadero Freeway, 148; *253. See also* Highways

Embassies, 116, 219

Emerald Necklace, Boston, Mass., *259*

Emotion, xi, 110–11

Empire State Building, New York, N.Y., 224; *265, 419, 423*

Enclosure, 7, 53, 156

Energy, 103, 157, 188, 190, 281, 288; *274*

England, 20, 45, 48, 90, 259; *38, 75*

Environment, xi, 31, 118, 157, 184, 187, 195

Environmental deterioration, 32

Environmental inversion, 184; *339–43, 345*

Environmental psychologists, x, 12, 72, 119

Epiphany, 234; *440a–d*

Equality, defined in Boston neighborhood, 99

Erikson, Erik, 73, 111

Esplanades: Brooklyn Heights, 223–26; *419–24*; Rotterdam, 159; *279*; Zurich, 182; *334, 338. See also* Waterfronts

Ethnicity, 122, 174, 213, 242, 257–58

Ethnic: neighborhoods, 71, 72, 75, 90–94, 95–96, 233; diversity, 75, 101

Ethnocentrism, 72, 111

Ethologists, 6, 59, 73

Ethology, ix, x, 109, 116

Europe, 37, 72, 103, 159, 166, 169, 174, 194, 242

Europeans, 150, 258

Evolution, 12, 73, 109–12, 177, 280

Expressionism, 159

Expressways, 90, 96, 119, 171, 225, 255, 270. *See also* Highways

Exurbanites, 146

Eyes and brain, xi, 178

Fabos, Julius Gy., 253

Fahnestock Memorial Park, 271; *502b*

Fallen angels, 114

Faneuil Hall, Boston, Mass., 94, 140–42; *170, 232, 237, 238*

Farmers' markets, 166, 244; *297*

Farmhouses, 47; *72–73*

Farsta, Sweden, 167; *300*

Far West, 272, 281; *505, 506*

Fashion, 17, 228

Fein, Albert, 259–60

Fences, 7, 8–9, 32–35, 55, 65, 280, 288; symbolic, 68, 70, 73, 74, 248; *11, 12a–k*

Fenestration, 4

Fenway Park, Boston, Mass., 259

Ferry Terminal, San Francisco, Cal., 148; *253*

Festival of the Virgin, Bolivia, 279; *523*

Feudalism, 161
Fiedler, Arthur, 236
Finn, Huck, 163
Fischer, Fred, 6
Floodplains, 285
Florence, Italy, 177−78, 179; *321−24*
Folk dancing, Amherst common, Mass., 245; *458*
Ford Foundation building, 157, 185; *275*
Forest products, 266
Forest Service, 266
Forests, virgin, New England, 285
Fortresses, residential, 56, 59, 85
Forum, Rome, 179; *326*
Founding Fathers, 72, 127
Fourth of July, 236; *444*
"Fourth of July in Maine," 246
Franklin Park, Boston, Mass., 259
Freedom,190, 220, 268, 270, 280
Freedom Trail, Boston, Mass., 94
French, Daniel Chester, 205
French Quarter, New Orleans, La., 65, 169; *121a−d*
French village, *194*
Friedman, M. Paul, 211
Frost, Robert, 108
Fulton Ferry, 223

Gabo, Naum, 160
Galileo, 261
Gans, Herbert, 94, 96; *Urban Villagers, The,* 94
Garden: Central Park as, 253; cities, 167; *299a−d*; district, New Orleans, 65; *122−30*; sculpture, Museum of Modern Art, New York, N.Y., 155; *269*; romantic, 259; plaza, Stockholm, 166; *296*; transition to, 45; *63−65*
Gateway: Arch, Saint Louis, Mo., 171; *308−13*; to house yard, 18; to North End, Boston, 92; *157, 158*; to Washington, D.C., 205; *390*
Gaudí, Antonio, 220
Gemeinschaft, 113, 114, 117, 120, 266
Genetic pool, 110
Genius loci, 82, 218
Gentrification, 74, 101−02, 117, 132, 145, 146, 150, 224
Geographers, 118
Germany, 20, 71, 118; *36*
Gerster, Georg, 88, 281; *151*; *Grand Design: The Earth from Above,* 281
Gesellschaft, 113, 128
Gestalt experience, xi
Gibson, James J., 8
Giotto, 178
Glasgow, Scotland, 60, 290; *106*
Global village, 120
Goetheanum, Switzerland, 260; *486*
Goldberger, Paul, 154
Golden Gate Bridge, San Francisco, Cal., 148; *252*
Goldfield, Nevada, 277; *513c, d*
Gorelik, Mordecai, 32

Gothic, 150, 174, 220, 221−22
Government Center, Boston, Mass., 94, 124, 137−40; *169, 227−34*
Granary Burying Ground, Boston, Mass., 127, 137; *206*
Grand Canyon, 262; *487−89*
Grand Central Station, New York, N.Y., 190; *357*
Greeks, 14, 99
Greeley, Horace, 154−55; *267*
Gresham's Law of Environment, 35
Grid. *See* Street grid
Grosse Point, Michigan, 74
Groups, 22, 73, 75−78, 84, 90, 112−13, 233
Gun control, 35

Habitat, 16, 63, 64, 73, 148, 280
Hadley, Mass., 245
Hale, Edward Everett, 259; *484*
Hall, Edward T., 86, 112, 216
Hall, Mildred, 216
Halprin, Lawrence, 250, 270
Hannibal, Mo., 169−70; *12j*
Hanover Street, Boston, 92; *57*
Haptic, defined 8−9; 33, 48, 54, 59, 82, 184, 188, 211
Harbor: as center, 146; Boston, 143, 160; *243, 244*; New York, 150, 160; *256, 257, 264*; Oslo, 168; *303*; San Francisco, 148
Hardin, Garrett, 35
Harlem, New York, N.Y., 253
Harlem, East, New York, N.Y., 59
Harvard Forest Museum, 285
Hatfield, Mark, 248
Haussmann, Baron, 218
Haymarket, Boston, Mass., 94, 140; *169, 235*
Heckscher, August, 117; *Public Happiness, The,* 117
Hegel, Georg Wilhelm, 114
Height-to-width ratios, streets, 48, 229, 272
Herald Square, New York, N.Y., 154−55; *266*
Heroes, 120
Hewitt, William A., 218
Hierarchy: dominance, 6−7; of mews and courtyards, 226; of needs, 113; of routes, 270; of streets, 36, 41; proxemic−distemic, 226; spatial, 58; in walled cities, 88
Highjacking, 116
Highlands, Scottish, 290
High-rise: housing, 22, 58−63, 83−84, 94, 162, 177; buildings disallowed, Stockholm, 166
Highways, 152−53, 166−67, 248, 266, 260−80; rules of, 115; water, 162, 189
Highway services, 277; *514, 516−20*
Hispanics, 257−58
Historic preservation, 6, 37, 186−87, 191, 223−26, 281
Hoffer, Eric, 118
Holland, 60, 159−63; *279−89*
Holy Family, Madrid, Spain, 200; *380*
Holyoke, Mass., 22, 31; Veteran's Park, *468*
Home, 2−7, 22, 58, 59, 88; motor, 279; single-family, 104,

166. *See also* Houses
Hood, Raymond, 229
Hoorn, Netherlands, 163; *288–89*
Hotels, 185–88; *344–49*
Houses, 3–21, 33–34, 45–46, 48, 51, 53–54, 64, 86, 87. *See also* Home
Housing projects. *See* High-rise housing; public housing; multifamily housing
Houston, Tex., 174, 188
Howard, Ebenezer, 167
Hudson River, 75, 152–53, 270
Hull Street, Boston, Mass., 93; *162*
Human scale. *See* Scale
Hungary, 270
Hunter–gatherers, 111
Huntington, Anna Hyatt, 248
Huntington Avenue, Boston, Mass., 132
Huxtable, Ada Louise, 188
Hyatt Regency. *See* Hotels

Idaho Falls, Ida., 228, 250, 281; *465–67*
Identity, 72, 182, 219, 244
Ideology, x, 117
Image, xi, 28, 65, 186, 195, 203, 269; collective, 215; systems, conflict of, 32; of childhood, 45, 290; self-, 218
Imageability, of rivers, 144
Imagination, 218, 288
Indians, 64, 81–82, 271, 281–82; *118, 133, 134, 526*
Individuality, 46, 114, 116
Industrial cities, ugliness of, 259–60
Information overload, 72, 155
Information seeking, 157
Innovation, 116, 118
Instinct, 73
Institutions, 137, 179, 205, 211, 244
Integration of public places, 117
Intellectuals, 144–45
Intelligence, 156, 160, 177
Intelligent beings, in space, 111
Interaction with others, relief from, 7
International relations, 111
International School. *See* Architecture
Interstate Highway System. *See* Highways, Interurban path systems
Interurban path systems, 189–99
Intruder, sense of, *9*
Involvement, 119, 211, 229, 251, 258, 261
Iran, 116
Irish, 90, 99
Irrationality, 117
Irrigation, 288
Islands, 146–48, 152, 164; *247–50*
Israel, 85–88; *140–50*
Italians, 37, 56, 90–94, 99, 177–81, 242; *56, 57, 97, 157, 165*

Jackson, J. B., 8, 281
Jackson, age of, 150
Jackson Square, New Orleans, La., 169
Jacobs, Jane, 58, 114, 137, 233; *Death and Life of Great American Cities, The*, 114, 137
Jamaica Pond, Boston, Mass., 259
Jamestown, N.Y., 242; *452*
Japan, 115, 213
Jefferson, Thomas, 65, 108, 158, 203
Jenkins Hill, Washington, D.C., 207
Jersey City, N.J., 75–78
Jerusalem, 85–86, 89, 227; *140–42, 428*
Jews, 85–88, 99, 161, 234
John Hancock, 127
John Hancock building, old, Boston, Mass., *222*
John Hancock Tower, Boston, Mass., 133–35; *221, 223–24*
Jordan, Vernon, 102
Jung, Carl, 2

Kallman, McKinnell, and Knowles, 137
Kansas, 275; *507–08*
Kaplan, Stephen and Rachel, 119, 211, 229, 258
Keefe, Frank, 228
Kennedy, J. F., 78
Kennedy Library, Boston, Mass., 102–03
Kensington, London, England, 20; *38*
Kevin Roche, John Dinkaloo, and Associates, 157
Kibbuzim, 88
Kinesthetic, 8, 33
King, Martin Luther, Jr., 117
Kirdi farmsteads, Cameroon, Africa, 88; *151*

Lakes, 182, 185, 208, 291; *338, 345, 539*
Land, agricultural, 281, 285
Land and buildings, 49, 53
Landmarks, 119–20, 121, 122, 146–47, 159, 166, 173, 177; Dubuque, Ia., 228; *430*; for nations 200–12; global, 158; national, 171, 191; New York, N.Y., 150, 153, 154, 223; *256, 265, 419, 421–23*
Land ordinances of 1896, 51
Landscape, ix, 28, 63, 188, 270, 273–75, 281–88; architects, 2, 12, 242, 250, 270, 288; architecture, 49, 52, 253, 257; Dutch, 288; New England, 272, 285; preferences, 119; Scotland, 290; *537*
Land-use: laws, 32; planning, 31
Langton, Jane, 146; *Dark Nantucket Noon*, 146
Language, 73, 109–10, 111, 156–57
Lapidus, Morris, 186
Las Vegas, Nev., 186, 249, 277
Latter-Day Saints, temple of, 250; *467*
Law, 43, 73; enforcement territorialized, 116
Law Enforcement Assistance Administration, 6
Legibility, 112, 115, 119, 258
L'Enfant, Pierre, 203–08
Leonardo da Vinci, 177

Levittown, Long Island, N.Y., 9–12, 54; *16, 17*
Lewis Wharf, Boston, Mass., 64; *119*
Leyhausen, Paul, 6, 7
Life-style, 7, 28, 32, 70, 82, 92, 97, 148, 156
Lijnbaan, Rotterdam, The Netherlands, 161; *283*
Limbic system, 110–11
Limmat, river, 182; *333–35*
Lincoln, Abraham, statues of, 205, 211, 248–49; *388, 396a–d, 463a–d*
Lincoln Center, New York, N.Y., 233; *437, 438*
Lincoln City, Ore., 248–49, 278; *461–63, 520*
Lincoln Memorial, Washington, D.C., 205; *389, 390*
Linday, Nancy, 257–58
Lindbergh, Anne Morrow, 261
Lindbergh, Charles A., 195, 261
Lindsay, Vachel, 178, 205, 272, 282
Loch Lomond, Scotland, 290; *537*
Logan Airport, Boston, Mass., 143; *244*
London, England, 150, 174, 178, 194
Look-alike buildings, 46–47, 229
Look Park, Northampton, Mass., *471, 472*
Louisburg Square, Boston, Mass., 56, 97; *99b, 177*
Louisiana Territory, 65
Lovins, Amory, 288
Lowell, Robert, 246–48
Lynch, Kevin, 75, 115, 119, 121, 130, 132, 137, 144, 258; *Image of the City, The*, 75–78, 119; *What Time Is This Place?*, 115

McHarg, Ian, 290, *Design with Nature*, 290
McKim, Mead, and White, 132, 192
MacLean, Alex, 90–91, 103; *154, 155, 192*
MacLean, Paul D., 110–11, 115, 117, 288
McLuhan, Marshall, 120
Madison Square Garden, New York, N.Y., 192–93; *361, 362*
Madison, Wis., 14, 18, 62, 104, 125, 208–12, 228; *32, 62, 92, 195, 393–98*
Madrid, Spain, 200–01; *378–83*
Mallet, David, 5, 9; "I Knew This Place," 5–6
Malls: Central Park, N.Y., 256–58; enclosed, 184–85; *339–43*; Madison, Wis., 212; *396e–f*; U.S. national, 205; *389*; Ramblas, Barcelona, 220; *411, 412*; Rotterdam, The Netherlands, 161; *283*; Stockholm, Sweden, 166; *295*
Mammals, 6, 111
Management, park, 258
Manhattan, N.Y., 77–78, 127, 135, 150–58, 153, 223–24, 228, 257; skyline, 223–24; *258, 259, 419, 421–23*
Manor, 45, 70
Mansard roofs, 4, 24; *3, 4*
Manship, Paul, 229
Marketplace: curtailment of, 227; distemic, 113; of ideas, 144–45
Markets, 142, 166, 177, 182, 184, 242, 244
Martha's Vineyard, 148

Marx, Karl, 113, 114
Masaryk, Thomas G., 174
Maslow, Abraham, 113
Massachusetts, state planning policy, 228
Massachusetts Turnpike, boundary of South End, 99; *181*
Mass production of houses, 4, 46, 48–49
Meadows, New England, 284; *532*
Mediterranean, 37, 61, 179
Megalopolis, 103
Melting pot, Jamestown, N.Y., 242
Memorial Bridge, Washington, D.C., 205; *390*
Menotti, Gian-Carlo, 290
Mesa Verde, Col., 81; *133*
Mestan, Anton, 37
Metropolitan Opera, New York, N.Y., 229, 233; *437, 438*
Mexico City, 82–83; *470*
Michelangelo, 177
Middle America, 150, 210, 233
Middle class, 32, 75, 84, 88, 103, 117, 118–19, 122
Midwest, 50–51, 281
Milde, Gordon T., 253
Military outposts, Roman, 174
Minneapolis, Minn., 169, 173
Mississippi, 65, 169–74, 182; *304–08*
Mobile homes, 104, 279
Mobility, 74, 117, 118–19, 213, 240
Moldau River, 174
Moline, Illinois, 213
Montague Street, Brooklyn, N.Y., 226; *425, 426*
Montreal, 63, 194
Monuments, 120, 159–62, 171, 190, 200–12, 247
Moon landing, 261
Moonwalk, New Orleans, La., 169
Moore, Charles W., 2, 5, 9
Moscow, 194
Moslem quarter, Jerusalem, 85; *142*
Motels, 146, 250, 277–78, 290
Motion picture, effect on public ritual, 232
Mountains as boundaries, 82; *135*
Mouse habitat, 59; *105*
Movement, 276
Muir, John, 260
Multifamily housing, 22–32, 55–62
Multinational corporations, 218
Mumford, Lewis, 159–61, 223; *Highway and the City, The*, 159–61
Museums: Modern Art, New York, N.Y., 155; *269, 270*; Natural History, New York, N.Y., 157; *273*
Music, related to landscape, 258
Mystery in landscape, 119, 211, 258
Mythology, 70, 71, 73, 82, 120, 150, 238
Myths, 50, 104, 108, 180, 216, 219, 270, 281; of city alienation, 113; egalitarian, 72; inverse to fences, 71; street design, 43, 51–52; suburban, 74

Nantucket, Mass., 146–48, 163, 246; *11, 12g, 71, 247–51*

Napoleon III, 218
Natchez, Miss., 17, 170; *27, 28, 307*
National Airport, Washington, D.C., 199
National Gallery of Art, Washington, D.C., 205
National Institute of Mental Health, Bethesda, Md., 109, 110
National Parks Association, 262
National Park Service, 102, 171, 261–68; problems of, 279
National Park System, 260, 268
Nature, 49, 168, 260–61
Neighborhoods, 7, 62, 71–105, 108, 112, 150, 280
Neocortex, 110–11
Neotribalism, 116, 210, 219
Netherlands. *See* Holland
Neutral ground, 6
Newark Bay, 78; *131j, k*
New Bedford, Mass., 77
New Deal, 205
New England, 47, 146–48, 244, 284, 285
New England commons. *See* Commons
New Englander, transplanted, 16
New Jersey Turnpike, 76, 271; *131a, 503a–c. See also* Highways
Newman, Oscar, 7, 31, 78, 84, 116, 226
New Mexico, 16, 281; *12d, 29, 134, 506a, 526*
New Orleans, La., 65–69, 148, 169, 170, 173; *121–30*
New South, 186
New towns, 163, 167, 177, 184, 255
New World, 158
New York, N.Y., 59, 89, 148–58, 188, 190, 193, 213, 220, 253–58; *103, 256–70, 273, 275–78, 363*
New York; State Department of Public Works, 271; milkshed, 284; *530*; parkway, 270; *502a–g*
New York Times, 75, 205
Niagara Falls, N.Y., 290
Nodes, 119, 121, 154, 173, 179, 182, 200
Nonconformity, 116
Norfolk, Va., 241
North America, 37
North End, Boston, Mass., 37, 42, 90–95, 122, 142; *57, 61, 154–66, 196, 240*
Norwegians, 168
Nostalgia, 127, 145, 187
Noyeau, 180

Object-oriented culture, 24
Office buildings, 150, 228
Old Custom House tower, Boston, Mass., 93, 124, 140, 142, 143; *163, 197, 233–36, 243, 244*
Old Faithful geyser, 266; *496a–d*
Old Faithful Inn, 266; *497*
Old North Church, Boston, Mass., 92–93, 122, 137, 143; *156–62, 196, 227, 243, 244*
Old State House, Boston, Mass., 127; *205*
Olmsted, Frederick Law, 53, 144, 253–60, 271
Olmsted, Frederick Law, Jr., 205

Openings, 4, 229
Open space, 74, 167
Oregon, 248–50
Oslo, Norway, 168; *301–03*
Ostia, Italy, 37, 56, 179; *56, 97*
Oxford, England, 178
Ozarks, 275; *509*

Parades: Easter, 234; *441–43*; of tractors, 237; *446c*
Paris, France, 150, 174, 194, 195, 218
Park Avenue, N.Y., 280; *524*
Parking in residential complex, 56
Parks: apartments on, 31; as neutral ground, 6; city, 207, 248–59; *392, 461, 463a–c, 464, 466–71, 474–84*; create street enclosure, 53; harbor, 94, 159, 168; *168, 279, 303*; in malls, 184–85; *342, 343*; national, 261–68; private, 213; *399*; riverfront, 94, 159, 168, 169–70, 223; *168, 233, 279, 303, 304, 307, 308*; state, 268, 270; urban, 228
Parler, Peter, 174
Parris, Alexander, 141
Parthenon, 14, 140; *21, 236*
Party walls, 21
Passport, control, 196; *371d*
Paths, 8, 51, 119, 121, 137, 258
Path systems, interurban, 189–99
Pathways, auto, 268–80; *500–24*
Patios, 28
Peachtree Center, Atlanta, Ga., 188; *352*
Peachtree Plaza Hotel, Atlanta, Ga., 185; *344, 345*
Pedestrian: malls (*See also* Malls, Streets, pedestrian) as paths, separated from vehicles, 255; plazas, 88; terraces, 229; *432a*; walkways, 167; *299d*
Pedestrians: accommodated with cars, 165; served by shopping centers, 184–85
Peekskill, N.Y., 271
Pei, I. M., 130, 135, 137
Peninsulas: Bayonne, N.J., 76; North End of Boston, Mass., 90; South Boston, 95
Pennsylvania Station, New York, N.Y., 191–93; *358, 359*
Penobscot Bay, Me., 143
Perception, 41, 43, 72
Personality, 4, 46
Perspective, xi, 54, 180
Petersham, Mass., 242, 244, 251; *451d*
Philistines, 144–45
Photography, xi–xii, 178, 229
Piazza della Signoria, Florence, Italy, 178; *322*
Picasso, Pablo, 159
Picture windows, 28
Pilotis, 87; *145*
Planned communities, 51, 98
Planned unit developments, 24–28; *46, 47*
Planners; as gardeners, 70; ban cars, 212; of proxemic places, 119; outlook of, 71, 94, 104, 109, 122, 178, 288; Park Service, 262; problems of, 245; stop middle-class

flight, 102; zoning as design, 188

Planning, 83, 160–61, 166, 190, 193, 212, 255; Commissions, 132, 223, 226; Massachusetts policy, 228

Playhouse, Amsterdam park, 60; *109*

Plazas, 6, 41, 159–60, 166, 168, 178, 229, 231, 242; *296, 324c, d, 433, 452*; Constitution, Hartford, Conn., 231; *435*; Plaza de España, Madrid, Spain, 200–01; *381–83, 468*

Pluralism, 32, 72, 75, 109, 218

Poets, 178, 211, 246–48, 272

Polders, 163

Police. *See* Social behavior, control of

Polis, 22, 108

Pompeii, 242; *451a*

Popko, Edward S., 82

Population, 111, 118–19, 165, 189, 244

Porches, 12–19, 36, 56, 65; *15–29, 31, 95, 122, 125, 126*

Port cities: American, 149–58; North European, 159–68; Ostia, Italy, 179

Portland, Ore., 248, 250; *464*

Portman, John, 186

Portuguese, 99

Post, George Browne, 208

Postmodernism, 186

Potomac river, 207

Power, 150, 174, 218

Prague, Czechoslovakia, 150, 174–77, 194, 277; *314–20, 367, 368, 429*

Prairie, 51, 171, 213

Prefabrication, 46, 48–49, 83; *137*

Preferences, landscape, 119

Preservation, wilderness, 281

Primary group, 112–13

Primates, 12, 110–11

Privacy, 4, 6, 18, 20–21, 28, 68, 73, 136

Private ownership of public places, 229

Private personality, emphasis on, 117

Private pond, New Salem, Mass., *473*

Professionals, 74, 117

Professions, 111, 112

Prometheus, 229; *432d*

Proprietary interest, 32, 84, 102

Protestantism, 161

Proxemics: defined, 112–17, 112n; control of behavior, 114–15, 257–58; headhunter, 280; in corporate setting, 213; neotribalism, 210; of age, class, and mobility, 279; of intelligentsia, 241; of town commons, 244; proxemics, warriors, 116; 112–267, passim

Prudential Center, Boston, Mass., 128–29, 137, 231; *210–12*

Pruitt-Igoe, 58, 62, 84, 102

Pseudo-species, 73, 111, 113

Psychologists, environmental, 72

Psychology, 8, 59, 270

Public Garden, Boston, Mass., 123, 136, 259; *197, 198, 484*

Public health and welfare, 24, 104

Public housing, 3, 7, 55–56, 83–84, 101, 102

Pueblo Indians, 64, 81–82, 281–82; *118, 133, 134, 526*

Puerto Ricans, 99, 101, 120

Pushkarev, Boris, 270; *Man-Made America: Chaos or Control?*, 270

Quincy Market, Boston, Mass., 94, 140–42; *170, 238, 239*

Racial prejudice, 117

Radio City Music Hall, 233

Railroads, 99, 174, 182, 189–95, 269–70; *131f, 180*

Railroad stations, 190–93; *355–60, 369*

Ramblas, Barcelona, 220, 234; *411, 412, 440*

Ramsay Gardens, Edinburgh, 56; *99a*

Range, American west, 50

Range, animals, 73

Rapoport, Amos, 36, 43, 65, 88

Rationality, 112, 114

Rats and mice, 111, 261; *105*

RCA Building, New York, N.Y., 155, 229; *431*

Redwoods National Park, 265; *492, 493*

Regions, 28, 150, 269

Rehabilitation, 101

Religion, 74, 82, 130, 161

Renaissance, 161, 177, 260

Reps, John, 207

Research, interdisciplinary, 111

Restaurants, 146, 186, 196; *56, 348, 353, 377, 426*

Retirement communities, 35

Revere, Paul, 92–93, 122; *196*

Revitalization of downtown, 228

Rhine, river, 182

Richardson, H. H., 132–35; *132*

Right to: home territory, 7; travel, 189, 194, 280

Risen ape, 114

Rituals, 75, 82, 117, 180, 196, 232, 234, 236

Rivers, 144, 169–83, 174, 177, 179, 189, 207, 285; *245, 246, 304, 307, 308, 314, 317, 321, 325, 333–35, 533*

Roadside stops, 277; *513a*

Roberts, Steven V., 75

Rockefeller Center, N.Y., 155, 193, 228–31, 233; *431–33, 439*

Roebling, Emily, 223

Roeblings, the, 153

Roebling, Washington, 223

Roles, 111, 112

Rolling Grass and High Hill, 24–28, 56; *46a–l*

Roman aqueducts, 127

Romantic landscape, 256, 259–60

Rome, 42, 73, 116, 179–81; *60, 325–32*

Roosevelt, Franklin Delano, 168, 205

Rotterdam, 159–62, 168; *279–83*

Rouse, James, 141

Rousseau, Jean Jacques, 114, 260
Row houses, 20, 48, 55; *31, 38, 76*
Roxbury, Mass., 99, 102, 103, 145
Rushing, Katheryn, 262
Russia, 118

Saarinen, Eero, 171, 196, 213
Safdie, Moshe, 64
Saint Augustine, Fla., 234; *441–43*
Saint Louis, Mo., 171–74; *308–13*
Saint Lucia farmhouse, 20; *73*
Saint Peter's Basilica, Rome, 130–32; *327–32*
San Francisco, Cal., 51–52, 89, 121, 148, 193; *87, 152, 252–55, 364*
San Geronimo Church, Taos, N.M., 82; *134*
Santa Fe Trail, 173, 272–73
Sasaki, Dawson, and DeMay, 131
Sasaki, Hideo, 214–18
Savannah, Ga., 53
Sawtooth alignment of houses, 54; *91*
Sawyer, Tom, 163; *12j*
Scale: of courtyards, 58; contrasts in Boston, 127; distemic, 115; Dutch sense for, 162–63; neighborhood, 31, 102; human, 22, 130–32, 183; reference for, xi; small is mammalian, 120; village, 84, 162
Scenic metaphor, 32
School integration, 117
Schumacher, E. F., 288; *Small is Beautiful*, 288
Science, 112, 156, 260–61
Scollay Square, Boston, Mass., 137
Scotland, 48, 56, 60, 290; *74, 99a, 106, 537*
Scott, A. C., 262; *489*
Scott, Dred, 171
Sculpture garden, Museum of Modern Art, New York, N.Y., 155; *269*
Sea-lanes as highways, 189
Seaport cities, 150–68
Seaports, 143, 162, 169
Seaport towns, 146–48, 163
Sears Crescent Building, Boston, Mass., 139; *230–31*
Seasonal flux of people, 147–48
Seattle, Wash., 270
Security in face of diversity, 113, 280
Self-image, 2, 16, 22
Self-interest, 113
Semiarid landscapes, 50
Sennett, Richard, 116–17, 128; *Fall of Public Man, The*, 116–17
Sense of movement, 270
Sense of place, 104, 218, 246–48
Sense of sky, 195
Sense of space, lost by wide streets, 43
Senses in haptic system, 9
Sex roles, 74, 111
Shantytowns, 82; *136*
Shelter, impulse for, 81

Shopping centers, 184–85, 187. *See also* Malls
Shopping corridor, 210
Shorelines as urban boundaries, 82, 90, 166; *135, 154, 290, 298*
Sidewalk position, 55; *92, 93*
Sideyards, 19, 20, 34
Sierra Club, 260
Silence, need for, 290
Single-family homes, 3, 5, 20, 28, 37, 55, 104, 166
Single-use spaces, 137
Site planning, 24–28
Skin as boundary, 3, 7
Skyscrapers, 257, 260
Slums, 84, 99, 290
Small-group identity, 108–09, 111, 113
Small towns, 70, 72
Smetana, Bedrich, 174
Social behavior, control of, 7, 9, 73, 114–16, 257–58
Social class, 72, 112, 119, 146, 213
Social engagement, civilized, 232–33
Social group as living thing, 70
Socializing: porches, 17; *31*; rear of house, 19; *33*; shopping centers, 184
Social justice, 118, 280
Social landscape, model of, 118
Social mammal, 280
Social mobility, 118–19, 213
Social neutrality, 261
Social order of individuals, 114
Social science: view of evolution, 109, 213; scientists, reaction to genetic origins of behavior, x
Social structure of resort towns, 146–48
Societies: gang, 74; pluralistic, problems of designing for, 245; traditional, 245; agricultural, 260, 281; consumer, 182; of inward antagonism, 180
Sociobiology, 109, 120
Sociologists, 12, 62, 73, 116–17
Sociology, primary and secondary groups, 112–13
Soglin, Paul, 211
Solitude, 261–62, 265
Song, city as, 128, 136; *209*
Sontag, Susan, xi–xii; *On Photography*, xi
South Boston, Mass., 95–96, 145; *171a, d*
South Dakota, 282; *527*
South End: Boston, Mass., 98–101; *171a, 180–91*; Springfield, Mass., 78, 120; *132a–l*
South Moluccans, 84
Space: conceptual, 111; transitional, 7–8; "waste," 88; *151*
Spain, courtyards of, 56; *100*
Spatial experience and speech, xi
Speech patterns, attitudes to street, 37
Spirit of St. Louis, 195
Sprawl, urban, 103
Springfield, Mass., 53–54, 78, 89, 242; *90a–d, 95, 96, 451f*
Square: Capitol, Madison, Wis., 212; *397*; St. Peter's,

Rome, 180; *327−30*
Squares: town, 174, 241−49; *316, 451*; height-to-width ratios, 41
Stage art, 120
Stage, Capitol steps as, 203; *385*
Stage design, ix, x, 32
Stage, public spaces as, 139, 182, 191, 205, 229
Stahl, Tad, 141
Stairway, must climb to see, 9
Stanley, Idaho, *82, 83*
Statehouse, Boston, Mass., 96, 124−25; *173, 202−04*
Statue of Liberty, 150, 153, 224; *256, 422*
Statues: Columbus, Springfield, Mass., 78, 120; *132d, e*; *David*, Florence, Italy, 178; *323*; Don Quixote and Sancho Panza, Madrid, Spain, 201; *382, 383*; Edward Everett Hale, Boston, Mass., 259; *484*; George M. Cohan, New York, N.Y., 155; *268*; Holy Family, Madrid, Spain, 200; *380*; Horace Greeley, New York, N.Y., 154−55; *267*; Abraham Lincoln, Lincoln City, Ore., 248−49; *463a−d*; man and bird, Zurich, Switzerland, 183; *338*; prefabricated family, Zurich, Switzerland, 183; *336*; Prometheus, Rockefeller Center, New York, N.Y., 229; *432d*; Franklin D. Roosevelt, Oslo, Norway, 168; *303*; Rotterdam, The Netherlands, 159−61; *279−82*; Union soldier, Castine, Me., 247; *459*; workingmen, Oslo, Norway, 168; *302*; World War I soldier, Springfield, Mass., 120
Steel, use in architecture, 213−14
Steinbeck, John, 279; *Travels with Charley*, 279
Steiner, Rudolf, 260
Stockholm, Sweden, 150, 164−67, 290−98
Stone Age, 109
Street: socializing, 37, 67; *57*; width encourages speed, 43; corridor, 42, 48, 55; crime, 7; grid, 51−52, 208; change with time, 221; *411−14*; life, Belgrade, 61; Life Project, 257; malls, 166, 170, 228; *295, 305, 396f, 430*; names define boundaries, 74; separation, 18; as setting, 46; spirit changed, 31; theater, 232−38; *439−47*
Streets: bicycle, *255*; building alignment, 53; confuse invaders, 87; *147, 148*; cultural differences in use of, 36−37, 65; cul-de-sac, 7, 55, 104; curvilinear, 53; *88*; height-to-width ratios, 41−43; *60, 61*; myth of, 37; as neutral ground, 6; pedestrian, 161, 166, 184, 212, 220−28; *199, 283, 295, 339, 340, 396f, 430*; safe for strangers, 114; radial, 200, 207; shopping, 222−26; *416−18, 427, 428*; as social territory, 36; walls of, 46
Streetscape, continuity of, 193
Stubbins, Hugh, 188
Subdivision ordinances, 42
Suburban boundaries, 103−04
Suburban prototype, 65
Suburbia, openness of, 187
Suburbs, 4, 9, 19, 74−75, 84, 88, 103, 104, 184, 253
Subways, 193−95; *365−68*
Sullivan, Louis, 14, 260; *485*
Summer resorts, 146−48

Sunderland, Mass., *93, 193*
Surplus value, 112
Surveillance, professional, 84
Suttles, Gerald, 74, 233; *Social Order of the Slum, The*, 233
Swedes, 150, 164−67, 242
Symbiosis, 146, 212
Symbolic exchanges, as substitute for war, 113
Symbolic systems, 73
Symbolism: of Boston, 122, 143; of corporate headquarters, 213; opening of the West, 171; of World War II, 160
Symbol: of Christian culture, 201; *380*; Lincoln as, 211; both proxemic and distemic, 201; Vatican as, 180; world, 158
Symbols: attached to buildings, 4, 89; *5, 153*; of education, 210, 248; of frontier civilization, 210; of joy, 160; *282*; imposed by one group on another, 96; *171c*; local and regional, 242; cities as, formations, 174, 200−12; distemic, 120; of suburbia, 74−75
Switzerland, 182−83, 190−91; *333−38, 355, 356*
Symphony Hall, Boston, Mass., 132
Syrians, in South Boston, Mass., 99, 101
Szarkowski, John, xii

Taconic State Parkway, 271; *502a−h*
Talent, 213, 246
Taos Pueblo, 81−82; *118, 134*
Tapiola, Finland, *76*
Technology, 111, 112, 156, 164−65, 214, 260, 280, 288
Tel Aviv, Israel, 87; *145, 146, 150*
Television, effect on public ritual, 232
Temple of the Holy Family, Barcelona, 220; *410*
Teotihuacan pyramids, 82
Terrace housing. *See* Row houses
Territorial imperative, x, 20, 65, 247
Territory, 65, 110−11, 117, 146−48, 244, 251, 288; conceptual, 155; in evolution, 73, 75, 116; mobile, of car, 190, 270; social, 6−7, 21, 56, 75, 88, 177
Texture in landscape, 8. *See also* Haptic
Thames, river, 174
Thanksgiving Day Proclamation, 71
Theater, civic, 117, 128, 165; of natural events, 266; street, 232−41
Theatricals, bicentennial, 128; *208*
Thompson, Bart, 141
Thoreau, Henry, 261
Thought, x−xi, 111, 288
Three-dimensionality, xi, 180, 229
Tiberius, 179
Tiber, river, 179; *325*
Time, 32, 46, 115−16, 137, 156, 191, 220−21
Times Square, N.Y., 155; *268*
Tiogo Pass, Yosemite National Park, 264; *490*
Tobacco landscape, 22, 285−87; *43, 533−35*
Tönnies, Ferdinand, 113−14, 128
Topophilia, 260
Tourists, 93, 115, 146−48

Tourists, distemic in proxemic neighborhoods, 115
Town hall: Dubuque, Ia., 228; *430*; Old, Stockholm, 164;
    291; Rotterdam, 161; *283*
Townscape, brought indoors, 184
Town squares, 164, 174, 175, 241–49; *292, 316, 451a–f,
    453, 454, 457–59, 461, 463a–d*
Towns, seaport, 146–48
Traditions, 48–49, 112, 227
Tranquility, 104
Transcendence of local differences, 113
Transcendentalists, 259–60
Transitional space, 7, 16, 22, 24–28, 48, 88, 185, 211, 226
Transitional zones, 6, 7, 43, 45, 54, 58, 159, 244
Transportation, 143, 153, 189–99, 269–80
Travel, 146, 189, 190, 193, 195, 269–70
Trees, 34, 37, 41, 65, 120
Tremont Street, Boston, Mass., 99, 127, 137; *182, 227*
Trinity Church, Boston, Mass., 132–35; *217–23*
Trinity Church, New York, N.Y., 127
Triune brain, 110–11, 288
Trust in environment, 118
Tuan, Yi-Fu, 260
Tuemmler, Fred, 223
Tunnard, Christopher, 270; *Man-Made America: Chaos or
    Control?*, 270
Turf, 5, 7, 32, 111, 112. *See also* Territory
Tuthill, Robert, 78
Twain, Mark, 150, 169–70

Uffizi Palace, 177–78; *322*
Uniformity, 49, 241
Union of states, 211, 269–70
Union Square, San Francisco, Cal., 148; *254, 255*
United Nations, 11, 120, 157–58, 180, 200, 245; *276–78*
Unity, 46, 47, 48, 210–11
Universality, 218
Universities as distemic centers, 144–45
University of: California, Berkeley, 210–11;
    Massachusetts, 102–03, 244, 288; *455, 456*; Oregon,
    248; Wisconsin, 209; *394–96a–d*
Urban design, 3, 6, 8, 137, 158, 171, 228–31
Urban renewal, 31, 129, 162
Urban-rural fringe, 32
Urban villages. *See* Villages, urban
U.S.S. Constitution, 93; *161*

Vallingby, Sweden, 167; *299a, b*
Vatican, 130–32, 180–81, 200; *327–32*
Vaux, Calvert, 257
Venturi, Robert, 186
Verandas, 15; *27, 28, 29. See also* Porches
Verbal thought, x, xi
Verrazano-Narrows Bridge, 153
Vertebrates, 110
Vicksburg, Miss., 170; *304–06*
Viet Nam War, 6, 210, 248

Vieux Carré, New Orleans, La., 65; *121a–d*
Village, global, 120, 237; peasant, 113; scale, 84, 162
Villages, 70, 94, 104, 116, 150, 178, 183, 234, 277; urban,
    73, 115, 117
Visual: discord, 46; logic, 51; metaphor, 33; system, 9;
    thought, x–xi; unity, 229
Vltava River, 174–77; *314*
Volga Deutsch, 118

Walden Pond, Concord, Mass., 261
Walls, 12, 70, 85–86, 89, 108, 119; Berlin, 189–90;
    354a–c; Jerusalem, 85–86; *140*; Prague, 177; *318*;
    Vatican, 181; *331, 332*
Wall, S.D., 237; *445–47*
Wall Street, N.Y., 41, 127, 150, 223; *258, 259, 421*
Washington, D.C., 125, 158, 194, 199, 201–07; *365, 366,
    384–92*
Water, 119, 231
Waterfalls, 250; *464, 466, 467*
Waterfronts, 90, 94, 143, 152–53, 159, 223–26
Water travel, 119, 159
Weinmayr, Michael, 253
Westchester County, N.Y., 270
West End, Boston, Mass., 94, 96–97, 121; *174*
Western ideas penetrate tall buildings, 62, 84; *115*
West Indians, 99
West Side Highway, New York, N.Y., 152–53
West 33rd Street, New York, N.Y., *360, 361*
Where's Boston?, 129
Whitman, Alden, 261
Whyte, William H., 220, 257
Wilderness, 260–68, 281
Wilkie, Richard W., 118; *100, 135, 136, 523*
Wilson, Edward O., 109
Wind Cave National Park, 266–68
Windmills, 288; *536*
Windows, 3, 4, 6, 7, 8, 59
Wisconsin, 208–12
Women's liberation, 74
Woolworth Building, N.Y., 152
Working class, 72, 74, 99, 104, 245
World Trade Center, New York, N.Y., 150, 158, 193;
    257, 265
World War II, 61, 159, 168, 242, 280
Worship of automobiles, 279; *523*
Wright, Frank Lloyd, 18, 33, 51, 218; *32*
Wyoming, 281; *525*

Xenophobia, 113

Yards, 16, 31, 36, 41
Yarmouth, Me., *91*
Yellowstone National Park, 266; *496–98*
Yosemite National Park, 264, 281; *490, 491*
Youth gangs, 184, 257–58
Yugoslavia, 61–62, 240; *110–15*

Zadkine, Ossip, 159, 168; *280, 281*
Zen and the art of motorcycle maintenance, 251; *472*
Zero population growth, 127
Zoning, 24–28, 31, 33, 41, 56, 104, 125, 132, 188
Zoo, Central Park, N.Y., 257; *482*
Zurich, Switzerland, 182–83; *333–38*
Zuyder Zee, 163